Violent Encounters

Violent Encounters

Interviews on Western Massacres

Deborah and Jon Lawrence

University of Oklahoma Press : Norman

Also by Deborah Lawrence

Writing the Trail: Five Women's Frontier Narratives (Iowa City, 2006)

Library of Congress Cataloging-in-Publication Data
Lawrence, Deborah.
Violent encounters : interviews on western massacres / Deborah and Jon Lawrence.
p. cm.
Includes bibliographical references and index.
ISBN 978-0-8061-4126-8 (hardcover)
1. Indians of North America—Wars—West (U.S.)
2. Indians of North America—Violence against—West (U.S.)—History—19th century.
3. Massacres—West (U.S.)—History--19th century.
4. Indians of North America—Interviews.
5. United States—Territorial expansion—History—19th century.
I. Lawrence, Jon, 1945–
II. Title.
E78.W5L38 2011
973.5—dc22

2010044188

The paper in this book meets the guidelines for permanence and durability of the Committee on Production Guidelines for Book Longevity of the Council on Library Resources, Inc. ∞

Manufactured in the U.S.A.

The manufacturer's authorized representative in the EU for product safety is the Mare Nostrum Group B.V., Mauritskade 21D, 1091 GC Amsterdam, The Netherlands, email: gpsr@mare-nostrum.co.uk

To the victims

Contents

Illustrations

Figures

Maps *Cartography by Tom Jonas*

Preface

In recent years, many people have called on historians to reach out to a larger public. *Violent Encounters* responds to that call. This collection of interviews with nine authors—Marc Simmons, Margot Mifflin, Will Bagley, Chip Colwell-Chanthaphonh, Michael Tate, Albert Hurtado, Robert Utley, Jerome Greene, and Ned Blackhawk—focuses on hostile interethnic relations in the multicultural frontier West. The interviews are designed to give a sense of the variety of opinion among current authors on the violence that accompanied the settling of the American frontier.

No period in our country's past has produced more historic encounters between Indians and whites than the years from 1840 to 1890. These interviews examine this era, with occasional forays into earlier and more recent times. They include a general discussion of the McComas Massacre; the Oatman Massacre; the Mountain Meadows Massacre; the Camp Grant Massacre; Indian-white encounters along the Overland Trail; violence in early California; hostilities between the frontier army and the Sioux, from the Santee Sioux Revolt to Wounded Knee; hostilities between the army and the Cheyennes, including the Sand Creek Massacre and the Battle of the Washita; and violence between the European Americans and the Shoshonean-speaking Great Basin tribes, including the Bear River Massacre.

As underscored by our book's subtitle, a special class of violent encounters consisted of those events in which innocent people—those under a flag of truce or those living peacefully and not bearing arms, including women, children, and the elderly—were mercilessly slaughtered. Adopting historical usage, we refer to such events as massacres, without distinguishing cases in which one or two people were killed from those in which large numbers were killed. Such massacres are viewed as heinous by almost every culture (especially by those of the victims). To participate in such killing requires a state of mind in which the victims are viewed as less than human.

Frontier violence was endemic. While many ethnic groups were involved, *Violent Encounters* focuses primarily on Anglo-Americans, Indians, and Hispanics. Whites massacred Indians, Indians massacred whites, Indians massacred Indians, Anglo-Americans massacred Anglo-Americans, and Mexicans massacred Apaches and vice versa. All ethnic groups were perpetrators, and all ethnic groups were victims at one time or another. None can claim complete moral purity. This book seeks to clarify what happened and, when possible, why.

Granted, hostile relations on the frontier were not necessarily the norm. Trade, mutual assistance, and friendship often prevailed between Indians and white Americans, especially prior to 1860. On the other hand, an assessment of the documented frontier conflicts attests that violence was endemic to the frontier period of the American West: these were not just minor instances of violence that grew out of a frontier environment filled with young men, alcohol, and freedom but serious forms of violence, including premeditated and carefully choreographed actions.

Our initial goal was to consider most of the major massacres, as well as representative minor massacres, that occurred in the trans-Mississippi West during the period 1840 to 1890. At the same time, our interviewees, whether academic (Mifflin, Tate, Hurtado, Blackhawk) or nonacademic (Simmons, Bagley, Colwell-Chanthaphonh, Utley, Greene), were to be professional scholars, adhering to exacting standards for the establishment of historical truth. Following these criteria, we have included discussion of such major events as the Clear Lake Massacre in California, the Mountain Meadows Massacre, the Santee Sioux Revolt, the Bear River Massacre, the Sand Creek Massacre, the Battle of the Washita, the Camp Grant Massacre, and the Wounded Knee Massacre as well as minor cases such as the McComas Massacre and the Oatman Massacre. We have had to leave out some significant incidents, such as the Marias River Massacre, the Warren Wagon Train Massacre, and the Osage-Kiowa Cutthroat Massacre. Overall, we present the reader with a discussion of a majority of the most significant massacres as well as representative smaller-scale instances.

Despite the focus on massacres, we make no effort in the interviews to define the term. One reason for this approach is that authors disagree over whether certain encounters are to be viewed as massacres, battles, or assaults. While the slaughter of noncombatants might euphemistically be called "collateral damage" rather than a massacre in some instances, we consider it reasonable to include such cases in a more general discussion of the phenomenon of interethnic violence. Indeed, the interviews proceed from discussion of specific massacres—the McComas Massacre, the Oatman Massacre, the Mountain Meadows Massacre, and the Camp Grant Massacre—to a more general discussion of Indian-white violence: relations between Indians and emigrants on the Oregon-California Trails, the destructive effect of the settlement of California on the Indian population, the whole course of history of the U.S. Army's encounters with the Sioux and with the Cheyennes (such as those at Sand Creek, Washita, Little Bighorn, and Wounded Knee), and the long history of colonial and postcolonial era violence in the Great Basin, including the Bear River Massacre.

Violent Encounters differs from most modern scholarship on the West by including a broad range of interviewees: academic historians, National Park Service historians, nonacademic professional historians, an anthropologist, and a journalist. The history of the American West is complicated, including different races and cultures and a variety of changing institutions. No one person's narrative can ever encompass the whole story. By incorporating different authors' approaches to western history and the writing of western history, our book acknowledges that diversity. This is particularly important for a discussion of frontier violence, because the voices of the victims, who were in some cases preliterate and unable to defend themselves in writing, need to be heard.

In an effort to give a deeper understanding of the historical background of the violent encounters, we questioned the interviewees both specifically and broadly. The result was that in several cases the interviews focus more on the overall history than exclusively on a given massacre. Furthermore, some authors are more interested in understanding the deep context of the frontier violence than in creating a narrative history of particular events. The gain is that we obtain coherent views by outstanding current authors toward a deeper understanding of the prominence of incidents in the frontier West in which innocent people, peaceful and at times unarmed, could be slain without mercy.

One of the virtues of the interview format is that the authors can be outspoken and give straightforward statements about their beliefs and speculations regarding these issues, allowing them to go beyond the constraints under which historians generally operate. In so doing, they challenge both traditional patriotic views of Western expansion and politically correct ideologies. We note also that we occasionally asked "leading questions"; typically, these were cases in which we thought we knew the response in advance but wanted to clarify the author's view for our readers. We note that the interviewees were quick to disagree with us when they thought we were wrong.

During the interviews, we have also explored a number of related themes. We examine the processes involved in "doing history," including questions about sources and interpretation as well as questions about personal experiences in the research process. We have also asked about how the interviewees deal with undocumented or poorly documented sources, such as the work of local and nonprofessional historians or the use of oral accounts given by Native American participants and their descendants. Every one of our authors has dealt with these issues, each in a different way.

Additionally, *Violent Encounters* allows the reader to reconceive what is meant by "history." The authors we interview discuss what it means to conceptualize a historical event, the ways in which history is used as a political tool, and the need for the incorporation of multiple viewpoints when reconstructing past events. This book is an effort in that same direction—toward inclusive historical frameworks. Unlike most books on western history, it includes an understanding of the role of literature in furthering historic understanding. While most historians are careful in pointing out the historical errors, both large and small, in the fiction about the frontier West, we find that they are often quite open to the insight into historical conditions that well-written literature can give.

Because our background, as well as that of a few of our authors (Simmons, Bagley, and Tate), includes participation in organizations that further the National Historic Trails (the Santa Fe Trail, the Oregon-California Trails, and the Old Spanish Trail), we have also asked for the authors' opinions about preservation of the historic sites associated with the events being discussed. As examples, Bagley points out that the Mountain Meadows site is threatened by commercial development, and Utley discusses how he engaged in legal action against the National Park Service for violation of the spirit and letter of key historic preservation acts.

Violent Encounters is divided into nine interviews, arranged chronologically in the order in which the interviews were conducted. We have chosen this ordering because questions asked at later interviews reflect authors' responses in earlier interviews. Each interview stands alone, however, so that the reader need not proceed in the order of the text.

We also include an extensive bibliography that will point the reader to texts giving the historical background for the massacres and campaigns and also to works cited and discussed by the interviewees.

In conducting these interviews, our methodology was as follows. Prior to each interview, we read the key texts that constituted the focus of the interview as well as a number of other background works by the same author and others. We formulated an initial set of questions, which we transmitted to the interviewee in advance. We used these questions as a guide during the course of the actual interview but typically deviated and asked new questions suggested by the interviewee's responses. We then transcribed the tape recording of the interview. We edited the transcription to remove redundancies, to complete sentences, and to remove awkward grammar. We often resequenced the order of the transcription, in the interests of a clearer exposition. We provided endnotes for the text. We submitted the edited transcript to the interviewee, who then made written corrections, additions, and deletions. This process helped us, as interviewers, to be reasonably well informed, ensured accuracy in the exposition of the interviewee's views, and allowed for an extended give-and-take beyond the actual interview.

As mentioned, our background includes participation in the work of organizations dedicated to the preservation and promotion of the National Historic Trails. Indeed, the first four interviews were initially published in *Overland Journal,* the periodical of the Oregon-California Trails Association (OCTA); *Desert Tracks,* the publication of the Southern Trails Chapter of OCTA; and *Spanish Traces,* the organ of the Old Spanish Trail Association. Because we are not historians, we view ourselves as educated laypeople who have done sufficient homework to raise questions that we feel will be of interest to an enlightened public. We sincerely hope that this book stimulates further conversations about the process of the historical imagination and that it encourages readers to think about the past in new and more inclusive ways.

This project is the product of many people. We are pleased to acknowledge the assistance of Robert Clark and Steven Baker of the Arthur H. Clark Company and the University of Oklahoma Press, who have enthusiastically guided the production of this book and provided much valuable counsel. Our thanks go to our copy editor, Kathy Lewis, whose insightful suggestions have enhanced the readability of this book. We are grateful to historians Robert Hine and David Weber, both of whom participated in previous interviews that we conducted and inspired and supported our work. Our appreciation also goes to Tom Jonas, who created the maps for each chapter. Finally, we are indebted to the authors we have interviewed, who welcomed us into their homes and offices and gave freely of their time and insight to help us toward an understanding of violence in the frontier West and the process of writing history. Their historical insights and ideas are the fabric of this book. We cannot thank them enough.

Violent Encounters

Judge Hamilton McComas, his wife, Juniata, and two of their children, on an outing shortly before the McComas Massacre. From the collection of Marc Simmons.

Chato, the leader of the Apache raid that resulted in the McComas Massacre. From the collection of Marc Simmons.

CHAPTER 1

The McComas Massacre

An Interview with Marc Simmons

IN 1880 JUDGE HAMILTON C. MCCOMAS, who had previously lived in Monticello, Illinois; Fort Scott, Kansas; and St. Louis, Missouri, went to the New Mexico Territory as an investor in and legal advisor to the mining business. He settled in Silver City, where he established a law practice. In March 1882 he brought his family out from Missouri. They lived in Silver City's Exchange Hotel until McComas bought a house at Sixth and Hudson.

In early 1883 Chato led a party of Chiricahua Apaches in a raid from the Mexican Sierras into southeastern Arizona and southwestern New Mexico. The Apaches were primarily seeking ammunition. More than thirty-five men—miners, teamsters, and others—had been killed by the time the Apaches reached the Burro Mountains, southwest of Silver City.

On March 27, 1883, at 2 P.M., the judge, his wife, Juniata, and their six-year-old son Charley set out from their home in a rented buckboard for a trip to Lordsburg, in the southwestern corner of New Mexico. They left their two daughters, Ada and Mary, with friends. On the night of March 27, they stopped at Mountain Home, a roadside hostelry about seventeen miles south of Silver City on the eastern side of the Burro Mountains. Another lodger at the inn that evening was John Moore, the Grant County deputy assessor. The discussion over dinner was about the Apache raiders and whether or not they posed a threat to travelers on the Lordsburg Road. The McComas party left Mountain Home at nine o'clock the next morning. Moore followed about forty-five minutes later.

In 1883 the Lordsburg Road did not follow the route that New Mexico Highway 90 does today but veered off west through Thompson Canyon. Several hours after leaving Mountain Home, the judge and his family had passed through the canyon. Just a mile beyond its western mouth, they stopped to have a picnic under a walnut tree. They were attacked by the Apache raiders. Evidence at the scene suggests that Judge McComas was shot in the buckboard but leaped out to return the fire of the Apaches in an attempt to protect his

The walnut tree in Thompson Canyon, where the McComas Massacre occurred. 1993 photograph by Marc Simmons.

wife and child before he was mortally wounded. Juniata was dragged from the wagon and bludgeoned to death. The Apaches stripped the bodies of McComas and his wife, took their guns and ammunition, the surviving horse, and Juniata's dress, and kidnapped Charley McComas. Before leaving the scene, they ripped up the judge's business papers and piled them on his naked back.

Army troops under General George Crook pursued the Apaches. So did militia units such as Captain James F. Black's Shakespeare Guards, formed in the mining town and stagecoach stop south of Lordsburg. On May 15, 1883, Crook's Apache scouts attacked a camp of Apaches in Mexico's Sierra Madres. Nine of the Apaches, including an old woman, were killed. Many of the others escaped into the mountains. Some of the Apaches who survived that assault said that Charley was among those who fled into the mountain wilderness. But Jason Betzinez, an Apache warrior and cousin of Geronimo, tells a different story in *I Fought with Geronimo*. Betzinez was not at the Sierra Madre camp when it was attacked, but he said that Apaches who were there told him that a warrior named Speedy, mad with grief because his mother had been shot to death during the fight, killed Charley with a rock. The army never found Charley's body, so the mystery about his fate persists.

Although today the McComas tragedy is only a footnote in the history of the Indian wars in the Southwest, the event was a nationwide sensation at the time and had a lasting impact on the lives of the Apaches.

Marc Simmons is an independent professional historian who lives in Cerrillos, New Mexico. The author of more than forty books on the history of New Mexico and the Southwest, he is widely considered to be the historian laureate of New Mexico. He is well known to emigrant trail enthusiasts as an authority on the Santa Fe Trail and has written the main guidebook for the trail, *Following the Santa Fe Trail: A Guide for Modern Travelers,* and several historical works, including *Murder on the Santa Fe Trail,* which received the C. L. Sonnichsen Book Award.[1] As a founding member and past president of the Santa Fe Trail Association, he has been a leader in preservation of trail sites, such as the Pigeon's Ranch building at the Glorieta Battlefield east of Santa Fe.[2] His long-standing interest in Kit Carson culminated in his book *Kit Carson and His Three Wives.* He has held both a Woodrow Wilson Fellowship and a Guggenheim Fellowship and received the Golden Spur Award from the Western Writers of America. He has also written a series of books for children that focus on heroic children of the Old West.[3]

We interviewed Simmons at the San Marcos Café, near Cerrillos, New Mexico, on November 8, 2004. The interview focuses on his book *Massacre on the Lordsburg Road: A Tragedy of the Apache Wars.*

DJL (Deborah and Jon Lawrence): Since you wrote *Massacre on the Lordsburg Road,* have you learned anything significantly new about the McComas Massacre?

MS (Marc Simmons): Little fragments have come up here and there, but I haven't gotten any big revelation. Several weeks ago, Sheila Tryk, the former editor of *New Mexico Magazine*, sent me a story from the newspaper in Joplin, Missouri.[4] It was by a feature writer who had found some new information. One thing she said that surprised me, and that I wish I'd known when I wrote *Massacre on the Lordsburg Road,* was that Judge McComas was already a specialist in mining law in Missouri before he left the Midwest for New Mexico. I thought that didn't happen until he came west and made some investments in mines, after which he became involved in the legal aspect. This new fact gives a little more depth to the story. The writer had been to Fort Scott, which

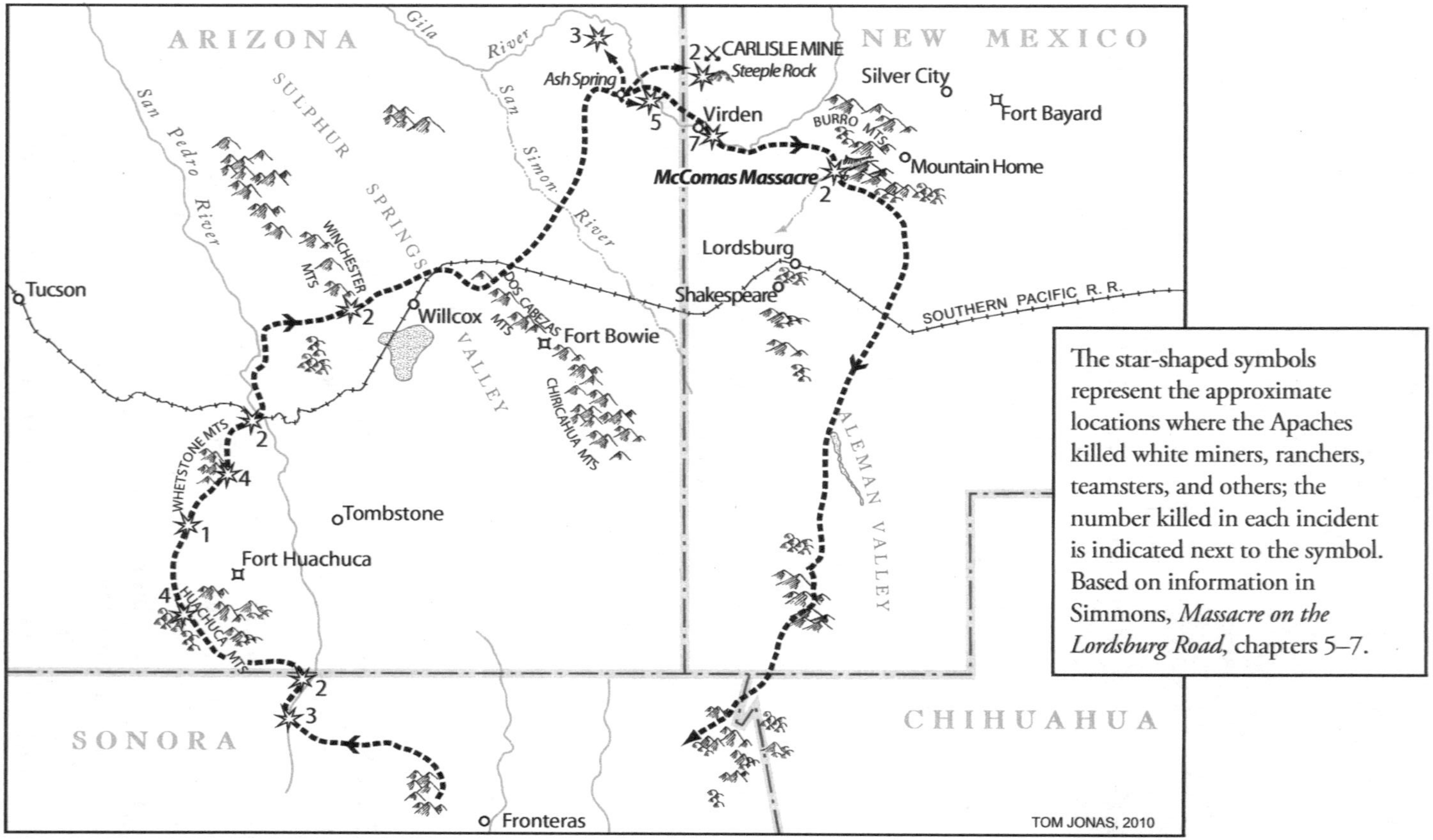

The route of Chato's raid, March 14–30, 1883.

is not far from Joplin, and may have learned about it there. I'd never been to Fort Scott. I depended on other researchers there to send me material; and I paid a photographer to make the photograph of the McComas tombstone in the local cemetery that was included in the book. I've also heard from other McComas descendants; I've got a large file on them that I'll probably donate to the Silver City Museum some day.

DJL: Of the mysteries and puzzles concerning the incident, which would you most like to have answered?

MS: There are both small and large puzzles. I'd like to know what was in Judge McComas's head when, in the face of knowledge of the Apache outbreak, he went ahead with that trip. With hindsight we can say, "How could he possibly take his family on such a dangerous venture?" If he'd gone by himself, maybe he could have braved it out and taken his chances, but how could he put his family in harm's way like that? I made a big issue over this question in the book. This brings up one of the fundamental keys that I use in writing history, when trying to interpret human behavior. And the key is simply this: people tend to believe what they want to believe rather than what the facts of reality dictate. It is second nature for us to validate our fantasies or engage in wishful thinking, the evidence notwithstanding. There is a good case to be made that the judge was doing something like that, and so brought disaster upon himself and his family.

DJL: At Mountain Home, a hostelry on the road, the guests were talking about the Apache outbreak over the dinner table and Juniata, the judge's wife, was so frightened that she didn't want to continue on the trip to Lordsburg.

MS: Yes, it is really astonishing. Perhaps there was something in Judge McComas's character, stubbornness or blockheadedness. But given this universal human trait that I just mentioned, it is quite possible that he talked himself out of the danger. And I explained in the book why he might have felt that way: he had taken this road many times, he was familiar with the territory, and he wasn't convinced that the Apaches were close to the area around Silver City at that time. He most likely saw it as a very small risk. Also, he was intent on his business. There are probably other factors, or something in his head that we don't even know about, that we can never know. Since history is always provisional, we take the evidence we have and make of it the best account that we can. Yet many points are left unsettled. That is what makes the study of the past so interesting—you are forced to speculate.

DJL: Another guest, John A. Moore, the county's deputy assessor, who was also at Mountain Home, left forty-five minutes later. Why didn't he and the McComases travel together?

MS: I know, that's almost incomprehensible. Maybe he wasn't well but got to feeling better later. Maybe he stayed behind because he was scared, but then his courage returned. We're trying to put ourselves into that kind of situation, but we don't know the circumstances. Nor do we know the motives of these people or their modus operandi. All those unknown factors enter in.

DJL: We're interested in the relationship of this incident to the history of the old emigrant trails. While the massacre occurred in 1883, essentially at the end of the trail era, there seem to be connections to earlier trail history. Of particular interest to us is the question as to how dangerous the Indians actually were to the emigrants. Some tribes may have been more kindly disposed than others. On the other hand, tribes such as the Comanches and Apaches were not benign at all. And incidents such as the Oatman Massacre in 1851 were not uncommon.

MS: The view that raids on the emigrants were not so common is one that we've been hearing recently.[5] Maybe on the Oregon Trail in particular the Indians were not as dangerous as is generally believed. But the Indians were always a hazard, and if an emigrant got complacent, he could run into serious trouble and lose his life and lose his family members' lives too. On the Santa Fe Trail there is no question that from the very beginning the Indians were extremely dangerous. A typical case was the incident at McNees Crossing in 1828.[6] Two men, Robert McNees and Daniel Monroe, went ahead of their party, stopped at the crossing, and lay down to take a nap. Indians came and shot them. McNees was killed outright; Monroe was picked up by the caravan when it reached the crossing but died shortly thereafter.

I tend to think that this emphasis on trying to paint the Indians in a better light, not paying attention to the evidence, is one of political correctness. The same sort of emphasis has been given to the captivity narratives, such as that of Olive Oatman. This is something entirely new in the last ten or fifteen years, people trying to say that the captivity narratives were sensationalized and exaggerated, that these women who were carried into captivity did not suffer as suggested in their published narratives. It is again an effort to put the Indians in a better light for politically correct purposes. Actually, the evidence that the narratives are essentially correct is overwhelming, but perhaps it's easy to gull people who haven't seriously studied the Old West into believing otherwise.

In *Massacre on the Lordsburg Road,* I couldn't decide, based on the existing evidence, whether poor Juniata was ravaged before or after she was killed. But the horror stories were so grim that even if the journalists who wrote up these poor women's experiences did tend to exaggerate for a popular audience, and there was a lot of that, it doesn't mean that the story essentially was untrue or that the captives had an easy time of it. Many captives were ruined mentally and physically by the experience.

DJL: There were a lot more incidents of theft of livestock than of murders, but this could be absolutely disastrous and affect the emigrants' ability to survive.

MS: It was pretty grim. Other things cumulatively might have been more important than massacres, but such fatalities were a serious issue. At times the trails certainly were quiet and a lot of people got through without having serious trouble, but that doesn't mean the danger wasn't there. They may simply have been lucky. Perhaps circumstances existed such that it happened to be a quiet time, for example, when the Indians were off hunting rather than raiding.

DJL: One of the strengths of your book is that you look at the situation from so many angles and you put it in a larger context. We love the way you have a chapter on the Apaches and then you move back into Silver City and give the history behind the McComases coming to the Southwest; you provide the army's point of view and the citizen's point of view. It must be a challenge for you as a writer to maintain balance.

MS: I wasn't consciously trying to maintain balance. I was trying to tell as much of the story as I could find. It may turn out to look like balance, but it was not a conscious effort. People have said something similar when reviewing the children's books that I'm doing now on heroic children of the Old West. They say, "Oh, look, he's got a girl in the first story, a Hispanic New Mexican boy in the second story, and an Indian boy in the third." It looks as if I'm touching all bases. My goal, however, is to build a story around a few historical events involving a real child, one that rings true to the time and place. And it's *hard* to find such stories in the existing record. These are the ones I've come up with. So I've taken some flack, but I wasn't attempting to be politically correct by touching all bases.

DJL: In trying to understand the Apache mindset, what do you consider to be the best sources?

MS: Asa Daklugie is probably the best, and I think that Eve Ball, when interviewing him, was pretty well attuned to accurately recording his story.[7] Daklugie learned English late in life. He was the son of Juh, who was a major Apache leader in the Sierra Madre of Mexico but didn't receive the publicity of Cochise or Geronimo. Daklugie had the Apache mindset. But the problem is, even then you have to be very careful because these Apaches often were not intending to tell what happened in an accurate manner. They were trying to protect their people. In everything they said, they were attempting to make their people look good. In trying to understand them, a historian is always working under that handicap.

In his book on the Pueblo Revolt, David Roberts reports asking the Indian lieutenant governor of Acoma, "Have you heard of the Pueblo Revolt?"[8] The reponse was "I'm not sure I've heard of it." Roberts questioned, "What do your children think of this?" The lieutenant governor replied, "Well, they don't know about it. Our elders say we shouldn't talk about that." If the young people ever asked about the Pueblo Revolt, which they probably almost never did because they most likely had never heard of it, the elders would say, "This is not for you to know." They just put it away. It was too far back. In trying to understand them, you get to a blank wall. They're thinking on an entirely different track.

And the Apache Indians, how different was the track they were on! In the book on the McComas Massacre, I even compare them to the Comanches regarding the cultural approval of cruelty toward others.[9] The Apaches were also cruel to animals. I give examples, trying to understand what was in their heads and why they acted the way they did.

Whereas today a common view of journalists particularly, but one that's filtering down and affects academics as well, is that anything an Indian says must be true just because an Indian says it. But the modern Apaches, having been influenced first through missionary teachings when they were held captive at Fort Sill and later through the American school systems, do not think like the old Apaches. The point is that you can't get a modern-day Apache or modern-day Pueblo to tell you something that will help you understand how their ancestors once thought. In the first place, they're not going to tell you. They're going to falsify deliberately in order to protect their heritage. And second, they don't necessarily say to themselves, "I'm speaking on something that's going into the historical record so I should be accurate." That's part of our culture, not theirs. They have a dozen other motives for saying something that's not connected with reality. They want you to believe it and they may even believe it themselves, but that doesn't mean it's true.

A related point was made by Grenville Goodwin, the anthropologist who is the subject of the recent book *Apache Diaries.*[10] When he was a young man, he worked for a trader at one of the reservations, Fort Apache or San Carlos. He learned to speak Apache and got as close to the Apache people as any outsider could get. This was during the late 1920s or early 1930s, when there were still a lot of older ones left. Somewhere in his diaries or journals Goodwin mentions that he once asked an elderly Apache to tell him what life was like for his grandparents before they had much contact with white men. The Apache looked at him and said, "I can't tell you that. I don't know how they lived—that was too long ago. You white men don't know how your grandparents lived either. There have been too many changes." What a revelation! It would have been during the 1850s, when he was a boy, that he knew his grandparents, and as to what their life was like prior to then he had only the foggiest notion. Whereas when anybody today asks, "Tell us what life was like in the old days," they assume that the modern Indians will know all that. But as the Indian informant said, "You white men don't know. How do you expect us to know?"

I was mildly amused by an article in the *Albuquerque Journal* about Geronimo entitled "Hail to the Chief."[11] To quote the article, "A memorial to Chief Geronimo was unveiled by his great-great grandson Harlyn Geronimo on a Saturday at the Gila Cliff Dwellings National Monument. 'My great grandmother talked about this area where the great chief was born,' he said." Now, we know Geronimo wasn't a chief. He was more of a second-tier war leader. He has gone down in history because he lasted longer than many other Apaches and he was particularly ferocious. But what was more interesting to me was the following quote in the article: "Local resident Jim Ransom, who completed construction of the monument, said working on the project was an honor." It would have been totally unthinkable to people of the nineteenth century who lived through the Geronimo period that it would be an honor to commemorate him. Ransom continued: "It is my hope that this monument to Geronimo's birthplace rekindles his spirit, that his love of freedom and his passionate resistance to tyranny rise up today, that it grows until it fills the hearts and minds of everyone everywhere." Nobody in the nineteenth century would recognize these lofty sentiments as being true of Geronimo. As a matter of fact, the army moved him and his people out of Arizona to get them away from the mass of vigilantes who wanted to lynch him once they had him under control.

I've heard many horror stories about Geronimo that are indisputable. During his later years before he died at Fort Sill in 1909, at which time he was pacified and belonged to a church—I think the Apaches at Fort Sill were Dutch Reformed—a reporter interviewed him and asked him what he most regretted about his early raiding career.[12] Geronimo replied, "It was all the children I killed." If you read some of the stories about how he killed them, it will turn your stomach. It is unbelievable. There are so many unimpeachable sources and so much collaborative evidence about what they did to children that you can't dismiss all of this as journalistic hyperbole. This is a white man's fantasy: "If I were an Indian, I would do this or that. I would engage in passionate resistance to tyranny." There's not a shred of evidence that was in Geronimo's mind; that was not an Indian way of thinking. Nor this "rekindle his spirit of his love of freedom." It was his love of raiding!

This so-called Indian point of view always amuses me. The view of Kit Carson has fallen afoul of that. Beginning in the 1970s, interviewers would ask young Navajos, "What do you think of Kit Carson?" The problem with this question is that the Indians' only sources of information on Kit Carson are white people's books. If they read the anti-Carson books, which is typically the case, they reply, "Oh, we hate that butcher." What many of these young people know is what they learned from VISTA volunteers who were teaching on the reservation. Most of these volunteers were eastern preppies who came out to save the Indians. They had read Dee Brown's *Bury My Heart at Wounded Knee*,[13] so they had a negative picture of Kit Carson. I started reading newspaper accounts of young Navajos who said, "We hate Kit Carson because of what he did to us. He was a butcher. We can never forgive him." I said to myself: "Boy, that quote 'We can never forgive Kit Carson for what he did to us' sounds familiar." I knew when I heard it that they'd gotten it from a non-Indian, and I think I found the source—*Bury My Heart at Wounded Knee*—though I can't swear to it. But then the newspaper people quote it as the tribal tradition. Well, it's not the tribal tradition. The tribal tradition is something else. It can be found in a book the Navajos did themselves. In it, you don't find any vitriol against Kit Carson. As a matter of fact, he's hardly mentioned. Their vitriol is against the neighboring tribes, the Hopis especially, but also the Yavapais, the Apaches, the Utes, who all took advantage of the fact that their old enemies the Navajos were under attack by the army and rushed in for the kill.

DJL: What book was this?

MS: *Navajo Stories of the Long Walk Period*, published by Navajo Community College.[14] It has been out of print for a long time, although maybe it has been reprinted in paperback. If you want to get the Indian mindset, this is one of the few sources that I know. The interviews were done back in the 1930s when people were still living who had been on the Long Walk as children. It includes input from people who were born later but had heard the stories from relatives who had been on the Long Walk. They recorded the stories in Navajo on tape, and then twenty or thirty years later they translated them into English at Navajo Community College, using Navajos to do the translating. There was no doctoring. They published the book themselves, so there was no Anglo editor. It is one of the few cases I know where a publication went through these various processes with only Indians involved. It's fascinating to read because it reveals the way the older Navajos thought. In particular, they were totally pragmatic when telling of the horrible things that were done to them. One old Navajo woman, who was captured and taken up onto the Hopi mesa, said almost matter-of-factly, "One of their medicine men came over and snatched my baby in his cradleboard and took him and threw him off the edge of the cliff." Stories like that! But the way they tell it is not as we would tell it: "I went through this wrenching emotional experience." The way the Indians remember those things is very pragmatic.

A similar pragmatism can be seen in the way that certain Plains Indians made peace among themselves in 1840 at Bent's Fort.[15] They had been making war and killing each other in a very brutal manner, torturing the captives they brought in, and so forth. But there had been such carnage on all sides that they finally decided it was in their best interest to make peace. They emptied Bent's Fort of trade goods to give as gifts to each other when just a few weeks before they'd been mass killing one another. They just put it out of their minds! We could never comprehend that.

That's the Indian mentality. You have to look closely and read between the lines of a lot of sources before the picture begins to emerge. And what you get is not a real understanding but rather a sense or a taste of what was in the Indian mind. Then you start despairing because you know you can never really grasp it. You're just getting the outer edges. But it makes you humble about giving the Indian point of view. I really get annoyed when people announce, "We're going to give you the Indian side." When people utter statements like "We can never forgive Kit Carson for what he did," they typically have gotten the picture from our side, from the army's point of view. When they learn what Kit did, they conclude, "If I were an Indian, I could never forgive Carson." But that's not valid at all as the Indian point of view.

Anyway, it is the journalists who build up these stories about 150 years of grieving over the travesties of the Long Walk. It certainly left a deep scar, but for different reasons than a modern white man would expect. I think I'm 95 percent correct in saying that there wasn't a bitter memory of Kit Carson. In the first place, Indians tended to respect an enemy if there was a reason to respect him from their point of view. Carson may have led troops against them, but they tended to have respect for him as a warrior. They didn't have such a bitter hatred of him and they didn't think that he was a butcher as these modern Indian kids think. What these youths are actually giving is a modern white man's view, in particular, a white man's view of what he would feel if he were an Indian. This view gets back to the Indians and gets transformed into the official traditional Indian view. But the Indian youths got it from their assistant basketball coach, a youth himself, who came from Andover, Massachusetts, and who got it from reading Dee Brown.

It's a struggle and really that's what I was trying to do in *Massacre on the Lordsburg Road*, to give you just enough so that you'd begin to see that the Apaches were working on a different level, that they had a different way of thinking at the time.

DJL: After murdering the judge and his wife, why would they proceed to tear up all his business papers and sprinkle them on his body? How can you understand that?

MS: Such things were not uncommon. In the massacre at Wagon Mound on the Santa Fe Trail in 1850, Ute and Jicarilla Apache Indians destroyed a stagecoach and killed ten men in a big fight.[16] When Lieutenant [Ambrose E.] Burnside and his troops arrived, they found the U.S. mail scattered all over the place. Why did the Indians bother to stop and do this? They did strange things, and we can't understand the reasons.

DJL: It seems to us that there's a quality of myth in the story of Charley McComas's captivity. The story kept proliferating and altering, to the point where there were rumors of sightings of him as a red-headed Apache leader down in the Sierras in the 1920s. It reminds us of the story that Frank Dobie tells in *Apache Gold and Yaqui Silver* about the lost gold mine somewhere north of Silver City.[17] The stories about the mine kept recurring and changing; prospectors continued to try to find this lost gold mine. The tales don't seem to have a lot of relationship to fact. The process kept going on and on. It's probably still going on!

MS: Yes, they're still doing it today. They've moved the location of the mine now up west of Socorro around the Tres Montosas Peaks, out of the range that has been searched so many times already. There have been recent books by people who have spent their entire lives searching for the mine after tracking down all the different versions of the story.[18]

I don't like to use the word "myth" in this context because it is so overworked. I think it doesn't serve a real purpose to call these things myths. It's not really helpful. What you get in any kind of incident like this is conflicting stories. Some of them are made up. In some cases, people heard the story from somebody else, embellished it, and claimed it as their own story. There are all these different ways stories filter down. Historical methodology has its techniques, not much used any more, to try to sift through conflicting stories and try to find a kernel of truth somewhere in there. And sometimes the stories are so conflicting, as in the case of Charley's captivity, that it is just impossible to come up with anything you feel comfortable with. So you end up doing what I did in the book, where I wrote up all the stories, or myths if you prefer, that I heard. They are all fascinating. I probably missed a few. This allowed me to do an entire chapter on what might have happened to Charley McComas. I think that it is one of the more interesting parts of the book.

DJL: Charley's sister Ada Hazleton died in 1963. What were her thoughts about her brother?

MS: What I heard, especially from Judge McComas's descendants, was that she tried to preserve Charley's memory and keep it pure. I think I mentioned in the book that she got into a fury when she first read a story in one of the men's magazines in 1944 that Charley had lived and become a raider with the Apaches. She thought that sullied his memory and couldn't possibly be true. She was completely disturbed by the story and from that point on she was very defensive about it. I've found in a number of cases that women are especially defensive when their family line has a black sheep. They are the first to hide it in the closet, if they can. They don't want to sully the family name. They take up the cudgel in defense of the family member.

DJL: Better that he'd be dead than to be an Indian.

MS: Yes, something like that. Ada lived through that era, and the horrors she heard about when she was a child would certainly have influenced her. She wasn't going to have anything to do with the twentieth-century maudlin regard for the Indians.

My way of viewing this is that the events have already occurred. If you want to deal with the history, then forget about emotions or making value judgments and simply tell what happened. Readers can come to their own conclusions. If they want to make a value judgment, that's fine. But today's value judgments have nothing to do with the events of that time. You can go another step and contrast values then with our values now, but that's a separate story. It's more related to how we've changed or how we've evolved. But when you're dealing with the story of that time, your primary duty is to stay in that period and try to figure out, to the best of your ability, what happened and then try to explain what it means. It's what it means, the interpretation, that gets you in trouble because nowadays academics say that there's no way anybody can be objective. Everybody has a hidden agenda or an axe to grind and may not even realize it, so everybody's interpretations are different. That has led to a denial that there's any such thing as objective truth. Well, that's the height of absurdity because events happened in only one way. We may not know how they happened, but that doesn't mean there's no such thing as objective truth. As a professor of mine once said, "History is the never-ending search for the closest approximation of the truth."

DJL: We're interested in your attitude toward nonprofessional historians, including those whose pamphlets you can find in local museums. You make very good use of their work in your book, but since they are not professionally trained, you must have to be careful in using such material.

MS: Oh, you do. I provide the source, but I don't say, "Regard it with skepticism." Anybody who is serious about history will know that, while what is reported may be hearsay, it may be all we have. Often in hearsay, or in recollections, there is a kernel of truth somewhere. You may not be able to tell where it is, but you tell the story because you want to preserve the kernel. Future historians may see something there that will lead them to find out what the kernel is or what the whole story is. So it is worth recording all these things and having them preserved, especially between the covers of books, so somebody can use it farther down the road.

DJL: One of the functions of the trail organizations is to work to preserve historic sites. In this regard, Shakespeare, New Mexico, is a truly valuable historic site.[19] It was used by emigrants, by the Jackass Mail and the Butterfield Mail, by the U.S. Army, and by miners. But it is currently in private hands: Janaloo Hill inherited it from her parents, and now she and her husband, Manny Hough, serve as caretakers. What's going to happen to Shakespeare in the future?

MS: We don't know. Janaloo asked me recently to contact Governor Bill Richardson as well as the head of State Parks and the head of the Legislative Finance Committee to support the state's acquisition of Shakespeare. I thought the chances were pretty small, simply because the last thing the state wants is another white elephant to fund while supporting all the other demands made on the budget. Anyway, I got nice letters from all of them, and it is going to come before this next legislature; there'll be an appropriations bill to acquire Shakespeare. I have the impression that the governor is favorable to the idea and might sign such a bill if it comes through. It will be part of some larger bill, and we don't know whether it will even pass through the legislature. If it does, that would be great.

DJL: History enthusiasts like ourselves and historians like you who write about trails encourage tourists to visit trail sites. This is a good thing, but it can be at great expense to the landmarks themselves, many of which are vulnerable. It's a double-edged sword. We read your book on the Santa Fe Trail, we drive the dirt roads, we walk in the ruts, and we probably do a little bit of damage in the process. In a recent incident at Independence Rock on the Oregon Trail, large numbers of people walked over the site and presumably did damage to the inscriptions.

MS: My suspicion is that historic trails are not going to bring in hordes of people. Most people are not really that interested in history unless it's in Disneyland, where they can go to have a vicarious history experience. The mere process of having to go a long distance on the trails helps weed out all but the more serious. Some of these sites are readily accessible to the public and that allows vandals in, but there's no way to avoid vandals as far as I can see. Even if a site is highly protected, it still can get vandalized.

DJL: As compared to your other books, you put a lot of yourself into *Massacre on the Lordsburg Road,* especially in the introduction. You talk about a high degree of serendipity, the pieces of the puzzle falling into place, almost as if the spirits of the McComases themselves want their story to be told.

MS: Something related, that I find most interesting, is that as I got into the story I continued to discover many very small things that Judge McComas did over the years that kept him on this course that led him to that fateful day on the Lordsburg Road. If any one of those little things had not happened, or had been done even slightly differently, he wouldn't have been there on that day at that time. Revealing the full story, which had never been done before, made it possible to trace back and to see this tissue of circumstances. I think that in all of history almost every significant incident has that kind of chain of circumstances. In this case, all the pieces were present that brought the judge to that particular place and moment, and we can look back and see the whole process. We all have, in our lives, this series of small events that leads us to this or that larger event. Sometimes it leads to tragedy, sometimes to greater things. But if any of these events, which can be almost infinitesimal, are pulled out of the chain, then the whole thing collapses and our lives come out totally different. It makes us all seem very contingent upon small circumstances. The big circumstances have to be there; but also if any one of those small circumstances is removed from the picture, the edifice collapses. In the life of Judge McComas, the beginning, middle, and end would all have been different if any little thing had changed. That really impresses me.

DJL: It's a historian's view of fate.

MS: Yes, it's a historian's view of fate. Fate or higher powers. We can't truly know about them and we can't factor them in. We can only wonder about them. As historians, we have to deal with cause and effect.

CHAPTER 2

The Captivity and Return of Olive Oatman

An Interview with Margot Mifflin

ON AUGUST 10, 1850, ROYCE OATMAN with his wife and seven children left Independence, Missouri, in a wagon train of Brewsterites, members of a Mormon splinter sect led by James C. Brewster.[1] The goal of the wagon train was Bashan, a new Zion that they hoped to found near the mouth of the Colorado River.

The emigrants followed the Santa Fe Trail into New Mexico. Dissension caused the group to split near Las Vegas. Brewster headed first to Santa Fe and then went to Socorro, where he founded a colony. Royce Oatman and several other families traveled directly to Socorro and took the southern route from Socorro to Tucson. Part of the company resolved to stay in Tucson, and the rest proceeded down the Santa Cruz River to the Gila River and the Pima villages. The Oatmans left the Pima villages on their own to make the trip down the Gila into California.

On February 18, 1851, west of Gila Bend, the Oatmans' wagon was attacked by Indians, probably Yavapais, and all but three of the family members were killed. Two of the daughters, Olive (aged thirteen) and Mary Ann (aged seven), were taken captive. Lorenzo (aged fourteen) was clubbed and left for dead but survived. He returned to the Pima villages and from there went to California, where he spent the next few years in an effort to find his sisters. In 1852 the Yavapais traded the girls to the Mohaves. Mary Ann died of starvation in the winter of 1853 or 1854, but Olive survived. While living among the Mohaves, Olive was tattooed on her face and arms.

In 1856 Olive was ransomed by the United States government at Fort Yuma, where she was reunited with her brother, Lorenzo. Following her ransom, Olive went to El Monte, California, and from there to Oregon Territory. Royal B. Stratton, a Methodist minister, met her and popularized the Oatman story in his book *Captivity of the Oatman Girls.* He took Olive on a lecture circuit in several cities in the eastern United States. Later she married John Fairchild and moved to Sherman, Texas, where she lived out her days. She was survived by an adopted daughter, Mamie. Lorenzo married and moved to Red Cloud, Nebraska.

(Left) Olive Oatman in her later years. Photograph courtesy of Patricia Carreon.

(Below) Painting of Mohave Indians by H. B. Möllhausen, made during the Whipple railway survey of the 35th Parallel. From the collection of Margot Mifflin.

MARGOT MIFFLIN is an associate professor of English at Lehman College of the City University of New York (CUNY) and directs the Arts and Culture program at CUNY's Graduate School of Journalism. She has written for the *New York Times, Salon,* and *Entertainment Weekly* and is the author of *Bodies of Subversion: A Secret History of Women and Tattoo* (New York: Juno, 1997; and Powerhouse Books, 2001), a feminist history of tattoo art. Her interest in tattoo art led to her work on the life of Olive Oatman. We interviewed Mifflin on February 9, 2005, in a telephone conversation between Nyack, New York, and Irvine, California. The interview focuses on what she learned while working on her biography of Olive Oatman, *The Blue Tattoo: The Life of Olive Oatman* (2009).

DJL (Deborah and Jon Lawrence): Could you tell us a little bit about the book you're writing?

MM (Margot Mifflin): It's a biography for a general-interest audience. I'm really interested in Olive Oatman as a historical first and as a cultural hybrid. She was not the only white captive to live with Indians—there were hundreds, even thousands, of captives—but she was the only one who carried the physical evidence of her Indian identity back into the white world with her, in the form of her facial tattoo. The tattoo is really the thing that sets her apart. She also has a very dramatic story, from the actual attack, in which most of her family was killed, to living with the Mohaves and learning about their culture. She was the only white to be immersed in Mohave culture for years, and this happened just before the onset of their near-extermination.

For me, the question of whether she married a Mohave or not (something that has been alleged over the years) is not central to her case—it's what her life was like with the Mohaves and how she adjusted once she returned. Most of what's been written on her focuses on her captivity. I'd also like to tell about her experiences while she was on the lecture circuit, whether she believed the derogatory things she said about the Mohaves, and her life as a married woman in Texas. And I'm interested in her personally because she did suffer from some kind of depression in her adult life.

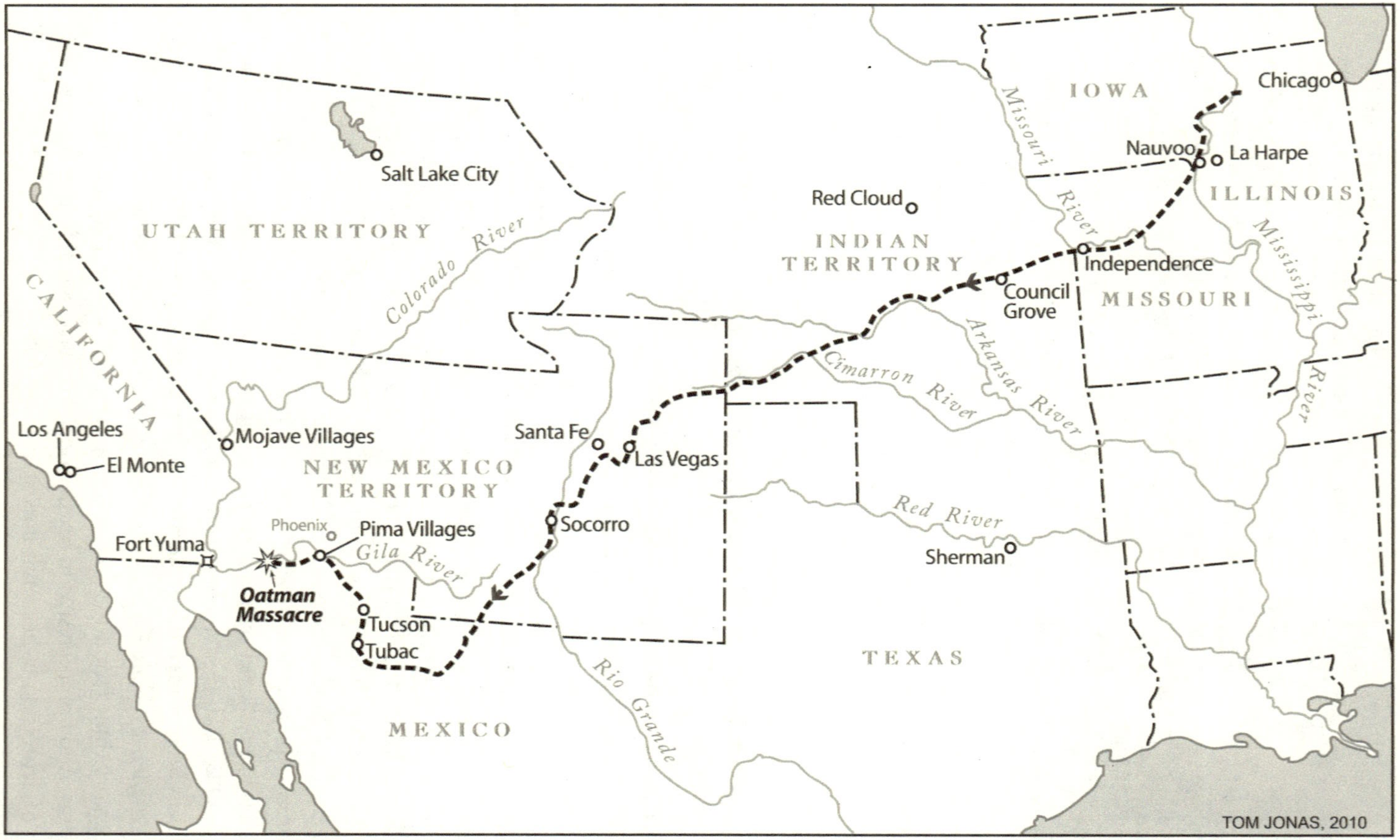

The route followed by the Oatmans from Whiteside County, Illinois, to the massacre site in western Arizona. Adapted from McGinty, *The Oatman Massacre.*

DJL: If you could ask Olive Oatman a question about her experiences, what would it be?

MM: Along with the question of "Did you want to return?" I would ask whether her difficulty in later life was due to post-traumatic stress as a result of the massacre, or if it was rooted in regret for having left her Mohave family, or both.

DJL: Oakley Hall put an Olive Oatman character in his historical novel *Separations.*[2] In the novel, the Oatman character didn't want to come back. She was really intimidated when she was dragged back to the white world.

MM: There are a lot of books and stories that were inspired by Oatman that I've discovered in this process. One of them, *So Wide the Sky,* by Elizabeth Grayson, is a romance whose main character is based on Olive Oatman. Also, Elmore Leonard wrote a short story called "The Tonto Woman" inspired by Oatman, which appears in *The Tonto Woman and Other Western Stories.*[3] The book has a photo of Oatman on the cover. The photo is not credited, and it's not identified as Oatman, but it's clearly her. Strangely, in addition to the chin tattoo, they've painted her cheeks.

These two books are interesting to me because they add a sexual dimension to her character. The thing everyone wanted to know when Oatman was ransomed was whether she'd been raped or not or whether she'd married into a Mohave family, which she said she hadn't. But the Mohaves were very sexually free. Children had socially sanctioned sex from puberty on. If Oatman was, as I believe, an acculturated Mohave, she was probably—ultimately—doing the same. The Mohave anthropologist Michael Tsosie confirms this possibility.[4]

Grayson and Leonard probably knew little about Mohave culture, but they picked up on this unexplored aspect of her character. She was probably much more sexually uninhibited than other white women of the Victorian period. Leonard's story reflects her sexuality through the eyes of a cattle rancher who falls in love with her; Grayson's is more about her Oatman character coming alive sexually when she meets another "half-breed"—a half-Indian, half-white scout.

DJL: There is even a *Death Valley Days* episode about the massacre! The cavalry officer who helped Lorenzo in the search for his sisters was portrayed by Ronald Reagan.

MM: Yes, and like a lot of these adaptations, it's a reflection of its era: it was made in the 1960s just after the Civil Rights Act was passed, and its drama is more rooted in the fear of miscegenation than in fear of Indians as any real threat to white power.

DJL: What about more scholarly works?

MM: A book just came out titled *María Amparo Ruiz de Burton: Critical and Pedagogical Perspectives.* There's an essay in it called "Rescuing the Past: The Case of Olive Oatman" by Andrea Tinnemeyer. Tinnemeyer argues that María Amparo Ruiz de Burton based her protagonist on Olive Oatman. Ruiz de Burton was a Mexican American author who grew up in California. She lived in San Francisco at the time when Olive Oatman was being ransomed. Her novel is about a Mexican Indian captive who lives with a New England family and the culture clashes that ensue.

Another recent book is by Doris Clark, an Oatman descendant. Clark's work started out as a genealogy, but she dug up some really good original documents and put them into a book called *The Oatman Story.* It's not scholarly or well documented, but she has some great material. Kathryn Derounian-Stodola, who edited the Penguin anthology *Women's Indian Captivity Narratives,* has done meticulous scholarly work on Oatman.[5] She has written about Oatman's celebrity, with an emphasis on how her story was filtered through her biographer, Royal Stratton.[6]

The best book on Oatman is by Brian McGinty: *The Oatman Massacre: A Tale of Desert Captivity and Survival* from the University of Oklahoma Press. McGinty has done serious, wide-ranging research, and his book is really fresh. Where a lot of amateur Oatman scholarship repeats the same questions and recycles the same language, McGinty sorts out the various tribes involved and raises new questions. His book is about the Oatman Massacre, not about Olive's whole life, and it's a scholarly analysis.

DJL: We are aware of several collections of material on the Oatman story: for example, the collection at the historical museum in El Monte, California, and the Pettid collection in Arizona.[7] Are we correct in assuming that there is a collection in Sherman, Texas? Also, it is our understanding that Lorenzo Oatman ended up in Red Cloud, Nebraska. Is there a collection of material in Red Cloud?

MM: There is not much material in Sherman and only a little in Nebraska. Genealogical and historical societies in several towns and cities in Arizona, California, and New York have Oatman information. I have in my research file a list of nearly a hundred museums and historical societies that relate to Oatman, her family, or her period.[8]

DJL: Is there any correspondence in the extended Oatman family that might be useful to your research?

MM: Yes. I've found two relatives who promised to share information and then simply vanished. One is in California and has a suitcase of things relating to Olive that was passed down through the family. If I remember correctly, the name of the other is Robin Brown, but I believe that whatever she has was published in Doris Clark's book. I'm hoping they both resurface at some point. I've done genealogy research on the Fairchilds in Michigan and found little beyond census documents—no letters or diaries. But an Oatman relative named Richard Nolan was helpful, and Walter Fields, the husband of an Oatman descendant, Dorothy Fields, helped me immensely, not just with resources but in thinking through the story.

DJL: We are interested in the way you use material from nonprofessional historians. For example, Stodola mentions that you have to be careful in using the Pettid collection in Arizona. Could you speak to that issue?

MM: The Pettid collection is an interesting case. Pettid actually wrote a complete book that was never published. For some reason, he threw out his notes. I asked Peggy Larson, who worked with him as his assistant, what he did with his sources, and she said that they are just not there. I use him very little in my book, and then only when I can cross-reference what he said, since his sources aren't documented. I think his research is generally solid. He didn't fabricate as far as I can tell, but he did use fabricated details to add color. Pettid had a bit of [Royal B.] Stratton in him: he overwrote and said things like "the weather was fickle as a woman." But he also added some interesting background about local history and plant life in the various areas he described.

Regarding sourcing, the same holds with Doris Clark, whose book is not well documented. The good thing is that she Xeroxed a lot of material and put it directly into her book, so you can see original letters and documents.

DJL: We have a number of questions about the Oatman story. The first: what was Royce Oatman's relationship to the Brewsterite party?[9] We have heard that both he and his wife, Mary Ann, had abandoned the Methodist Episcopal Church for the Mormon Church. What encouraged him to join the marginalized Brewsterite sect? Did he actually believe in "Bashan," Brewster's vision of a Zion in the vicinity of what is now Yuma, or did he join the party only for the purpose of traveling with a wagon train that was headed in the right direction . . . toward the goldfields of California?

MM: The Oatmans were originally Methodists. McGinty explores this in his book. He doesn't say exactly why and when they converted to Mormonism, but the town where they lived in the late 1840s, La Harpe, Illinois, was a Mormon stronghold. I found a diary of Mary Ann's cousin, which tells of Royce arguing with Mary Ann's father about who they were going to follow as the new Mormon leader after Joseph Smith's death. Royce wanted to follow Sidney Rigdon—the early Mormon leader who contested Brigham Young's leadership—to Pittsburgh, while his father-in-law (Joy Sperry) was going to Utah with Young.[10] And Royce, who apparently could be very hot-headed, told the old man that if the Sperrys went west, their throats would be cut by Indians—ironic, considering what happened to Oatman's family.

By the time the family left for the West, Royce was riding around the countryside preaching and trying to round up people for the trip. He already had the religion. On the other hand, Lucy Oatman's friend Susan Parrish, who later wrote about the trip, said that her family was going specifically to find gold, though her father claimed to be searching for Bashan as well.[11] So not everyone on the journey was religious. They organized it as a religious exodus, but they needed everybody they could get to join the wagon train. I'm not even sure that Royce's religion survived the trip, because there are hints that at some point during the journey he abandoned the religious idea and just wanted to find gold. But that's hard to verify.

The destination of the wagon train was revealed to them by Brewster's prophecy. Brewster was reviled by the other Mormons. He was only eleven years old when he had his first revelation. Joseph Smith thought he was a phony and probably didn't like that Brewster opposed polygamy, considering that Smith had many wives. Smith actually made a statement saying, "We have lately seen a pamphlet written and published by James Brewster purporting it to be one of the lost books of Esdras, and we consider it to be perfect humbug."[12] The Mormons excommunicated the Brewsterites in 1837. So Brewster never rose to the status of Joseph Smith. But he still pushed on and went west. And he's the one who had the idea of going to the mouth of the Colorado River. He said it was beautiful and warm, and I'm sure that, for an excommunicated Mormon, it helped that it was 600 miles from Salt Lake City. It probably seemed like a nice place for him to start his own club, so to speak. But in the end, it was a dry, barren, and basically horrible place, and no one from the original train settled there—even the few who made it that far traveled on farther west.

DJL: It is our understanding that it was Alfred Kroeber who first identified the Yavapais as the Indians responsible for the Oatman Massacre and not the

Apaches.[13] Is it possible that his informant was wrong? Are there any other sources of information on this issue?

MM: It is possible that this is wrong. McGinty maps out the possibilities in his book, explaining that the Yavapais lived closest to the site of the massacre, but he also theorizes that it could have been other tribes and says the question can't be settled definitively. The Mohave identification is obviously much simpler.

This brings up the one thread I want to pursue: the Mohave connection. I've talked to Michael Tsosie, a Mohave scholar who gave me a sense of Olive's life and place among them. I've asked Pamela Munro, a linguist at UCLA, a number of questions about words that Olive used or words that were used to describe her when she was with the Mohaves.[14] For example, Olive was called "Spantsa." That was her nickname. It has always been translated as "rot womb," as in "rotten womb." I asked Munro whether this was the case, because if it does mean "rot womb" and Olive was at a marriageable age when she was with the Mohaves but she didn't have children, and then she grew up and adopted a child, maybe she was barren and couldn't have children. The name could confirm her infertility.

DJL: That would imply that she had had sex with a Mohave and they found out that she was barren.

MM: Which might also imply that she had been married, although there was no formal marriage ceremony for the Mohaves. But it all falls apart for the following reason. Munro told me that the name literally translates not as "rot womb" but as "rotten vagina." She theorized that the nickname wouldn't really be about fertility. It would be about hygiene. She pointed out that the Mohaves were extremely hygienic and bathed every day, unlike whites, who didn't. Not to get too crude, but maybe they thought when they got her, "She's kind of skanky," and gave her the nickname because she didn't smell great. Or she might have been menstruating when they got her. It doesn't really work with the fertility theory. Tsosie proposed something entirely different: he says the name implies that she was having so much sex that she was worn out. A Mohave elder named Betty Barrackman told me that the name translates more literally as "sore vagina," which would be a fairly lewd, humorous nickname. Tsosie also sees the nickname as evidence that she was considered a member of the tribe, not a captive. As an outsider, she wouldn't have merited a nickname.

DJL: Does Pam Munro know the Mohave language?

MM: Yes, she compiled a Mohave dictionary that's useful in analyzing some of the words that are coming up in my research. I see McGinty has also used it. There are other interesting examples of relevant Mohave customs. People have said that Olive always put her hand to her chin when she met someone new. That seems to make sense because she was most likely embarrassed about her tattoo. But then I read in Kroeber that the Mohaves had a compulsive tendency to cover their chin—it was a gesture they often made. Now it's unclear to me whether she did that because she was tattooed or because she had become Mohave.

DJL: The article by Kroeber, who interviewed a Mohave at the turn of the twentieth century . . .

MM: Musk Melon.

DJL: Musk Melon claimed that the Oatman sisters were well treated by the Mohaves. Do you agree with that? Were they treated like slaves or were they treated well?

MM: By all accounts I've seen, they were well treated. My theory about the Oatman sisters is that the Yavapais were cruel to them and treated them as slaves, but the Mohaves took them in order to help them. Tribes had various reasons for taking captives, from vengeance to simply building up their own community. Supposedly Olive and Mary Ann were taken in by the Mohaves at the prompting of the chief's daughter. Olive said that they were adopted, and so did Musk Melon in that interview. He said that he lived a few hundred yards from where the Oatman sisters lived, that they were happy, and that the chief—they didn't have only one leader—said things like "They're one of us, so treat them well." There are many stories indicating to me that they were considered family. Their Mohave mother cried when Mary Ann died. She gave Olive food when they were starving, even though she could have saved it for her own children, who were also starving. The two sisters were given a little plot of land and a garden and like Mohave women they were able to plant crops. And the Mohaves resisted her ransom.

DJL: Were the Oatman sisters' facial tattoos the same as Mohave women's facial tattoos? Or as Olive herself claimed when she went on the lecture circuit, were they "slave marks" so that if the Oatman girls ran away, any other tribe would recognize them?

MM: The tattoo was supposedly done as a way of ensuring that they would get into heaven. The Mohaves apparently believed that if they weren't tattooed they would descend into a rat hole. The tattoo wasn't, at least not by any reliable account that I have found, a slave tattoo. When I was in Arizona I interviewed a Mohave elder, Llewellyn Barrackman, the former chair of the tribe, who said the girls' tattoos were no different from anyone else's. He saw the tattoos on people himself when he was a child. I also found a photo of a Mohave figure dating from the late nineteenth century, showing traditional Mohave garb, which has a tattoo identical to Oatman's, confirming that Oatman didn't wear a particular slave pattern as she said she did in her book.

Royal Stratton perpetuated some of this negativity about the Mohaves. He saw the potential in using Olive's story and used it to deride Indians, whom he himself detested. His racism is vicious, not only in her book but in some of his other writings as well. There are surviving texts of sermons he gave over the course of his career where he made it clear that he believed that it was the whites' privilege under manifest destiny to stamp out the Indians and continue westward to take the land.

Although in her lecture notes Olive says the Mohaves lived crudely in some ways, she never says they were mean. I think she had to say negative things about them to indicate that she wasn't really one of them. Once you were captured by Indians and returned to white society, you couldn't really say, "I wanted to stay." You'd be reviled by your own society, and it was just unladylike. But, despite the fact that it was socially suicidal to be an "Indian lover" in that period, Oatman made it as clear as she could that she was among family with the Mohaves.

DJL: Are meanings attached to specific Mohave tattoos? For example, Olive had tattoos on her arms as well as on her face. At home we have a lithograph of a Richard Kern painting of the Mohave village, from the Sitgreaves expedition.[15] In the drawing the women have some simple facial tattoos, but they have no tattoos on their arms. Did the different tattoos mean different things?

MM: The tattoos were largely decorative, not symbolic, and the shape of the face determined the design. For example, they valued a long face, so someone with a long face was given vertical lines to make it appear even longer. As for the arm tattoos, I think they came as a package with the chin tattoos, but the arm tattoos were only for women. The arm tattoo involved either one or two vertical lines. Interestingly, the same pairing exists among the Maoris in New Zealand—chin and arm tattoos, called *moko,* though the chin tattoo was (and is—the practice continues) specific to women. The arm tattoos that I saw when I researched this there a few years ago were more complicated than simple lines.

DJL: In 1854 the Whipple railroad survey brought many whites to the Mohave area.[16] Why do you think they didn't hear about the captive girl?

MM: I've wondered about that too. Olive may have looked enough like a Mohave that they didn't notice her because she blended in. Or they may have hidden her with or without her consent. I think it's more likely that she looked like an Indian at that point and passed as one. This could easily be true, considering that when she was ransomed they thought that they had the wrong person because they thought that she *was* an Indian. She was tanned and tattooed, and they'd dyed her hair with mesquite. But McGinty raises a very interesting point about this: she doesn't mention the Whipple party in *Captivity of the Oatman Girls;* nor does she mention being away from the Mohaves for any period. It's a vacuum in her story, which suggests she left it out for a reason: she had a chance to reconnect with whites and didn't take it. If she'd been hidden against her will, it would have fit with her story and added even more drama; if not, she wouldn't have advertised that she stayed willingly.

DJL: It appears that you believe that she didn't want to return.

MM: Olive was with the Mohaves for four years, a fairly long time, at a formative age. Joseph Heard's book *White into Red* tries to quantify the reasons for and patterns of assimilation by white captives into Indian culture, using age, culture, education, and so forth as variables. No clear pattern emerges, but Heard does say that after age twelve most captives increasingly resisted assimilation. Oatman was thirteen when she was taken, but she had four years with the Mohaves, lost her native language almost completely, and believed she had no family left. She didn't know that her brother Lorenzo had survived the massacre. All that combined with the fact that the Mohaves treated her as family—her Mohave mother wailed when she was sent back—leads me to believe that she was fully acculturated and didn't want to return.

DJL: Tell us what you've learned about her return to American society.

MM: The striking thing to me is to think of her coming out of this beautiful valley where she lived with the Mohaves, fishing, swimming, and, except when the drought occurred, enjoying a rich life. Then she was marched to Fort Yuma, a desolate, understaffed, and undersupplied army outpost with almost no women, except prostitutes, that was blazing hot and sinfully ugly. There's a double irony here: this was the site of both her return to "civilization" and Bashan, the area that Brewster had so romanticized.

DJL: When she got to El Monte, California, didn't the hotel keeper there and the cousins from Oregon compete for the right to tell her story?

MM: After Olive's ransom, her cousin Harvey Oatman went to El Monte, where she was living with some of the members of the original wagon train, the Thompsons. There wasn't a struggle about who would tell her story but rather about who she should stay with—Ira Thompson didn't see why Harvey just appeared on the scene when he hadn't tried to find Olive or help Lorenzo previously. But Harvey persuaded Olive and Lorenzo to go back with him to Phoenix in Oregon Territory. That was where they met Stratton. It was a Deadwood-type town that had just been started. Harvey was running a hotel called the Oatman Hotel, which must have been pretty flashy for its era. There's a local diary that describes a light show there where images of Europe were projected on the walls of the hotel by burning lime—thus the term "limelight."[17] Apparently this was a big draw for the hotel at the time. Harvey had four children. His wife died giving birth to the fifth, and then he just disappeared. He took off and nobody ever knew what happened to him, though he turned up years later in Arizona to mark the Oatman Massacre gravesite.

I found a letter sent to Olive and Lorenzo, after they left Phoenix with Stratton, from Harvey's brother Harrison, who later became a real estate mogul in Oregon. He sounds like a real character; he is very funny. He writes about living in his cabin when his wife was sick and was staying with relatives and friends. He gives a great blow-by-blow of what kind of bumbling bachelor he was without his wife there. He describes how he put his dishes in the sink and only washed them at the end of the week. It's fun to get a little taste of what this character was like. He calls them "Len n Olive," and the letters indicate that they were all close. The Oatmans had apparently chided him for not writing, and he responded with something like "Let's not accuse each other, let's express the same feelings in writing we expressed in person." And he tells Olive, "I love you as devotedly as any brother loved a sister."[18]

DJL: Have you found new sources of information on Olive's later life?

MM: I've stumbled on a few—mostly journals and letters. The most notable new piece of information that I've found is on Stratton. It turns out that, at the end of Stratton's life when he was back East and preaching in Massachusetts, he was at the center of a scandal in which he was charged with both bribery and adultery, though the charges weren't proved. He left his post as minister after this accusation was batted around for two years. Later he went crazy and died in an asylum. You have to wonder what his relationship with Olive was like.

DJL: Especially when they were on the lecture circuit together!

MM: Yes. And Olive lived with his family for a while on the East Coast. They stopped communicating about the time she got married.

DJL: We have seen a transcript of the lecture that Olive gave that is in the San Bernardino County Museum.[19] Do you have transcripts of other lectures?

MM: As far as I know, just that one transcript exists. Bowling Green University has the original, in her handwriting. I got a copy of it and compared it with the transcript that's floating around, which is probably the same one that you saw. I was hoping that there was something in the original that wasn't transcribed, but the transcription looks pretty true.

You can see Stratton's hand in the lecture notes and in the book. He was very flowery in his speech. There's a clear distinction between the tone that Olive used in her letters, which is flat and declarative, and the tone she used in the lectures and in the book. Stratton really manipulated her story and injected his own style into it.

DJL: In Lynn Galvin's article "Cloudwoman: The Life of Olive Oatman," there's a photograph of Olive where she's wearing a dress that has the same markings as her tattoos. She must have done this to advertise her lectures.

MM: I think that reinforces the notion that, with Stratton, Olive promoted her story; the dress was clearly designed to mimic the tattoo pattern. You can see in the lecture transcripts how she withheld information to entice people to buy her book. She'd say, "You can read more about this episode in my book." They sold photos of her at her lectures. There are enough photos of her around today to suggest that she must have sold a lot of them on the lecture circuit. A few years ago one sold on eBay for over $2,000.

My theory is that until she met her husband she worked with Stratton and was willing to promote her story because that was her meal ticket. As a single woman with no family, she had no other way to provide for herself and her marriage prospects were poor because of her tattoo. Certainly Lorenzo was having trouble supporting himself. He was unskilled and had never finished school, and he also had no family. He was just doing manual labor while she was in captivity. You see in their early letters how fractured their writing skills were.

DJL: Where was Lorenzo while she was on the lecture circuit?

MM: He started out with her on the East Coast then went back to Illinois and married a girl who lived on the farm next to the aunt and uncle that they had stayed with earlier, the Abbotts. I think it became clear that Olive was the star. There was at least one lecture where Lorenzo was along or where he spoke, but he dropped out early on and went back to the farm, married, and moved to Nebraska. And he opened a hotel. Olive was with Stratton for seven years while she was lecturing, from 1857 to 1865, and then she met John Fairchild.[20] They married and moved to Texas. So the coincidence seems to be that her lecture career ended when she got married. And her husband burned all the copies of her books that he could get his hands on.

DJL: Lorenzo's hotel was in Red Cloud, Nebraska, wasn't it? That was where Willa Cather lived.[21]

MM: Apparently Cather was a customer. Somebody sent me a bill or receipt of hers, proving that she frequented his restaurant. I haven't been out there, and I don't know whether there is anything in her letters or journals about this.

DJL: Is there any correspondence between Lorenzo and Olive when he was in Red Cloud and she was in Texas?

MM: There are few if any letters from him in Nebraska. I saw one she wrote to one of her relatives, complaining that Lorenzo didn't write and saying that she hadn't heard from him in two years. I don't know what he was up to, but there is an unconfirmed bit of gossip that I want to pursue: Doris Clark claims that Lorenzo had a secret family. She says that she has tracked down relatives who are descended from Lorenzo through another woman, other than his wife, Edna. He and Edna had four children, but only one survived. Clark says that she has interviewed women who say Lorenzo was their grandfather or great-grandfather.

DJL: And does she say that this relationship happened in Illinois or in Nebraska?

MM: In Nebraska. That may explain why he was out of touch with Olive.

DJL: There is an original letter from Lorenzo to his family members in Illinois in the El Monte Historical Society Museum. Have you seen this letter or others like it?

MM: Yes, I've seen some that he wrote after the massacre, telling what happened. I find it really sad. He says things like "You haven't written me." I can't figure out why the family wouldn't have tried to help him after the massacre. He spent all those years in California and nobody from the family ever came after him, the poor guy.

DJL: We've heard that when Olive was in Texas she wore a veil to cover her face. Is there any truth to this?

MM: Yes. Even in her obituary they mention that she wore a little veil.

DJL: Did her husband try to have her tattoos removed?

MM: People have said that, but I haven't seen any convincing evidence of it in writing. I think this is just a rumor. I don't think that in those days they would believe that they could remove a tattoo.

DJL: Did Mamie, Olive's adopted daughter, die shortly after Olive?

MM: No, she lived into old age. Olive died in 1903. John Fairchild lived a few years after Olive and then died in bed. That's when Mamie moved to Michigan, where she got married and started her own life. Mamie had a daughter whom she named Olive, but sadly the child died within a couple days of birth.

DJL: Earlier you mentioned that Olive suffered depression later in her life. Where did you hear about that?

MM: In her letters to her aunt and uncle, Asa and Sarah Abbott, in Illinois. They became like parents to her after her ransom. She corresponded with them over the years, saying things like "I'm so nervous. I've been feeling badly lately. I have terrible headaches." And she mentioned that her eyes hurt. Some of the letters have news in them about Mamie. In one she tells about Mamie's sixteenth birthday and her piano lessons. There was one point when Olive left Texas and went to a spa in Canada, the Springbank Hotel. It was a combination hospital/spa where they used mineral cures. She went for months, for some kind of therapy, and she was actually bedridden there for a month. All this came from a letter from her husband to her aunt and uncle, saying she was going and that she would be okay. But it clearly wasn't just a vacation. It was some sort of treatment she was undergoing, possibly a "rest cure."

I've tried really hard to find correspondence that would shed more light on Olive's personality, but so far I haven't succeeded. Olive sent a photo to a friend named Abi Colver in Phoenix, Oregon, addressing her as "my sister," so they must have been close, but I haven't found any return correspondence. There was someone in Oregon who said that Olive looked wrecked, that she looked much older than her years, and that she never smiled. But that is inconsistent with what other people said. In most of the photos she looks fine, if a bit stern. Although the tattoo was obviously a bizarre marking, especially in its day, aside from that Olive looked like any girl or young woman of her era, at least to me, in the photos that I've seen. But psychologically, she was clearly in pain.

DJL: Wasn't this kind of stress common for captives who returned to white society? We've recently read the book *Comanche Bondage*, about two women who were captured in Texas in the 1830s.[22] When the women were returned, they both soon died, presumably due to the hardships they had suffered.

MM: I know it is the case for some of the women captives chronicled in Derounian-Stodola's *Women's Indian Captivity Narratives*. There are definitely a few women in there who were never normal or happy again when they returned. And in some instances it was because they didn't want to return, but in others it seems as though they had trouble adjusting or had post-traumatic stress. Some of these cases are documented in Heard's *White into Red*. Some never readjusted. One, who couldn't even remember white culture because she'd been taken so young, adjusted with no problem. Some went back and forth between the two cultures. Some became Indian haters. One readjusted but claimed he loved his Indian mother better than the white mother he was returned to. There's no pattern, except that people who lived longer among Indians generally had more trouble reassimilating.

To me, Olive is such a tragic character, even though she's a survivor. She kept losing family over and over again. First, her family was killed on the trip west. Then the Yavapais took her. After a year, she was traded to the Mohaves. She lost her sister Mary Ann there, which was another major adaptation. And then four years later she was ransomed back and she had to leave her Mohave family behind. She wrote letters to her aunt in Illinois saying that she mourned her lost mother, but you can imagine that she probably mourned the loss of her Mohave mother and sister as well.

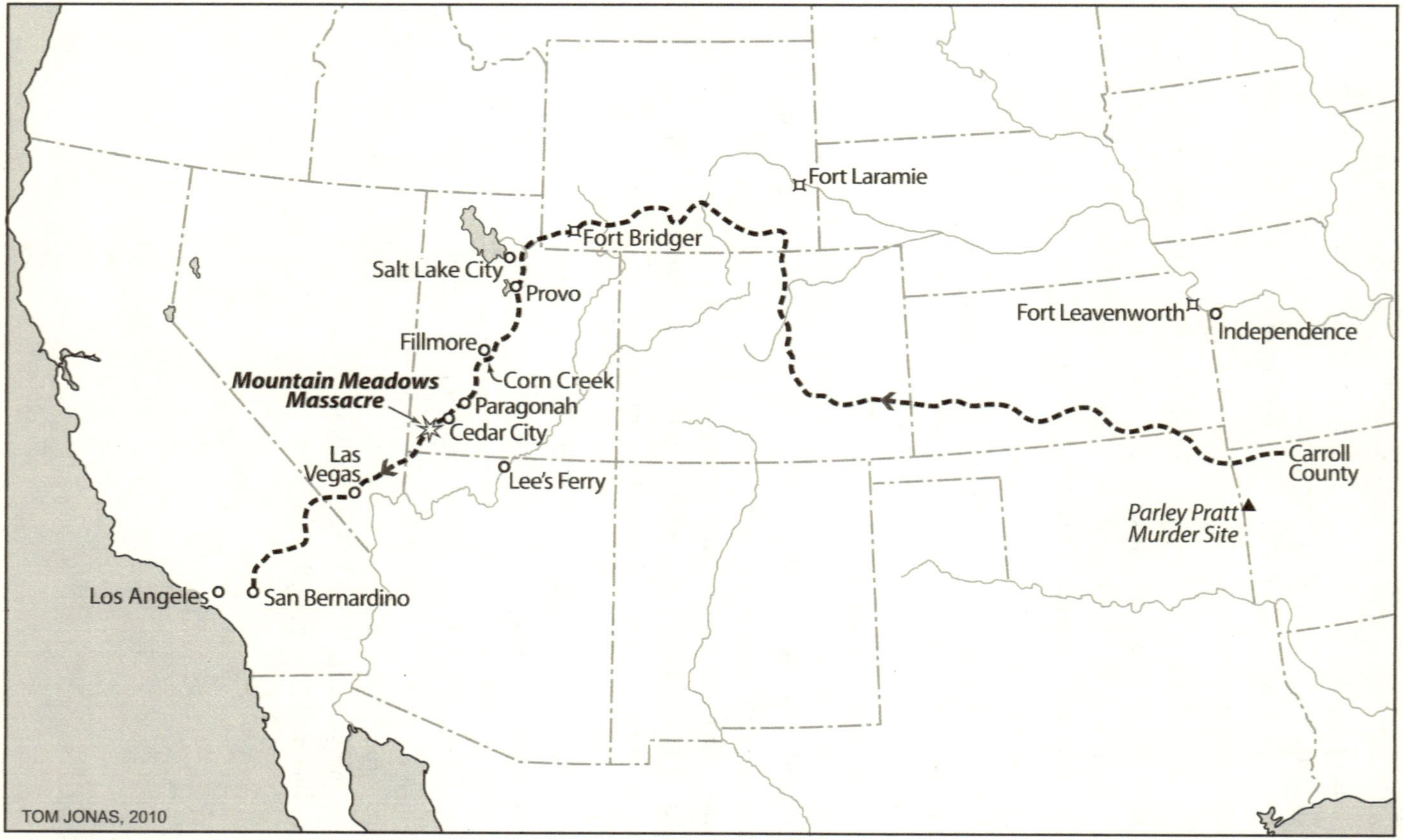

The route followed by the Fancher party from Carroll County, Arkansas, to the Mountain Meadows Massacre site in southwestern Utah. The eastern portion of the route coincides with the Cherokee Trail. The trail from Mountain Meadows to San Bernardino was the Salt Lake–Los Angeles wagon road, which coincided with the Old Spanish Trail. Adapted from Bagley, *Blood of the Prophets.*

CHAPTER 3

The Mountain Meadows Massacre

An Interview with Will Bagley

THE FANCHER-BAKER PARTY consisted of emigrants from Arkansas who were traveling to California in 1857. At the Mountain Meadows site in southern Utah, they were massacred by a party of Mormons from nearby settlements. This was the most violent incident associated with the emigrant trails.

Throughout the summer of 1857 the Mormon settlers in Utah were anticipating the arrival of federal troops under the command of Albert Sydney Johnston. The troops were sent to establish the authority of the U.S. government in Utah Territory, in the face of what was perceived to be Mormon defiance. The Mormon citizens feared another replay of the events in Missouri and Illinois that had led to their exile to Utah.

An unusually large wagon train, the Fancher-Baker party included some 130 emigrants, mostly from Arkansas, over a thousand head of cattle, and 200 horses. They arrived in Utah in the late summer of 1857 and decided to take a southern route to California, the wagon road from Salt Lake City to Los Angeles. As they traveled through Provo, Nephi, and Fillmore, they encountered hostility from the local Mormons, who sought to prevent them from grazing their cattle and refused to sell them provisions. The Mormons also resented the emigrants because Parley Pratt, a beloved Mormon leader, had recently been murdered in Arkansas.

When the Fancher party arrived in Cedar City on Friday, September 4, the Mormon settlers in the area refused to sell them food. The caravan then reached the Old Spanish Trail (their road to southern California), went through the village of Pinto, and passed by Jacob Hamblin's crude summer ranch house on Meadow Creek at the northern end of Mountain Meadows. The weary emigrants intended to graze and rest their stock at the meadows before undertaking the long stretch of desert that lay ahead.

On the morning of September 7, 1857, Mormons from Cedar City and nearby areas disguised themselves as Indians and opened fire on the Fancher camp from a nearby arroyo together with their Southern Paiute allies. After a four-day battle and siege, the Mormons, under the leadership of John D. Lee, pretended to come as rescuers under a flag of truce. All the members of the wagon train were marched into the field about a mile from their campsite and—with the exception of seventeen children under the age of seven—were massacred. These seventeen children were taken into Mormon homes. The remains of the victims were hurriedly thrown into shallow depressions and ravines and subsequently scattered over the immediate area by storms and wild animals.

On May 20, 1859, Major James Henry Carleton and his men, who were sent to investigate the massacre, buried bones from thirty-four skeletons in a grave and erected a rude conical monument. It was surmounted by a red cedar cross with the carved inscription: "Vengeance is mine: I will repay, saith the Lord." The U.S. Army forces at Camp Floyd helped return the seventeen children to relatives in Arkansas.

Investigation of the massacre was delayed by the Civil War. After several abortive attempts to bring the leaders of the massacre to justice, John D. Lee was arrested, tried, sentenced to death, and executed in 1877.

John D. Lee in late 1857, shortly after the Mountain Meadows Massacre. Courtesy of the Utah State Historical Society.

Will Bagley is an independent historian living in Salt Lake City, Utah. For a number of years, he wrote the "History Matters" column for the *Salt Lake Tribune.* Since 1997 he has been series editor of the Arthur H. Clark Company's *Kingdom of the West: The Mormons and the American Frontier,* a prize-winning multivolume documentary history currently consisting of ten published volumes. In 2003 Bagley's book *Blood of the Prophets*, which is the topic of this interview, won the best book award from Westerners International, the Caughey Prize from the Western History Association, and the Caroline Bancroft History Prize from the Denver Public Library.

Blood of the Prophets was followed by *Innocent Blood: Essential Narratives of the Mountain Meadows Massacre* (2008), a collection of key primary sources about the massacre that Bagley co-edited with David Bigler. Bagley's current project is a four-volume series titled *Overland West: The Story of the Oregon and California Trails.* The first of four volumes, *So Rugged and Mountainous: Blazing the Trails to Oregon and California, 1840–1848,* was published in 2010. The Utah Arts Council recently awarded its publication prize to the manuscript of the second volume, *With Golden Visions Bright before Them: The Oregon & California Trails and the Creation of the Mining West, 1849–1852.* Bagley hopes to complete the series by 2012.

Bagley describes himself as a "heritage Mormon" whose ancestors were among the early pioneers to Utah. We interviewed him in a telephone conversation between Salt Lake City, Utah, and Irvine, California, on October 22, 2005.

DJL (Deborah and Jon Lawrence): What inspired you to take on Mountain Meadows as a book project?

WB (Will Bagley): I was hired to do it. I had been reluctant to tackle the subject because I knew that the sources were so problematic. In fact, a lot of the so-called evidence about the massacre was actually *created* years later, while solid contemporary evidence was destroyed, so the problems with the evidence were immense. In April 1995 an ad appeared in the *Salt Lake Tribune* looking for a historian to do two years' research on the Fancher party. Thirty-five people applied for it, and I got it. It's one of the reasons that I consider myself the world's luckiest historian.

When I began the research I thought it would be very difficult, if not impossible, to go beyond the conclusions that Juanita Brooks reached.[1] The summary of her conclusions in her book *The Mountain Meadows Massacre* is really a masterpiece. Mormon historians like to say that she vindicated Brigham Young, but she did nothing of the kind—she said Brigham Young and George A. Smith "set up social conditions that made it possible." All the heated debate over whether Brigham Young was directly responsible for the atrocity is in many ways a distraction: once you determine who was morally responsible for the crime, what else do you need to know? Brooks concluded that the evidence indicated Young had not ordered it and would have stopped it if he could, but she stressed that this was based on the evidence available to her at that time, whereas the LDS church had hidden an enormous amount of material from her. As Brooks turned up more evidence on her own, she held Brigham Young directly responsible for the massacre. She believed that "John D. Lee would make it to heaven before Brigham Young."[2]

But I still thought that it would be very difficult to push the story beyond two obvious interpretations. One, to put it quite simply, is that it was a conspiracy to murder and that the Fancher party was doomed from the moment it entered Utah. The subsequent cover-up and all the lying and obfuscation about the crime certainly support this conclusion. The other interpretation is that it was simply one damn thing after another. I'm very much a one-damn-thing-after-another historian: events often cascade out of control and what starts out seemingly with a clear objective often winds up a complete muddle. There's certainly evidence to support both arguments. I didn't believe that I would find definitive evidence that would allow me to pick between the two alternatives. And I knew that people would say, "All the evidence against Brigham Young is circumstantial. There's no smoking gun; there's nothing that *proves* anything." Well, in fact, you wouldn't expect that. The orders for such actions were generally couched in either code words or very ambiguous phrasing. I certainly didn't expect to find orders from Brigham Young to kill the Fancher party. So I really was very surprised when I learned how Eleanor Pratt got to Utah,[3] and suddenly it was clear to me what had happened.

DJL: At the OCTA [Oregon-California Trails Association] 2005 Conference in Salt Lake City, you stressed the importance of the fact that Eleanor McLean

Pratt was rushed to Salt Lake in time for the Pioneer Day celebration by none other than Porter Rockwell.[4] Can you expand on this: how does it function as compelling evidence?

WB: That the circumstances of her arrival were so effectively hidden for generations convinced me her presence in Utah was the catalyst for the Mountain Meadows Massacre. The fact that it was Porter Rockwell who brought her to Utah was buried so deeply that even my dear friend Harold Schindler, who spent forty years turning up everything available on "Port," never learned about it.[5] But when I saw an entry in Elias Smith's 1857 journal that noted Rockwell's arrival on July 23, 1857, with the widow Pratt, I was amazed. All of a sudden I knew what had happened. Although I'm very much a one-damn-thing-after-another historian, the discovery that such a telling fact had been so carefully suppressed convinced me that the massacre *was* a conspiracy. I'm sure the Mormon church's historians will argue that Eleanor's arrival was an insignificant detail, but it wasn't: it gave away the ball game.

DJL: So the compelling evidence is not simply that Rockwell brought her to Utah but that they covered it up.

WB: At the trial of John Peter Zenger in 1735, which helped establish a free press in America, Andrew Hamilton made an astute observation: "The suppressing of evidence ought always to be taken for the strongest evidence."[6] Why do you suppose Mormon diarists tore so many pages from their 1857 journals? Why are so many documents and letters missing from Mormon records? Somehow I don't think it's because they vindicate Brigham Young in a case that has his fingerprints all over it.

So it's the cover-up. And that, I think, is the key to really understanding the Mountain Meadows Massacre. You can support either thesis; but when historians try to come up with an interpretation of history, it should be the one that is simplest and answers the questions most consistently. Well, the thesis that the Mountain Meadows Massacre was a calculated, ordered mass murder is easy to support because all the subsequent actions fit that pattern. But the thesis that, no, one thing led to another, Brigham didn't want it to happen, and he sort of sent orders down to stop it, but then afterward he had to protect the guys who had done it raises question after question. And the enormous lie that was manufactured to protect Brigham Young is an indictment all by itself. His alibi is just too complicated and convoluted—and often silly—to be believable.

DJL: Since you wrote the book, have you learned anything significantly new about the history of the massacre?

WB: I've been working on a documentary history, *Innocent Blood: Essential Narratives of the Mountain Meadows Massacre*, with David Bigler.[7] He's indexing it right now, so it will be out this fall if not sooner. New materials—newspaper reports, items hidden in previously unavailable Mormon documents, and the sudden opening of the Brigham Young Collection at LDS Archives—have produced a lot of surprises. We've turned up new information on some of the story's most colorful characters, such as songwriter George Armstrong Hicks and Montana pioneer James Gemmell.[8] Most surprisingly, we've come up with direct evidence of the systematic bribery and corruption that Mormon officials used to obstruct justice. We arranged the documents in chronological order, and it is remarkable how unambiguous that makes the story. If you look at the sequence of how the story grew and was manipulated and how the cover-up worked, you begin to see the actual machinations that made it happen. It makes it very difficult to buy the "Well, we'll never know what happened" approach. The documents show that what happened was no mystery.

DJL: So it's not so much that you've got new documents but that you put them together in a more compelling way.

WB: No, the book includes much material that was unknown or suppressed before David and I started working on the awful tale, and it presents several Paiute voices that have never been heard before, so it will be new to most historians. We are presenting the hard evidence itself, rather than trying to write an interpretive history where you have to adhere to a strict set of rules, acknowledge other possibilities, and question any kind of a certainty. I'm very pleased that the hostile reactions to *Blood of the Prophets* validate that I did achieve my goal, which was to tell the story and let it speak for itself. I said in the preface that I would hold my own personal opinions until the very end, and I think that the conclusions expressed in the afterword to *Blood of the Prophets* are more than justified by the evidence. It's the simplest explanation of the crime. And I defy anybody to come up with one that is more consistent and doesn't require ignoring critical evidence.[9]

DJL: Carleton's report seems to have the basic outlines of what happened.[10] Given official prevarication and the veil of silence surrounding the murders at the meadows, how did Carleton reach such a comprehensive overview so early, and what were his sources?

WB: Hal Schindler once said to me, "Murder will out." You don't commit a mass murder and have everybody remain silent about it. It was such a horrific act that there were decent men who were appalled at what happened—as were the vast majority of the Mormon people. When the federal authorities showed up in southern Utah in 1859, these men confessed, telling what they had seen and done. The very best evidence that we have on the massacre comes out of the reports of Major Carleton, Marshal William Rogers, and Judge [John] Cradlebaugh, because their inquiries were the closest to the time of the massacre.[11] Eyewitness accounts by Americans passing through southern Utah in 1857 also showed up in the newspapers. If you want to know what happened at Mountain Meadows, you need to look at this early evidence. The name of John D. Lee appeared in the *New York Times* with the details of the massacre in July 1858.[12] Now, part of the Mormon explanation of the cover-up is that Brigham Young just never knew who did it or what happened. Well, if it was in the *New York Times* and was then published in Salt Lake in the *Valley Tan*, it's silly to pretend that he didn't know what was happening.

DJL: Did Carleton and Cradlebaugh cite their sources?

WB: Carleton named names, and Cradlebaugh named his sources when doing so wouldn't get them killed. He indicated that most of the men who confessed to participating were so terrified that they came in the middle of the night when they hoped they wouldn't be seen. Some men also came up from the south to Camp Floyd, the army camp; they seem to have brought some of the first reports. It's not clear whether they participated in the massacre, but some of the informants did. It was foolish of the Mormon leaders to believe that they could keep such a secret. It was too horrific an act and there were too many decent people involved for them to keep this dark and evil secret forever.

DJL: Lee's *Mormonism Unveiled* is a fascinating account of the early history of the church, the kinds of religious experience common to LDS and members of other churches of that era, and early Mormon history (Haun's Mill, Nauvoo). At the same time, Lee obviously distorts his own culpability at Mountain Meadows. How did you use such information?

WB: Lee's *Confession* is really two books. Lee's autobiography, which only runs up to 1848, is one of the most reliable and excellent sources on early Mormonism. There are few other documents that capture the feelings and the passions of these people.

DJL: He even he talks about the Mormon culpability in the Missouri "Mormon Wars."[13]

WB: And his *own* culpability. [*Laughs*] I stand in awe of the *Confession of John D. Lee.* Here's a book in which the protagonist admits that he engineered the murder of 120 people, most of them women and children. He accepts responsibility for running the show. But at the same time he somehow manages to make you feel sorry for him. In all of Lee's writings, right down to his journals, it's always, "Poor, pitiful me. I'm such a nice guy, and the world just treats me badly." [*Laughs*] "People are always taking advantage of me. Nobody appreciates my true righteousness." It's comical—or at least very black humor—if you step back and look at it.

DJL: You suggested that the second book starts in 1848. Did his lawyer play a big role in editing that part of the autobiography?

WB: That's quite controversial, but I don't believe it for a minute. There's no break in style and I believe that the story in *Life and Confession* is John D. Lee's story—a lot of it's a lie, but it's the lie that Lee settled on after trying out many alternatives. The notion that it was all made up and inserted by William Bishop is contradicted by the surviving evidence.[14] Juanita Brooks also believed that Lee wrote the massacre account. Apparently the manuscripts were destroyed in the San Francisco earthquake, so the best evidence that would let us settle the question definitively no longer exists. But there were people at the time who, in response to the charges that Bishop had written it, did look at the manuscript and compare it to the finished book; they said that the confession was in John D. Lee's handwriting. And as the *New York Times* commented when it reviewed the book, it was "hastily put together, and has every mark of being the work of an uncultivated mind, but its very roughness only adds to the credibility of what it vouches for."[15]

DJL: Could you clarify the distinction between the pre-1848 and post-1848 parts of the book?

WB: The pre-1848 material is not about mass murder; it is Lee simply telling the chronicle of his righteous work for the Kingdom of God. He ran out of time and wrote his account of the massacre, with a few reports of his life in Utah, not long before his execution, and he wrote several different versions of it. I was able to turn up two basic newspaper accounts, both of which differ in slight but significant ways from the one that was published in the book in about May 1877.

The book's purpose was to create a story that portrayed Lee as a sympathetic, even heroic, victim. And to do that, he could not admit the most significant fact about the massacre: that it was organized and executed by the Mormons under the direct command of John D. Lee. If Lee had told the truth and said, "Oh yeah, me and my friends went out and recruited the Paiutes, then we attacked the party and killed them all," it would have been an invitation for a lynching.

Lee had a different purpose: he wanted to shift blame to anyone else who was available. Partly, he shifted blame to George A. Smith and Brigham Young, but the key victims of his blame shifting were the Southern Paiutes. Now, in 1876 and 1877, when he was being tried, there was a tremendous fear and hysteria about Indians in the United States. Right before Lee's first trial, Custer had died at Little Bighorn. But the notion that the Paiutes could attack and overwhelm a wagon train, and in the meantime intimidate their Mormon neighbors into doing something the Mormons didn't want to do, is simply preposterous. It denies the nature of the Paiute people, their style of warfare, and the basic power equation between the Mormons and the Paiutes. The Mountain Meadows Massacre was not caused or directed by the Paiutes. It was an operation organized, orchestrated, and executed by Mormons.

Lee also tried to blame the crime on the victims, by suggesting that their atrocious behavior brought it on them. No one outside of Utah believed that the emigrants had poisoned pools, wells, springs, flowing creeks, and ox carcasses when the stories appeared shortly after the massacre. When the first report appeared less than a month after the murders, the *Los Angeles Star* wrote, "We can scarcely believe that a party traveling along a highway would act in the manner described, that is to poison the carcass of an ox, and also the water, thus endangering the lives of those who were coming after them."[16]

As I began looking closely at the "Evil Emigrant Stories," as I call them, they became increasingly silly—especially the ones invented years after the fact. I once heard a Mormon historian do a paper trying to prove that the Fancher party included the Missouri Wildcats. This relied on Thomas Cropper's reminiscence, which was written *seventy years* after the event.[17] The memoir, which is quoted by Brooks, described an event that led to the Gunnison Massacre in 1853, not the Mountain Meadows Massacre four years later.[18] So it was clear in this particular case that it was a conflation. All the conflicts that had happened in southern Utah between Mormons and emigrant parties—and there were many of them—were conflated and tacked onto the Fancher party. Unfortunately, most of the contemporary record of what the party actually experienced was destroyed. The emigrants' documents were destroyed in the massacre, and the Mormon journals that would have documented their presence were destroyed. David Bigler found the only one that specifically mentions the Fancher party, the Pitchforth diary.[19] All the rest of the stories about the evil emigrants were concocted. The Missouri Wildcats do not appear in the historical record until 1873. Believe it or not, most of the horrific stories of the emigrants' behavior date from the 1890s. This is not credible historical evidence.

The new materials that surprised me most were the narratives of the surviving children. The best of them is by Nancy Saphrona Huff, who was five or six years old when the massacre happened. Her account was published in 1875, which means that the huge publicity from Lee's trials and execution had little chance to infect her story of the massacre. You can see the influence of this publicity on the stories of the other survivors. But Huff's version is simple and direct and powerful. As I look at the children's narratives, they have something that none of the accounts of the perpetrators, or of those that were making up excuses, had. They have consistency. Virtually every one of the survivors mentions seeing "Indians" go to the creek at Hamblin's ranch, wash off their paint, and become white again.[20] For me that was one of the most surprising and satisfying products of my research. It gives voice to these people. It provides evidence to the surviving families that their kin had done nothing wrong but show up in the wrong place at the wrong time.

DJL: We agree. We think that one of the strong points of your book is the sympathy that you show for the Fanchers.

WB: And I hope that there is also sympathy for the perpetrators. One element of the story that I was very surprised and pleased to be able to present was the letters from the murderers themselves, trying to find some sort of spiritual solace. George Spencer, who became a schoolteacher in St. George, wrote an impassioned letter to a church leader in southern Utah: it wound up in the Brigham Young Collection. In it he pleaded for spiritual advice and help. I later learned from Ken Sleight, a descendant of Spencer who is a legendary character on the Colorado River and is the model for Seldom Seen Smith in *The Monkey Wrench Gang,* that Spencer killed himself.[21] These men were essentially thrown away. They'd done the bidding of their leaders, but they were betrayed and abandoned.

So I hope that the book does justice to three groups of people who have been vilified and abused unjustly—the victims themselves, the Paiute nation, and the decent men who got caught up in this event and followed orders, sincerely believing that they were doing God's work.

DJL: We are curious as to why the Fanchers were so unvigilant when they arrived at Mountain Meadows. Didn't they face a lot of conflict before arriving there that would have put them on their guard?

WB: The contemporary record makes it clear that there were conflicts over grass, which would be absolutely credible because of what we know about overland travel and conditions in Utah. Every party that went through southern Utah had a hard time. The journals very consistently express relief to get out of Utah, especially when they went through southern Utah, because the hostility was so blatant and the government was so authoritarian. Many emigrants commented on how decent the individual Mormons themselves were but complained about how the authorities would use laws to run the equivalent of a frontier speed trap. People could be arrested for swearing on the territorial road or for letting their animals graze on private ground or even on public ground. There were many, many ways that the Mormons would extort money out of visitors, and they applied them very cleverly. So the conflicts were much more extensive than the Mormon records might pretend.

DJL: Given the hostility they faced in Utah, why do you think that the members of the Fancher party were relaxed enough at Mountain Meadows that they didn't even bother to circle their wagons or post scouts in the area? The Mormons were close enough to hide in the surrounding bushes and watch the Arkansans set up their camp.

WB: That was something that puzzled me very much. How do you explain the fact that the Fanchers hadn't even formed a wagon corral? It led me to do something I'm very reluctant to do, which is to look at the facts and then to speculate. And I'm very adverse to speculating. There are real problems in figuring out how the massacre happened. As I got more and more into this research, I learned that the Mormons' initial plan was not to attack at Mountain Meadows but rather to attack the train as it was making the descent from the Santa Clara plateau down into Santa Clara Canyon. You can still see today where the old wagon trail went down the hillside; it's very steep and treacherous. I believe that if they'd carried out their plan and attacked the train when it was strung out in that situation, they could have started with a party at either end; by the time the two attacking parties got to the middle, there would have been no survivors who could have given an account. Why did Lee decide to abandon that plan and do something else? And why would the Fanchers not have organized some sort of defensive camp?

Another question was, when did the Fancher party *get* to Mountain

Meadows? In the Mormon accounts, the Fanchers arrived there several days before the attack. I'm not sure whether this inaccuracy was because people's memories were bad or whether it's another diversion inserted into the historical record. But, in tracking the chronology of the Fancher party's locations, there are two reliable sources on where they were when. On August 15 they were just north of Nephi, Utah, which we get from Samuel Pitchforth's diary; ten days later, on August 25, they had traveled about eighty miles south to Corn Creek near the Indian farm. They were traveling very slowly: they were going about eight miles a day. So we can see how slowly they had been traveling from Salt Lake. That would be consistent with their desire to get their cattle ready to make the crossing of the Mojave Desert and with the fact that they didn't want to get there in September when it was too hot. The later they reached the Mojave—ideally in late October—the more advantageous it would be for them. Based on that, I tried to figure out where they camped as they went down to southern Utah. Despite the very contradictory and sometimes dishonest reports of when the Fanchers arrived in southern Utah, I concluded that Jessie N. Smith, who was a Mormon official, was accurate in saying that they arrived at Red Creek [present-day Paragonah] on September 3.

The chronology really is an important way to interpret all this. David Bigler did the first real analysis of "when they got where." A critical question is when the Fancher party arrived in Cedar City. We have many reports that the Fanchers were in Cedar City on a Friday. That tracks to September 4. Cedar City is thirty-five miles from Mountain Meadows. These people, after they camped with George A. Smith and his Indian allies on August 25, suddenly upped their pace from about eight miles a day to about twelve and a half miles a day—and that last push was even faster.

DJL: They were frightened.

WB: They seemed to be very concerned about what they had seen. When they got to Cedar City, there clearly was some sort of conflict. What exactly it was, I was unable to tell from any of the sources. The Mormon accounts of the Fanchers' depredations in Cedar City are told years later and are completely inconsistent; nobody tells the same story. I think the Mormon authorities took hostile action that created some sort of conflict between the emigrants and the locals, but even the LDS church's historians now admit that, whatever it was, it was over in a few hours. The trouble could have been over the grass, or where they could camp, or swearing. But then what happened the next two days? On Saturday they pushed hard to get as far away from Cedar City as they could, and on Sunday they made a second big push so that in two to three days they went thirty-five miles. For a well-organized train in good terrain that would not be a hard pace, but this was tough terrain, and it's clear that they were making a special effort. I believe that this effort is the key to understanding why there was no wagon corral. Groups of wagons pulled into Mountain Meadows late on Sunday, so that it was dark before everybody was into camp. They felt that at last they had gotten away, that they were now outside of the main Mormon settlements. They must have felt that they were beyond the main threat. Because otherwise they would have made the extra effort to fort up. When Lee saw how vulnerable they were, he changed his battle plan and attacked the next morning.

DJL: You state in your preface that the massacre is a "watershed event" and the most disturbing episode in the history of the LDS church. Yet there seems to be much in the story that is relevant to the more general history of the trails. Can you speak to this?

WB: It's the singularity of Mountain Meadows that makes it such a difficult event for historians. Historians are very reluctant to criticize an ethnic group or especially a religion. The Mormons had such a hard history of being unfairly treated and even persecuted that it is difficult for historians, especially non-Mormon historians, to step back and say, "This conflict really was about religion and politics." Nevertheless, the Mormons did something on the trail that nobody else ever did. The Mountain Meadows Massacre couldn't have happened anyplace else; where else in the West would a substantial body of white people dress up as Indians and attack a wagon train? There were white criminals who disguised themselves as Indians, but those were simply criminal operations.[22] Furthermore, the action was backed up by the Nauvoo Legion, the territorial militia. That's what makes it difficult to relate Mountain Meadows to the broader trail experience.

On the other hand, it's easy to appreciate how important the Mormons were in the history of the trails. Once the Mormons were in Utah, they provided huge advantages as well as big problems to overland emigrants. They offered travelers the chance to take a break. And, for the first time, there was a place on the trail where emigrants could resupply. Remember, when early emigrant trains tried to buy flour at Fort Bridger or Fort Hall, or even Fort Laramie, the traders would just laugh at them because they didn't *have* any flour. But once you had an agricultural community of very hardworking, determined pioneers in the Salt Lake Valley, they were able to provide pretty much anything the emigrants needed. It was a symbiotic relationship. The Mormons arguably couldn't have succeeded without the physical, material support that the emigration brought to them, especially in 1849. Furthermore the Mormons were very good pioneers; they opened up several trails and were very significant in the evolution of the overland wagon road.

Remember, the Mormons had come to Utah to establish a Kingdom of God, an independent theocracy. The nature of their religious passions and beliefs dictated that conflict with the federal government, which had its own notions about who was going to govern the Great Basin, was inevitable, and the Mountain Meadows Massacre was the product of that collision. You can see these conflicts come to a head in 1857 when the federal government felt compelled to send the army to Utah to reassert its authority. This was a function of this confrontation—and Brigham Young's decision to close the overland road and stage a horrific Indian "massacre" is part and parcel of that struggle.[23] It's significant because it shows see how difficult it is for a democratic republic to deal with a religious theocracy. The consequences of not dealing with it can be horrific events, like the Mountain Meadows Massacre.

DJL: It also could be viewed as a precursor to the Civil War, where we fought over secession. It was really a kind of secession.

WB: Oh, it was, absolutely. I just came across a statement by Daniel Boorstin in which he calls it America's unsung and inglorious first civil war, which is exactly what it was.[24]

DJL: What new information did you get from your interviews with the descendants of the Arkansas emigrants? In what ways did they contribute to your understanding of the Fancher-Baker party?

WB: The survivors' families preserve a feeling and a passion about this that impressed me most of all. They still have a sense of loss about what happened and a bafflement as to why it happened. I once had a Fancher family member, who was a Disciple of Christ, a very devout evangelical Christian, ask me, "What did these people"—meaning the emigrants—"do wrong that God would punish them?" I said, "They didn't do anything wrong, except be in the wrong place at the wrong time." But there's still, among the descendants, a puzzlement as to how and why this could happen.

DJL: A book that we really like is Judith Freeman's *Red Water*. Based on your research, how close to reality is Judith Freeman's take on Emma, Rachel, and Ann Lee, the three narrative voices of *Red Water*?[25]

WB: I think the book is inspired. But that's not an unbiased opinion. I helped Judith with the research, and I gave her the memoir of Ann Gordge Lee (who, I like to say, was the last thirteen-year-old that John D. Lee ever married). Freeman's novel fascinates me, because, as a historian, I'm so constrained by certain rules. There are very clear boundaries that surround what we can do. Whenever you speculate, whenever you step over those boundaries, you almost always, almost inevitably, get into serious trouble. As a historian, you have to stick with the evidence. You have to seek that most consistent, dispassionate answer. But that also tends to discount a lot of life that is very hard to quantify through historical evidence: feelings, social position, the differences between men and women in the West, the complicated nature of Mormon polygamy, the realities of how life worked in America's most successful theocracy. One of the revelations in *Red Water* that I thought was most revealing was that, in the story, Ann Gordge Lee only knew how to read the Deseret alphabet, the alphabet that Brigham Young created.

DJL: We saw the alphabet at This Is the Place Heritage Park in Salt Lake City.

WB: Allegedly Brigham Young promoted it to simplify English spelling and make it easier to teach. Some of the published academic studies of the Deseret alphabet raise the possibility that it had another purpose besides simplifying spelling: it was to control what people could read. If people could only read the Deseret alphabet and if all that was published in the Deseret alphabet was the *Deseret News,* the *Book of Mormon,* and the Mormon scriptures, that would mean you wouldn't have to worry about people going off and reading a bunch of things that might disturb them or that might give them ideas that you didn't want them to have.

DJL: This comes up in academic writing?

WB: Oftentimes they'll say, "People have proposed this, but it's just not true." Well, it *is* true. Of course it's true. Brigham Young was definitely obsessed with control and power, and he didn't put all this cockamamie system together just to simplify spelling. It did have that other purpose. It's silly to ignore it. But it was only when I read Judith's use of that fact and saw how it shaped Ann Gordge Lee's world that I really came to understand what a potent interpretation it is. By creating a character that has that limitation, Judith is able to show how real it would have been. Simply to ignore that, as one of the historical alternatives, is dishonest. She also was able to capture the passions and the feelings and, more than that, the struggle between these English and American pioneers and their environment. They had come out of humid, green climates, and they were suddenly dumped in the middle of the Great Basin in one of the harshest environments in the world. It was an incredible ordeal.

DJL: Last June we visited Lee's Ferry, Arizona, where we spoke with Allen Malmquist, the U.S. Park Service interpreter who discovered the "Lead Scroll" on January 22, 2002.[26] What is your opinion regarding the authenticity of the artifact? If it is authentic, what do you think would prompt Lee to write his confession on lead rather than, say, paper?

WB: Did Allen express an opinion?

DJL: No, he did not.

WB: Well, the problem with the artifact is that it has no provenance. When I first heard the story, I thought that this was an obvious fraud. We have no explanation of how it wound up on the floor in the rat droppings. Without a good knowledge as to how it got there, it's very hard to have any sort of definitive opinion about it. But, despite my initial skepticism, when I read the text, I thought, "Oh, my God, that's John D. Lee." So far, the hard scientific analysis has shown one thing, which is that the scroll appears to be made using lead that came from a mine that closed around 1870. The mine was used again after 1980 or so, but this lead seems to be an artifact of the nineteenth century.

DJL: Mark Hofmann was very good at making historically accurate forgeries.[27]

WB: But Hofmann didn't do this; his ex-wife assured me of this. My take on the "Dead Lee Scroll" is that, if it's a fake, they'll prove it. History is too complicated to create an artifact 150 years later that doesn't include some fatal flaw. The Drake's Plate that all the experts in the 1930s authenticated didn't stand up to modern metallurgical analysis.[28] And, in fact, the Clampers, who actually perpetrated the fraud, had pretty much published and announced that they did it very soon after the joke got out of hand, if anybody had been paying attention. So if the scroll is a forgery, it is likely the forgers will be unable to keep the secret, because otherwise what's the point? If they never get credit for it, why go to all that trouble? At the same time, I think that the text sounds authentic. There are Mormon handwriting experts that disagree with me, but I think that what's on the scroll itself is exactly what John D. Lee would have wanted to leave behind. Using a metal plate is something that would be very attractive to a nineteenth-century Mormon. But until we know where it came from, well, we'll never know. One thing is, you'll never prove it's authentic. All you can do is prove that it's a fake. But if it is a fake, I think they'll prove it.

DJL: One of the most important goals of trail organizations such as the Oregon-

California Trails Association is to help preserve key trail sites. What is the status of the preservation of the Mountain Meadows site?

WB: Mountain Meadows is a critical example of how a very important historic site is being threatened by our modern consumer society. There are vacation homes going up all over it, and there may be a golf course there someday. It would be a crime against history to transform that haunted spot into another trashed American landscape. Here the nation's obligation to its past is in danger of being derailed. Part of the problem is that the subject makes the leaders of the Mormon church so nervous that they want to control it. They've done that in part by buying up a good bit of the property. They seem to have control of a significant amount of the immediate site. What they need to appreciate is that this historical site is important for reasons that extend beyond the interests of the Mormon church. If the massacre had never happened at Mountain Meadows, I think it's entirely likely it would already be a National Monument, simply because it was such a significant historical place. It was so important in the history of the Spanish Trail, in the story of the emigration to California, and in the pioneering of the Southwest. It was highly praised by John C. Frémont, had an influence on trappers and explorers, and preserves dozens if not hundreds of ancient archaeology sites. The fact that the largest violent loss of life in the history of the Oregon-California Trails took place at Mountain Meadows means that the federal government should assume responsibility for the site and should protect it and help maintain its historic integrity. The trick will be for the leaders of the LDS church to realize that it is in their best interest to have a third party manage the site. If they simply stand by and let the place be trashed, they'll look as if they're calloused and indifferent to anyone's history but their own.[29]

DJL: Do you have anything to say in conclusion?

WB: Yes. The inescapable fact about the Mountain Meadows Massacre is that there's a dark question that looms behind all these studies: "Did Brigham Young do it?" I don't think that is the most important question about the massacre. The most important question is, what can we learn from this event about human nature? For me, the most difficult question is, what makes decent men commit horrific crimes? Mountain Meadows is an especially troubling example of that because these men were so completely convinced that they were doing God's will. I gave a series of talks in Arkansas last fall and I finally came up with a statement that summarizes my conclusions: "God save us all from men doing God's work."

The Camp Grant Massacre site in recent years. Photograph by Chip Colwell-Chanthaphonh.

CHAPTER 4

The Camp Grant Massacre

An Interview with Chip Colwell-Chanthaphonh

ON APRIL 30, 1871, A VIGILANTE GROUP of approximately six Anglo-Americans and fifty Mexican Americans from Tucson, Arizona, under the leadership of William Oury and Jesús María Elías, together with nearly a hundred Tohono O'odham allies, massacred more than a hundred Pinal and Aravaipa Apache men, women, and children near Camp Grant on the San Pedro River. From eleven to thirty-five Apache children were also taken into captivity.

Under the leadership of *haské bahnzin* (Eskiminzin), these Apaches came into Camp Grant in early 1871, suing for peace. Lieutenant Royal Whitman, who was temporarily in charge at the camp, recognized that he was not authorized to make a treaty but agreed to allow the Apaches to stay near the army post as prisoners of war. By early April 1871 some five hundred Apaches were settled about five miles east of Camp Grant in a traditional Apache farming area along Aravaipa Creek. The army issued rations to these Indians on a regular basis.

Whitman reported what he was doing to General George Stoneman, commander of the Department of Arizona, who was residing in California. Some historians claim that Stoneman returned those reports unread because Whitman did not file them properly. Later in April Captain Frank Stanwood, the actual commander at Camp Grant, returned to the fort and approved

Haské bahnzin (Eskiminzin) in 1888. Courtesy of the National Anthropological Archives, Smithsonian Institution, Washington, D.C.

of what Whitman had done. Soon afterward Stanwood left on a field mission.

In late March and early April a series of raids occurred, for which the Apaches at Camp Grant were blamed. On April 10 at San Xavier, southwest of Tucson, the raiders stole considerable livestock. In a second attack along the San Pedro River on April 13, four innocent Anglos were killed. These attacks aroused anti-Apache sentiment in the territory. John Wasson, editor of the *Arizona Citizen,* played a key role in fanning the flames.

On the afternoon of April 28 vigilantes met in the outskirts of Tucson to prepare for the secret attack on the Apaches at Camp Grant, which occurred early on the morning of April 30. The Indian encampment was several miles from the fort, so the officers there did not learn about it until later in the day.

The Camp Grant Massacre, which was one of the worst massacres in the history of the American West, caused an uproar in the eastern United States, especially among those seeking a peace policy with the Indians. In December 1871, under threat of martial law from President Ulysses S. Grant, the vigilante members were indicted and brought to trial in Tucson, Judge John Titus presiding. After five days of trial and only nineteen minutes of deliberation, the jury found the accused not guilty.

Having grown up in Tucson, Chip Colwell-Chanthaphonh became interested in the history and culture of Native Americans in Arizona and in the Camp Grant Massacre in particular. He received a B.A. in anthropology from the University of Arizona in 1996 and a Ph.D. in anthropology from the University of Indiana in 2004. He is currently curator of anthropology at the Denver Museum of Nature and Science. His books include *History Is in the Land: Multivocal Tribal Traditions in Arizona's San Pedro Valley* (with T. J. Ferguson, 2006), *Ethics in Action: Case Studies in Archaeological Dilemmas* (with Julie Hollowell and Dru McGill, 2008), and *Inheriting the Past: The Making of Arthur C. Parker and Indigenous Archaeology* (2009). His book *Massacre at Camp Grant: Forgetting and Remembering Apache History* (2007) won the 2009 National Council on Public History Book Award. We interviewed Colwell-Chanthaphonh on October 27, 2007, at the museum in Denver, focusing on his work on the Camp Grant Massacre.

DJL (Deborah and Jon Lawrence): We are impressed by the similarities between the Camp Grant Massacre and Sand Creek Massacre.[1] In both cases, armed civilians massacred camps of Native Americans who had sued for peace. In both cases, there was not only a strong reaction in Washington to the horror of the massacre of innocents but also righteous indignation against the Indians on the part of the local citizens and press. Can you comment on the similarities and differences between the two cases?

CCC (Chip Colwell-Chanthaphonh): I agree that there are many similarities, and you have outlined some of the main points—the role of the government and how each of the massacres was perpetrated by American citizens. I also think that the level of brutality in the two attacks was similar, which speaks to the genuine rage that a lot of Americans felt toward Native peoples during that period.

But I think that there are also a lot of differences that come across in the specifics of the events. For example, the Tucsonans recruited the Tohono O'odhams as allies in the Camp Grant Massacre. There are also differences in the role of the government in each case. In the Camp Grant Massacre, the

Sites in southern Arizona relevant to the Camp Grant Massacre. The massacre site was known to the Apaches as "Big Sycamore Stands There." The group from Tucson that attacked the Apaches traveled through Redington Pass, down the San Pedro River, and then bypassed Camp Grant to get to the massacre site. The area marked "Camp Grant Reserve" was set aside for the Aravaipa and Pinal Apaches by peace commissioner Vincent Colyer shortly after the Camp Grant Massacre. By 1872 most of the reserve had been subsumed in the Gila River Reservation. Based on information in Colwell-Chanthaphonh, *Massacre at Camp Grant*.

Apaches not only had sued for peace but were literally living as prisoners of war in the shadow of the military camp, which was there to protect them.

Other similarities come across not just in the specific events but in the broader historical scope or trajectory for each of those Native communities. For both of these communities in Colorado and in Arizona, the massacres represented a loss of land and a loss of a way of life. These were really turning points for all the tribes that were involved. I also think that in the longer trajectory of these events there are differences in historical memory, in how they have been remembered and forgotten. The case of the Sand Creek Massacre is relatively well known. There are a number of books; archaeology has been done there; and the site is now under the stewardship of the National Park Service.[2] Whereas today, even in Tucson and in southern Arizona, the Camp Grant Massacre largely remains unknown, forgotten, except in the memory of a few Apaches and a few people who live in the area. So to me there are some real differences in terms of how those two massacres have been remembered.

DJL: Perhaps another difference is the involvement of not just the Tohono O'odhams but also the Mexican Americans in the Camp Grant Massacre. Both of those groups had long-standing animosity toward the Apaches. Something like that was not the case in the Sand Creek Massacre.

CCC: Perhaps, but I'm a little less certain who the participants were at Sand Creek, whether all were Anglo-American or not. Since Colorado was part of Spain for a long time and then part of Mexico, some of those longer-termed animosities may have existed there as well.

DJL: The comparison to Sand Creek brings up another point. Can we understand the settlers' behavior (without trying to justify it) by realizing that they had been subjected to vicious attacks by the Native Americans and were understandably fearful to the point of paranoia?

CCC: We can recognize the situation of and even have an empathy for the American settlers in Colorado and southern Arizona in terms of their own historical experiences. Being a settler on the frontier was not an easy life. And certain Apache groups undoubtedly committed horrible crimes against innocent people.[3] But the level of brutality at Camp Grant is something that is very difficult for people like us really to understand. We face the same problem when we try to understand mass murderers or serial rapists. We can study them and try to dig into their psychology, but can we truly understand people who perpetrate those kinds of acts? I'm not sure that it's entirely possible.

Their behavior *is* in some ways understandable. Given all the events that led up to the massacre we can understand how the settlers would come to their conclusions and why, in some sense, they would do what they did. But, on the other hand, the acts were so incredibly vicious, and they were so unjustified on so many levels, that those kinds of acts are really hard to understand. It wasn't just a matter of going out and killing *haské bahnzin*,[4] who they thought was guilty: we are talking about the murder of scores of women and children and quite possibly some rapes as well. The O'odham accounts and the soldiers' reports tell of people being hacked apart with their limbs stuck vertically into the sand. That's more than revenge; it goes far beyond any kind of simple reaction to the Apache raids that were going on at that time. It's an extreme kind of behavior that is very difficult for us to understand.

DJL: Historian Marc Simmons points out several features of Apache culture that contributed to conflict.[5] First, the Apaches had what was essentially a raiding and warfare culture. Being a raider and a warrior brought high esteem. Second, they had an explicit concern for revenge. Third, when seeking revenge both Indians and settlers did so indiscriminately against all members of the enemy group, without determining the actual guilty parties. Didn't this last trait in part reflect a deep ignorance of the other group's culture?

CCC: Simmons's work is relevant here, but a better beginning point in thinking about Apache history is the work of Grenville Goodwin and Keith Basso.[6] Both of these anthropologists talk about the clear distinction in Apache culture between raiding and warfare. They were two very different things. Raiding was a survival strategy when the stores of meat were getting low, the children were crying from hunger, and times were getting desperate. Warfare was, as you were saying, more along the lines of revenge or to undertake violence that they considered socially justified in some sense. I think that's an important beginning point in trying to understand the Apaches' view of what was going on. And, indeed, when the Apaches were raiding, almost any outsider was a potential victim. Anyone could be raided. One Apache group could raid another Apache group—Apaches weren't even excluded from their own practices of raiding. And equally in warfare Apaches fought with one another. Different bands fought with others. There were different alliances. It is very difficult to peel apart the complex history of Apache warfare in southern Arizona.

I think it *is* true, though, that in the mindset of many of the groups involved during that period an attack on one of your own was an attack on the whole group. Reciprocally, you could attack anyone in the other group to obtain some kind of appeasement or revenge. Maybe this was not so much ignorance of the other culture but a way of seeing the world. For some individuals during that period, an attack on anyone in the other group was seen as legitimate revenge.

It is certainly true, however, that the Anglo-Americans and Mexican Americans completely misunderstood Apache social organization. We see over and over again in the historical record that governments, citizens, and others didn't understand that the Apaches were not one people. They weren't one nation. They were multiple bands with multiple leaders and multiple foreign policies. There wasn't one unified Apache foreign policy. That led to all kinds of complications. In the case of the Camp Grant Massacre, historical evidence suggests that it was Chiricahua Apaches who were perpetrating the raids that the Apaches at Camp Grant (who were predominantly Aravaipa and Pinal Apaches) were blamed for.[7] The Apaches who had surrendered at Camp Grant probably had nothing to do with the raids for which they were ultimately blamed.

I think, too, that it is important to recognize that even in the 1860s and 1870s the American government had a sense of justice that was different from that of the Apaches. For example, the formal government policy at that time wasn't to punish just anybody from another group when someone from that group committed a crime. There was recognition of the importance of the individual; the system of law and justice in the United States, even at that time, was such that the individual who committed the crime was the individual who should be punished. To excuse or explain away the massacre on the grounds that the Anglo-Americans and Mexican Americans thought it was okay to kill *any* Apache doesn't really take into account the American culture of justice for that period.

DJL: Apaches had a reputation for excessive cruelty. Although this is controversial for scholars, it is crucial to an understanding of the hatred that the whites and Mexican Americans felt toward the Apaches. Can you comment on the Apaches' treatment of captives? Did Apache cruelty become increasingly vicious in response to mistreatment at the hands of Mexicans and whites?

CCC: This is such a complex question, because the stereotype of Apaches is so engrained in the American consciousness. For more than a century now, Americans have cultivated the image of the Apache as a cruel, inhuman creature who was willing to mutilate and attack Americans almost at random. It is very difficult for us to get underneath that stereotype. It is part of the scholarly challenge of trying to address these histories.

Did the Apaches mutilate people that they killed? Yes. There is plenty of evidence for that. Were they crueler, more vicious, than the Spaniards, Mexicans, and Americans? That is a much harder argument to make. And that is where we have to look quite closely at the historical record. For example, in the year before the massacre the *Arizona Citizen* published a notice that the governor of Sonora was offering several hundred dollars—I forget the exact amount—for each Apache scalp that was brought to him. The scalps of women and children were less valuable than the scalps of men, of course. We can contrast this to Sherman Curley's version of the Camp Grant Massacre.[8] He actually survived the massacre, and he commented on his shock and dismay that the attackers at Camp Grant scalped women and children. He couldn't make sense of it. Why would they scalp them?

Here you have a very clear contrast between how the Mexican government, the American government, and the American citizens at that time were viewing mutilation versus how Apaches viewed it. The stereotype is that the Apaches were doing the scalping—not the Americans, not the government of Mexico! But in reality the Americans and Mexican government were condoning and even encouraging scalping. So there was viciousness on all sides. I think we have to be very careful about how we frame these questions because our stereotype that the Apaches were the more violent people has been so strongly entrenched over the decades.

DJL: Massacres on the western frontier often were precipitated by very tough characters, such as the border ruffians who led the slaughter of Mormons at Haun's Mill in Missouri.[9] After all, not everyone has the stomach to murder innocent women and children. Tucson had a reputation for being full of such characters. What kind of people were the Tucson citizens who were involved in the planning and cheerleading of the massacre? What were their motivations?

CCC: Again, to make a living on the frontier was certainly difficult. It took tough characters to do that, to make a living in Tucson, not to mention the San Pedro Valley. But to me, there is tough and then there is crazy. For example, the documentary record shows that plenty of settlers in the San Pedro Valley made friends with and were sympathetic to the Apaches. They lived peaceably as neighbors. But I'll bet those people were just as tough, in the general sense of "tough," as people like William Oury and Jesús María Elías who participated in the massacre.[10] I'm making a distinction between characters who were simply tough and people who had extremist views or who reacted in extreme ways to the events of the time.

You asked about their motivations. As I said earlier, I think it is hard to understand what psychologically motivated the murder of the Camp Grant Apaches in such a brutal way. But as for the general sense of what motivated them, I think that many of the Tucsonans really did feel that they were under siege, that their lives and their livelihoods were being threatened, and they really did have to do something about it. They felt compelled to try in some way to curb the raiding and the violence.

DJL: Maybe this was particularly true in the early 1870s; the problem had been building up for some time.

CCC: Perhaps. You used the term "paranoia" earlier, and I think this is a good way of putting it. When we look at the historical record more closely what we find is that the Apaches, in fact, were being disproportionately killed and enslaved compared to the Americans. For example, there are army documents from the mid-1860s to the mid-1870s that cite how many soldiers were killed versus how many Apaches. By the army's own accounting, the ratio is thirteen to one; for every thirteen Apaches who were killed, only one soldier was killed. At the same time, almost no solders were taken captive, whereas hundreds of Apache women and children were taken captive. And yet when a single soldier was killed, the Tucson papers and the territory papers went crazy. "We can't stand another day of this—the Apaches are wiping out the soldiers!" But when the soldiers went out and killed thirteen Apaches in one swoop, people celebrated.

DJL: What role did the newspapers and journalists, take Wasson as an example, play in contributing to the paranoia and hysteria of the settlers?[11]

CCC: They contributed in a huge way. Wasson is a central figure in trying to understand the history of the massacre. People who have written about the massacre, even Oury himself, often emphasize that only six Anglo-Americans were at the scene. That is probably a more-or-less accurate number—there might have been one or two more. But whether it was six or ten, people point out that it was a relatively small number of Anglo-Americans directly involved, compared to the number of Mexican Americans and Tohono O'odhams—the latter formed the largest group in the attacking party. But I think that number dismisses the fact that a lot more Anglo-Americans were involved in cultivating a deep fear and hatred of Apaches and excusing the murder and enslavement of Apaches. There was not only John Wasson, whose vitriolic journalism validated the massacre and inspired it, but also the jurors who shirked their duty of justice.[12] Hundreds, if not even thousands, of Tusconans welcomed the attackers back in jubilation. So focusing on the single-digit number, whether six or slightly more, of Anglo-Americans involved at the scene of the massacre dismisses the much larger participation of Anglo-Americans in Arizona territory who condoned it.

DJL: The testimony of nineteenth-century white settlers and twentieth-century Apache descendants is often unreliable and contradictory. Anglo-Americans justified their own savagery as part of what they viewed as an essentially just cause. Native Americans, when given their voice (as at the new museum at Fort Apache), often gloss over their own past cruelty. When you were researching Apache-white relations for your book, how did you determine which sources were trustworthy?

CCC: That's a really good question, because we need to have a deep skepticism of all historical claims, whether they come from the army, from the Anglo-American writers of the time, or from the Apache or Tohono O'odham perspectives. I think we need to be acutely skeptical about the historical validity of the truth claims embedded within these versions. For me, the best way to try to understand events is by incorporating as many perspectives as possible, an approach of multivocality. This is particularly important for the Camp Grant Massacre because for generations writers have only looked at the documents of the Anglos, many of whom were greatly invested in it themselves. So for me, an important way of trying to understand the massacre is by trying to understand it from as many perspectives as possible. And when we do that, we sometimes find striking congruencies between different kinds of historical claims.

One congruency that amazed me when I found it—and it amazes me to this day—is the narrative of an Apache woman, *bija gush kaiyé,* who related her version of the massacre in 1932 to Grenville Goodwin.[13] She talks about the events that led up to the massacre and describes coming into Camp Grant. Then, in a very specific statement, she tells how the women and children went out to cut hay and brought that hay back to sell to the soldiers, in return for tickets that they would exchange for calico. A historical document written by Lieutenant Whitman in 1872, some sixty years earlier, describes this same process, almost word for word, detailing the bringing in of the hay and the exchange of tickets for cloth.[14] To me, this is a really strong congruency. These two narratives are separated by time, by perspective—they are separated in almost every single way. And yet they both relate almost identical historical facts. Given that, we can have strong confidence that this one historical event probably did happen.

At the same time, in her narrative *bija gush kaiyé* says, and I'm paraphrasing: "I guess about one thousand of us were killed." No other historical document even comes close to that number. Indeed, the total number of Aravaipa and Pinal Apaches surrendered at Camp Grant was probably around five hundred. But do we disallow the rest of *bija gush kaiyé*'s narrative just because of this one statement? In the past, that is what has been done: "Oh, that's just Apaches relaying myth!" Or do we look critically at the specific facts related in narratives—as well as the narratives as a whole?

I think what we need to do is, first, get as many different perspectives as we can. Then we should critically evaluate where different narratives relate similar facts and where they relate dissimilar facts and try to explain both the similarities and the differences. And I think we need to be deeply skeptical of *all* these claims.

In regard to your statement that the Apaches gloss over their own cruelty, in my experience in working with Apache elders I have actually found that the Apaches are very up front about their history. They don't gloss over the acts of raiding and warfare that their ancestors participated in. What they resist is the one-sided story that dominates history books, movies, and dime novels. I think that what you saw at the Fort Apache Museum Heritage Center is in part an attempt to counteract some of those stereotypes that so dominate American consciousness. In my experience, the Tohono O'odhams also are very open to these difficult histories. And indeed they are difficult histories for all of us to confront. For example, the new museum of the Tohono O'odhams has a long wall with a series of panels about protecting the homeland, and one of those panels is about the Camp Grant Massacre.[15] It says, in plain English, that their ancestors killed unarmed women and children. To me, it's a brave confrontation, a brave way of addressing what are traumatic pasts for the whole community. Contrast this to Tucson, where the massacre perpetrators are implicitly celebrated in names such as Sam Hughes Elementary School, Carrillo Elementary School, Wasson Peak. Go into the Arizona Historical Society in Tucson and show me the lengthy exhibits on the Camp Grant Massacre.

So, quite to the contrary of what you suggest in the question, I find that the Apaches and the Tohono O'odhams have been much more willing to confront these difficult pasts compared to non-Indians in Tucson.

DJL: Some of the oral accounts that Goodwin collected, as given in Basso's book, tell of raids where the western Apaches wiped out whole villages, Navajos, Yavapais, Pimas, women and children, as if they were proud of it.

CCC: Basso's book gives good examples of this. But I don't see it as pride. It's reality. This is what happened. This is what we did. And, again, I think you would be very hard pressed to find a parallel "this is what we did" attitude in contemporary American history books or local books about Tucson.

DJL: You suggested earlier that it was Chiricahua Apaches who were responsible for the raid on San Xavier, south of Tucson, on April 10, 1871, and also perhaps for the raid near the San Pedro east of Tucson, on April 13.[16] What is the evidence for this? To what extent do you think that the Tucson citizens believed that the Aravaipa Apaches were the perpetrators?

CCC: For your readers who aren't familiar with the massacre, basically what happened was that Apaches came into Camp Grant in early 1871, suing for peace. The army officers at Camp Grant agreed to have the Apaches there as prisoners of war. By April of 1871 they were settled about five miles east of Camp Grant in a traditional Apache farming area known as *gashdla'á cho o'aa* (Big Sycamore Stands There). By April of 1871 about five hundred Apaches were settled there, almost all of the Pinal and Aravaipa Apaches.

During that same period, the Apaches at Camp Grant were blamed for a series of raids and depredations. One of the key events that really made people point toward Camp Grant was a raid that occurred on April 10, 1871. This was at San Xavier, southwest of Tucson. But even at the time, in 1872, an officer named Robinson said that to prove the innocence of the Indians at Camp Grant all you had to do was go back and look at when the rations were given out to those at Camp Grant and when the raids occurred.[17] He suggested that what you would find is that the raids were on the same days that the rations were given out. Now, to give out rations—coffee, sugar, meat, corn, and flour—for five hundred people, to each man, woman, and child, would have taken hours and also would have increased the scrutiny over the camp by the army on those days. It would have been almost impossible for an Apache to slip away unnoticed. The officers swore up and down that they did those counts, and on the days of the counts they never found large numbers of Indians gone. Occasionally Apaches would be allowed to leave the reserve to gather agave or to go hunting. But especially on the days when they were receiving rations, Apaches would know to be there.

DJL: The chart in your book, which makes such a detailed comparison of the dates of raids and the dates of rations, gives very strong support for this line of reasoning.[18] Furthermore, it is highly improbable that they could have been at Camp Grant for the rations and then raided at San Xavier on the same day, over twenty-four hours of constant travel away.

CCC: Yes, that's the second point. If you look at where those raids occurred, especially the raid on April 10, you will find that's at least a thirty-six-hour horse ride away from Camp Grant. For the Apaches both to commit the raid on April 10 and to be at Camp Grant to receive rations and to be counted on the same day would be a physical impossibility. The attack on the San Pedro, in which four innocent Anglos were killed, was on April 13—again a day that rations were being given out. There you will find that it was an attack not just by a few people but by one hundred Apaches. Every single Apache man at Camp Grant would have had to have been away on the day of April 13 when rations were given out to commit that depredation on the San Pedro River. And I think that it is clear that there is no reason for the army officers to have been lying.

So who was committing these crimes, the raids and depredations? Cochise and other Chiricahuas were known to be in southern Arizona during that period. I'm fairly certain that the evidence would suggest that these were Chiricahua Apaches who were committing all these depredations in April 1871. And we know that there were no Chiricahua Apaches at Camp Grant at that time.

DJL: Why were the victims of the massacre mostly women and children? Where were the men? If the attack had occurred during or right after a dance, as suggested by the oral narratives, the Apache men would have fought hard to protect their women and children and would not have run away, leaving them exposed to the attack. At least one source, Schellie, suggests the men were out hunting.[19] What do you think?

CCC: I think first we need to understand why this was such an important historical claim for the perpetrators. They tried to justify what they did by saying that the fact that so few men were killed was clear evidence that the men were out raiding. Hence, to accuse the Apache men of raiding, the Tucsonans had a vested interest in saying that it was mostly women and children who were killed. On the other hand, the army officers writing their reports had no reason to make any such justifications, and they made it clear that it was mostly women and children that were killed.

However, the fact remains that we don't know exactly how many men, women, and children were killed. The historical evidence suggests that about eight men were killed, so let's take that as a true statement for the sake of argument. I think we can explain that small number in several ways. First, in April of 1871 we know there were approximately five hundred Apaches at Camp Grant. During the massacre, about one hundred of them were killed. We also know from army documents that there was one man for every four women and children. If you take a random sample of one hundred people out of the five at Camp Grant, it would include about twenty men and eighty women and children. That gets us down to a more reasonable number of men involved to begin with.

Second, from the Apache versions, we consistently hear about a dance that was going on that night. It is possible that the men and women were separated because the men were dancing and the women were on the outskirts of the dance area watching. So on the morning of the massacre the men and women might have been sleeping in slightly different areas. But that's just a possibility.

Third, a simple answer as to why it was women and children who were killed is that they were easy targets. And as you say, the expectation is that Apache men would stick around and fight. But they must have seen the writing on the wall: it was going to be a massacre. When you are surrounded, when people are moving through your camp with war clubs and guns, you're human—you run. I think the men ran. But in the Apache accounts we find another explanation as to why men survived this event. In the narrative of Sherman Curley, who actually survived the massacre, what is so distinctive is that he fought back. As he relates, he was chased by Mexican Americans and Tohono O'odhams. He had a bow and arrow, so he actually was able to scare them off. Eventually they left him alone and went back to the camp. This is easy to imagine: would the attackers try to kill a man with a bow and arrow or maybe a rifle? Probably not. They would go find a young woman, an elder, or a child to kill.

So when we look at these numbers a little more closely, first we see that in a random sample of one hundred, you would only expect about twenty men to be involved. Given some of these other factors, it is understandable and realistic to see the death of only eight men as truly representing events as they unfolded.

DJL: There have been few new accounts of the Camp Grant Massacre, and indeed no single scholarly book on the topic, prior to yours.[20] Furthermore, most works recycle a small number of documents—the trial transcripts, military records, Oury's articles, newspaper accounts, and so forth. What is new in Camp Grant scholarship?

CCC: Grenville Goodwin's work about the massacre has been out there a long time, but it hadn't been used by historians.[21]

DJL: That's one of the new things you did, incorporating the oral accounts given to Goodwin by surviving Apaches.

CCC: Yes. For basically more than a century, what has happened is that the newspaper accounts, some of the military accounts, and the writings of Oury have been used over and over and over. If you read everything from Don Schellie's *Vast Domain of Blood* to even Sinclair Browning's sympathetic account of *haské bahnzin* in *Enju,* you find it is essentially a retelling of the narrative from the perspective of the Anglos. I think that the Apache narratives are central in trying to understand this event. And the Tohono O'odhams' calendar stick or event stick, which Ruth Underhill recorded in the 1930s and which again no one has used, provides a Tohono O'odham perspective that, in fact, fits with a lot of the other narratives in important ways.[22] That's what is new at this historical juncture: the appropriation of information that has been out there for a long time but that hasn't been well used.

DJL: Are there any more oral accounts other than the ones you treat in the second chapter of your book? Did anyone else besides Goodwin collect these narratives in the 1920s and 1930s? Of course there was Eve Ball, but she was over in New Mexico.[23]

CCC: There was Richard van Valkenburgh's narrative of Lahn from the 1940s.[24] Are there more pieces of information out there, more narratives that remain hidden? I think that it is quite possible, and we need to keep looking. Certainly, there is a lot more oral tradition. Oral tradition is different from oral history in that oral tradition consists of narratives that are passed between generations.

DJL: What about recent archaeology?

CCC: Excavations were done in 1962 when the highway was being realigned—it actually went right through a portion of Camp Grant. The objects and field notes from the excavation are at the Arizona State Museum but have never been published. So there is some work that needs to be done there, which might elucidate what was going on at Camp Grant.

DJL: Nothing has been done at the massacre site itself?

CCC: No major work has been done. There were some surveys. According to what some locals tell me, a big problem is that people have been illicitly collecting objects through the years.

DJL: That was true of Sand Creek as well. But they managed to go in there a few years ago and find a great deal of new material.[25]

CCC: Yes, there very well could be artifacts still underground, but I think it would be a very complicated political undertaking at this juncture. Not the least of reasons is that there are four different kinds of landowners right at the massacre site; so to negotiate with the landowners would be very complicated.

DJL: To what extent can we trust the picture of Whitman promoted in Elliott Arnold's book—that he was a man of peace, with altruistic motives—when most of what we know about him comes from his own accounts?[26] After all, some sources assert that he was a drinker and a womanizer. A similar question arises concerning John Clum.[27] According to David Roberts, John Clum was nicknamed "Turkey Gobbler" because he gloried in his own self-importance.[28] How reliable is Clum's account of *haské bahnzin?*[29]

CCC: I don't necessarily agree with the characterization that Whitman was a man of peace with altruistic motives. For example, he reports telling the Apaches in February of 1871 that, paraphrasing, "if you didn't come in for peace, then I'm going to wipe you off the face of the earth." That's basically what he said. I think he was a soldier first and foremost, and he was a soldier at a time when the expectation of the army was that either the Apaches were going to be peaceful or they were going to be killed. There were really no two ways about it.

The historical evidence suggesting that Whitman was a womanizer and a drunk mostly came from the Tucson newspapers and territorial papers after the massacre. This contrasts with what they wrote earlier, in December of 1870 when Whitman arrived in Tucson, when he was portrayed as quite a valiant soldier. I think we need to contextualize those later characterizations of Whitman as in part an effort by the residents of Tucson and other territorial towns to show the negligence and the incompetence of the soldiers at Camp Grant. They claimed he was drunk and lying down with the laundress at the fort. If Whitman was drunk, he could not have been counting Apaches and giving out rations—that is the subtext of those claims. I am skeptical of those characterizations of Whitman, and I think that we need to understand the historical context of where they were coming from.

It is a similar kind of thing with Clum, who, like Whitman, wrote about himself and what he did, and others wrote about him negatively. Clum is less relevant to the Camp Grant Massacre because he wasn't around until after it occurred. But he does, as you mention, talk a lot about it, and he wrote two lengthy articles about *haské bahnzin*'s life, trying to rescue *haské bahnzin*'s reputation.

What is significant for me is that it is not just Clum who paints a relatively positive picture of *haské bahnzin.* There were Americans living on the San Pedro who talked about peaceful transactions with *haské bahnzin.* After the massacre and some years later, *haské bahnzin* came to live on the San Pedro. He lived there peacefully. He had something like $3,000 in an account at a Tucson store. He is represented by Stoneman in positive ways.[30] Apache accounts talk about *haské bahnzin* trying to make the best out of very difficult circumstances. For me, Clum's account of *haské bahnzin* doesn't and shouldn't stand alone. When we look at it from the perspective of all of these other accounts, then we actually do find quite a bit of congruence as to *haské bahnzin* being a leader who was trying to do his best.

DJL: What do you think General Stoneman's motives were for not responding to Whitman's letters to him regarding the situation at Camp Grant?[31] Do you think he actually didn't read Whitman's report because it was improperly filed? Or do you think that he actually did read the letters but used the "improper filing" as an excuse not to respond to a situation that might reflect poorly on himself if it were to fail? Do you think Stoneman approved of Whitman's actions regarding the feeding station at Camp Grant?

CCC: Whitman reported what he was doing and sought orders from Stoneman. The story goes that Stoneman returned those reports unread because Whitman didn't file them properly. I think that the army records suggest that Stoneman probably didn't read those initial reports. However, while he may not have had all of the details that were in the reports, he probably was well aware of what was happening at Camp Grant, especially by the end of April 1871.

What Whitman was doing wasn't something new; it had been going on for quite some time: Apaches coming into camps, seeking peace, and then being recognized as prisoners of war. And it wasn't really a "feeding station." The Apaches agreed to surrender and they were prisoners of war. It was referred to by the derogatory term "feeding station" by the Tucsonans because they wanted to avoid calling the Apaches prisoners of war of the United States government and portray them as being in transit, just being fed by the federal government, which didn't know what it was doing.

I think that Stoneman implicitly approved of Whitman's actions, if not explicitly. Whitman was smart. He knew that as an army officer he could not have a treaty with the Apaches. Only the United States Congress can enact a treaty with an Indian nation. The Apaches came in and wanted a treaty, and he told them, paraphrasing again, "I can't do a treaty. You can be prisoners of war, and we can proceed from there." To me, that defines Whitman's competence. As a counterexample, in 1866 a captain at Camp Grant did promise a treaty and created a treaty with Aravaipa and Pinal Apaches. But of course the government couldn't uphold the treaty because it was made by an army officer and not by the United States Congress. In that case it was a false treaty or a treaty under false pretenses that the Aravaipa and Pinal Apaches entered into. To me, Whitman was smart, and he knew what he could and couldn't do. Could he accept Apaches as prisoners of war? Yes, he could. And so he proceeded carefully and cautiously and appropriately.

DJL: Captain Frank Stanwood came and took charge and approved of what Whitman had done. Then he left on a field mission. Did the Tucsonans know that Stanwood was going to leave the camp, and did they wait for him to go before they made the attack in order to make it easier for themselves?

CCC: I don't think so, because even though Stanwood and an attachment were gone at that point, there were still plenty of soldiers at Camp Grant. I think the attackers anticipated, correctly, that the camp was too far away from where the Apaches were living to find out what was going on. They were five miles away. Anyone who has been out in Aravaipa Canyon knows that sound doesn't carry far. Even a gunshot doesn't carry more than a quarter of a mile. I think that they anticipated that they could attack the encampment and know that the solders wouldn't hear about it until it was too late. And that's exactly what happened.

DJL: General Crook had negative feelings toward Whitman.[32] Why did Crook disrespect Whitman? What was the source of his animosity?

CCC: That's a tough one. I'm not sure that we have enough evidence to really know what Crook was thinking. Crook is out of my area of expertise too. But from my light reading of Crook, maybe saying he was a "perfectionist" is going too far, but he strikes me as a man who liked order, who had a very clear sense of how he thought the Apaches could be subdued and a strong sense of self-confidence that he could get it done. One possibility is that he objected to what he saw as incompetence in Whitman and the others allowing the massacre to happen, that they could let things get to that point. But this is just an idea I have—I don't know whether there is enough evidence to say one way or the other.

DJL: Ironically, some of the army officers, such as Crook, Bourke, and Davis, who were most effective at bringing the Native Americans to bay were also among the most articulate in expressing sympathy for the Indians, in defending the Indians' fundamental humanity, and in seeking a more humane treatment of their past enemy.[33] They were part of a historical development that has led to a more humane view of the Indians and their history. Can we similarly view the outcome of the Camp Grant Massacre in a positive light by seeing it as an early step in the evolution of an ethos that views such ethnic cleansing as completely reprehensible?

CCC: You are right that some of these army officers thought, uniquely for their age, about the humanity of Indian peoples. However, many of these same people mistreated Indians in different ways. As I said, Whitman was pretty clear about what he was willing to do to the Apaches if they didn't fully capitulate. Crook was pretty clear too. I'm not sure that we can go back to those individuals as the beginning of that historical trajectory.

But you are right about the significance of the massacre, and I think that this is one of the things we can take away from it. While it is hard to take away anything positive from a massacre, it is true that in later years we realize that these are not the kinds of events that we, as Americans, could ever be proud of or that we could ever condone. So in that sense I think the Camp Grant Massacre is an exceptionally important story for us to confront, to address, and to think about, because these kinds of events are still going on all over the place. Whether in Dafur, Iraq, or elsewhere, massacres continue to go on in our midst.

Additionally, I think that there are still a lot of tensions between American Indian communities and non-Indians in Arizona and elsewhere. It's gotten a lot better, and we aren't going to see a massacre of Indians anytime soon, but the Apaches are still living with the consequences of the massacre. They are still fighting for their land. They are still fighting for access to traditional places. They are still fighting for respect. They are fighting for recognition of their humanity. For Apaches, indeed for all of us, the legacy of the Camp Grant Massacre lives on.

So have we made progress over the last 137 years? Yes. Do we still have a long way to go? The answer is, again, yes.

Undated William Henry Jackson painting, *Crossing the South Platte,* in which Indians are depicted trading with the emigrants and helping move cattle across the river. The ford was at what was known as California Crossing, in the vicinity of present-day Julesburg, Colorado. Courtesy of the Scott's Bluff National Monument.

CHAPTER 5

Indians, Emigrants, and the Army on the Overland Trails

An Interview with Michael Tate

In the 1840s, the early period of the Oregon-California Trails' use, reasonably amicable relations prevailed between the westering emigrants and the Indian communities they encountered en route. At that time the emigrants were typically traveling in small parties and in families. The Indians therefore did not consider them to be a threat. The most important relationship between the two groups was one of trade, where the emigrants provided processed food (flour, coffee, sugar), hardware (knives, hatchets, tools, metal pots), manufactured clothing and blankets, and luxury items (pipes, beads, tobacco) in return for moccasins, bison robes, and freshly killed game. The trans-Mississippi Indians had become accustomed to such trade through fifty years of contact with French, English, Spanish, and American trappers and traders. Trade in livestock was also important and was often crucial for emigrants whose cattle, horses, and mules were exhausted by the journey. In addition, Indians provided services to the emigrants by assisting at river crossings, acting as guides or informants as to the geography the emigrants were traversing, and indicating the locations of good campsites with adequate grass, firewood, and water. On occasion Indians rescued emigrants from being lost or trapped by bad weather or injury, and at times emigrants behaved in a similar manner toward the Indians. Both groups engaged in gift exchange and in entertaining members of the other group with feasts and parties in their respective camps.

Despite this relatively positive assessment, most emigrants began the long journey west with strong preconceived notions about the character of the Native people. Indians were frequently viewed either as noble savages or as evil and/or ignoble savages. These perceptions had their origin in the literature of the era. Captivity narratives, which had begun appearing in the 1600s, spoke primarily of the travails of white Christian women captured by Indians in the eastern United States. The Leatherstocking Tales of James Fenimore Cooper embodied both stereotypes. Indeed, Cooper's protagonist, Leatherstocking, is a problematic blend of European, American, and Indian elements. Travelogues by Washington Irving, Josiah Gregg, Francis Parkman, George F. Ruxton, John C. Frémont, and Thomas Jefferson Farnham, trail guides by Lansford Hastings and Captain R. B. Marcy, anti-Indian articles in frontier newspapers, and the overall ethnocentrism of the times contributed to the emigrants' initial outlook. While some overlanders were able to change an initially negative view of the Indians, many continued to process their experiences entirely in the light of their preconceived ideas. The Indians were equally uncomprehending of the emigrants' culture. This cultural divide led to misunderstanding of each other's motives and often to unnecessary confrontation and violence. Wild rumors and fabricated tales of violence were widely circulated, and emigrants often greeted reasonable requests from Indians (such as recompense for helping at river crossings) with extreme hostility.

Unfortunately, the overlanders left a very strong footprint on the land. Large numbers of cattle and horses required extensive use of grasslands and water. The emigrants also needed firewood and game. These resources were obtained on lands that the Indians considered their own, while the emigrants considered the land to be public property. The resource depletion was exacerbated by the emigrants' tendency to indiscriminate bison hunting, where large numbers of animals were killed and left to rot on the prairie. The resulting destruction of the Indians' resources was particularly deleterious in the fragile ecology of the semidesert West, especially in the Great Basin, where the Shoshonean-speaking Indians were subjected to conditions of starvation as time progressed. As a consequence, the Indians increasingly began to demand some form of recompense from the army, from government agents, or from the emigrants themselves, often in the form of raids on the emigrants' cattle and horses.

The overlanders also brought diseases that were particularly fatal to the Indian communities. This process had already begun much earlier: northern Plains Indians had suffered great population loss due to diseases such as smallpox brought by the early European American traders and trappers. During the trail era, cholera was a particularly deadly disease, affecting both emigrants and Indians in large numbers.

Ultimately, under these conditions, conflict was inevitable. This became increasingly true after 1848, with an enormous increase in the number of overlanders during the California gold rush. While Indians would sometimes attack lone individuals who were away from their party, most Indian attacks on wagon trains involved stampedes to obtain cattle. Sometimes Indians would kill one or two emigrants in the process of such raids. Following loss of their cattle to an Indian group, emigrants often attacked the next group of Indians they encountered, whether these Indians were the guilty party or not. Many hardened frontiersmen had the attitude that any Indian they saw should be killed. The emigrants never remained in one place, so the Indians often retaliated on the next wagon train that came along. There were also a small number of massacres. Most of these, such as the Ward Massacre of 1853 and the Utter Massacre of 1860, occurred in the Great Basin and involved Indians who had become increasingly desperate in the face of extreme resource depletion. Overall, however, the number of people killed was small; roughly four hundred emigrants and an equal number of Indians were killed during the period 1840 to 1860.

The U.S. Regular Army's role prior to the Civil War was to protect both emigrants and Indians. While the army occasionally accompanied emigrant trains, the soldiers provided a greater service at standing bases, such as Forts Kearny and Laramie, where emigrants could obtain supplies and some measure of safety. Following the Fort Laramie Treaty of 1851, the army also had the responsibility to maintain the peace by providing Indians with gifts and annuities and preventing white emigrants and settlers from encroaching on Indian lands. Unfortunately, the army was not very effective in this dual role because it was badly undermanned and had no legal rights to arrest citizens who violated the treaties.

The Civil War led to an enormous increase in the frontier violence. Farmers began moving into the western plains and miners into Colorado in the late 1850s, putting increased pressure on the Indians' resources. Volunteer troops massacred Indians at Bear River in 1863 and at Sand Creek in 1864. While the Bear Creek Massacre led to a cessation of violence in the Great Basin, the Sand Creek Massacre led to retaliation by the Indians, who attacked ranches and stage stations along the Platte River and the rivers of western Kansas. This retaliation set the stage for counterattacks and ultimately for the large-scale conflict between the Indians and the army in the post–Civil War era.

In addition to its military program, the frontier army played a very strong role in the settlement of the West. Soldiers acted as explorers and scientists, built roads and bridges, defended the construction of the railroads and telegraphs, and performed limited service as lawmen. Contracts with citizens to provide agricultural products, livestock, and services such as carpentry and blacksmithing to the army were essential to the growth of western towns and cities. The army's support of settlement sped up the process of the elimination of the Indians from their previous territory and their confinement to reservations. Ironically, in their later years, a number of the most effective Indian fighters, such as Generals Benjamin Grierson, Nelson Miles, and George Crook, became key advocates for the rights of the Native communities.

Custer's 1874 expedition into the Black Hills, with photographer W. H. Illingworth in the foreground. The expedition was connected to the mining activity that violated the Treaty of 1868 and led to the Sioux War of 1876–77. Courtesy of the South Dakota State Historical Society.

Michael Tate holds the Charles and Mary Martin Chair of Western History at the University of Nebraska, Omaha, where he has been Graduate Program chair and head of the Native American Studies program. His book *The Frontier Army in the Settlement of the West* (winner of the Nebraska Book Award) discusses the multitude of positive contributions outside the battlefield that the frontier army made to the settlement of the West. *Indians and Emigrants: Encounters on the Overland Trails* (winner of the Great Plains Distinguished Book Prize for 2006 and the Parmly Billings High Plains Book Award for 2007) cites diaries, journals, and oral histories to challenge conventional stereotypes concerning the relations between emigrants and Indians during the era of the overland trails. His book *The American Army in Transition, 1865–1898* deals with the social history of the army, including issues such as black and Indian regiments and the army family. His recent article "The Artist and the Entrepreneur" on William Quesenbury and John Wesley Jones is being prepared as part of a book, in conjunction with the Nebraska State Historical Society. Tate's current project is to edit a set of unpublished diaries, letters, memoirs, and government documents relating to the overland trails. We interviewed him in Omaha on February 2, 2008; our focus was on the book *Indians and Emigrants: Encounters on the Overland Trails.*

DJL (Deborah and Jon Lawrence): Your book makes a completely convincing case that the threat to emigrants by Indians on the Oregon-California Trails has been overblown. Indeed, we have read a number of emigrant diaries in which there is no mention of serious problems with Indians. Our question is, why were the Indians so benign? Their cultures were based on raiding and warfare. If another tribal group came into their territory, they would try to annihilate them as enemies. Why were the Indians as kind to the emigrants as they were?

MT (Michael Tate): What they often were fighting for in intertribal warfare was the right to control resources—hunting and grazing grounds, timber, and so forth. And they saw great profit to be made in raiding each other, for horses

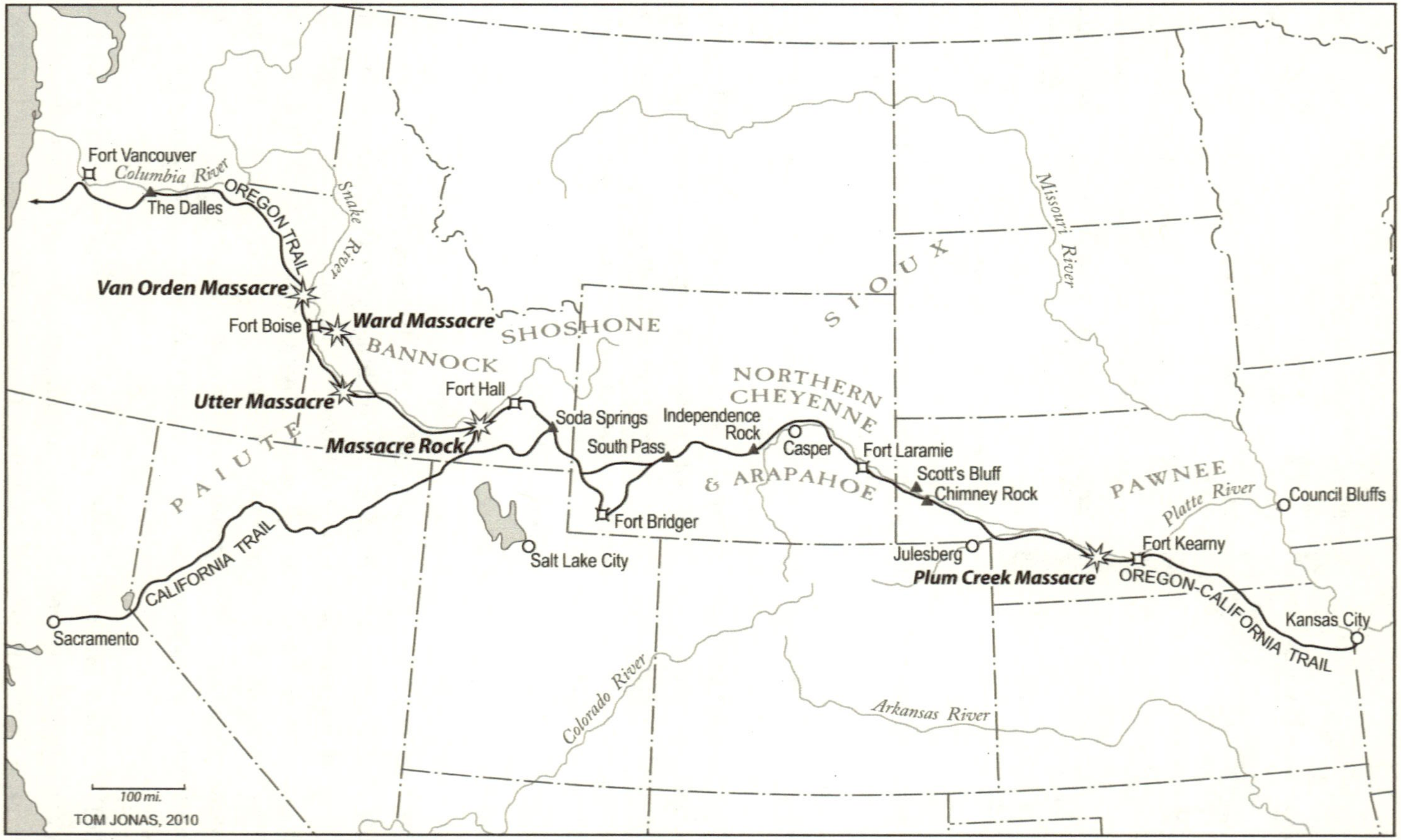

The Oregon and California trails, showing trail landmarks (solid triangles) and the locations of massacres. The territories of several tribes are also indicated. Based on information in Tate, *Indians and Emigrants.*

in particular. Raiding was also a way for a man to prove himself and to gain the right to marry. These were traditional cultural patterns. Initially in the 1840s, when the number of emigrants was small, they didn't see the overlanders as being natural enemies. First of all, the emigrants were just passing through the land. They were not making an attempt to take over the resources of the tribes. So the emigrants were not perceived as the same sort of threat as the enemy tribes.

More importantly, the Indians saw advantage in alliance with white people. That trend goes all the way back to the beginning of North American Indian-white contact on the East Coast and in Spanish and French areas. Alliance with whites brought them trade, making them richer, and brought military alliances and access to advanced weaponry. In the period that proceeded the trail era, the Plains Indians already had made contacts with whites—the fur traders, who had brought the first trade goods. Many of them had intermarried with the traders. So when the Bidwell-Bartleson party started across in 1841, the Indians were already in the mode of trading with white people.[1]

True, the emigrants left a rather heavy mark on the land, even early on, that was not the best for the Indians. In the long run, it led to serious conflict. If the Indians had had a crystal ball in the 1840s and had seen what was going to be the outcome in the long run, they might have had a very different reaction. But sometimes we get a little too myopic today in making judgments such as "This was so devastating to Native Americans. How could they have allowed these people to come through their land?" Well, in the short run, it didn't look like it was a disadvantage.

DJL: Your book does indeed stress that a key reason for the relatively good treatment of the emigrants was that at mid-century the emigrant/Indian relations were based on "mutually beneficial trade, cooperation, and friendship." You also state that the Indians were "shrewd traders who usually acquired the prized items they sought."[2]

MT: In the 1840s an Indian on the trail was there largely to trade with white people. He wasn't there on the Platte River to fish, but because people coming through were bringing things he didn't have in sufficient quantities. And these were very valuable commodities, labor-saving devices: sewing needles, pots, traps, woolen shirts, guns, flints for guns, gunpowder. In other cases, they were materials that could be taken into the vast interior to trade to other tribes for equally valuable items.

People sometimes assume that Indians always got bilked in these trading agreements—as though it was the sale of Manhattan Island all over again. Perhaps the trade items were mundane things, as we see them today, but from the Indians' perspective, those items were worth a king's ransom because they couldn't easily be obtained. Indians often felt victorious in the trade. "Boy, did we put a good one over on that guy! Look at what we gave him—moccasins and a broken-down mule. We were hot traders and he was naïve."

The Indians were not passive, constantly exploited players in this story. They had their own agendas. Through trade, they enriched themselves, made themselves more powerful, and made their societies more stable. In the short run, it was a natural thing to do. In the long run, it made them more dependent on white people.

DJL: An important point that you raise in the book concerns the Indians' concept of gift exchange and reciprocal obligation. Did this mean that they often expected wagon train members to accept an obligation of reciprocity that was frequently not understood by the emigrants?

MT: The concept of reciprocity was nearly universal among North American Indians. In the tribes that were on the western overland trails, it was a mainstay of life. "Reciprocity" meant that when you received a gift, a kindness, or some help, you gave back in some way. It didn't have to be immediate—it might be three years later. It was not a "this for that" kind of exchange. Rather, you performed an act of kindness or brought a gift in place of the kindness shown you. It wasn't to be looked upon as an obligation. It was to be done with a glad heart. It wasn't just to make you a big man or to belittle somebody. Quite the opposite. It was to enrich the other person, who then would enrich you. Unfortunately, perhaps, this process was cyclical. It just kept going. You never reached a point where you had returned all of the favors, but it integrated the relationships between members of that society and encouraged the extension of personal honor.

At the most basic level, it was done among kin. But it also went higher to other members of the band, then to the broader tribal structure, for example, to other bands of Sioux, and then sometimes to other tribes, when the two tribes were on good terms. With the arrival of white people, it was just an extension of that process. Starting from early in the century, Indians had relationships with mountain men that were based on reciprocal understandings. When mountain men married into these tribes, such relationships were strengthened even more. Some of the mountain men just played the game because it was necessary to do it, but others understood and participated in these reciprocal relationships.

So when the overlanders began coming, the Indians had no reason to assume that white people knew nothing about reciprocity. They considered it universal. And that's why, I think, whites often would receive gifts, sometimes very large ones, from the Indians. The Indian was honoring them for something that they had done—which in their mind might have been trivial.

The problem for the emigrants was that they hadn't read a book on Indian etiquette when they stepped out onto the trail. Mostly they were reading pretty negative things. "Don't let the Indians come into your camp. Watch out! They are after you and your livestock." When Indians would ride into the camps, in twos or threes, hardly a menace, they would ask for food. Guidebooks of the 1850s would warn the emigrants not to let Indians come into their camps.[3] But all that these peaceful Indian visitors were looking for in that food, perhaps, was a payback from these people who were using their resources as they traveled across the tribal domain. The emigrants may not have been physically taking something out of the Indians' pockets, but they were using vital resources that belonged to the tribes.

There was clearly cultural misunderstanding about reciprocity. Too often whites saw it as begging. "They are coming in. They want food. They are just a bunch of beggars. We had better fire a shot at them and chase them away. We don't want them to get too close to our children or to our property." I think Indians must have been mystified by the whites' belligerent responses. Three wagon trains treated them nicely and then a fourth wagon train a few days later started shooting at them just as they appeared on the horizon. The white people's actions made no sense, particularly because they would not acknowledge the reciprocity needed to pay for what they was using. So culturally, white people and Indians were on two different wave lengths.

Another problem was that, since the overlanders were just passing through, they were not going to achieve a long-term relationship whereby they came to understand this reciprocity. So the Indians quickly came to understand that to get back the reciprocal gift they had to get it *now*. It couldn't be a year from now or even next month, because these people were going to pass on to points farther west.

The most successful overlanders were those who figured out that they were far better off playing into this cultural world rather than trying to resist it. Of course, the problem was that as they traveled farther along the trail, Indians continued to ask for gifts. When emigrants began running short of supplies, the demand became hard to meet. Some of the people were generous in what they gave to Indians as they crossed Nebraska, but by the time they got to western Wyoming, where the obligation was being asked by Shoshonean people, they had to say, "We just don't have these things. We can't give you any more." That was a problem of supply and demand that was not solvable.

DJL: Emigrants brought their prejudices with them. However, as evidenced by the diaries and letters of overlanders, the journey west often was transformative. To what extent do you feel that emigrants' encounters with Indians on the trail encouraged their ability to see beyond cultural and racial distinctions?

MT: Most people who arrived at a jumping-off town on the Missouri River brought negative concepts of the Indians. Back east, there were two views of Indians: James Fenimore Cooper's noble red man and the fearsome savage.[4] But clearly the savage image, brought on by popular culture, including the dime novels, outweighed the other image. Most people were very apprehensive about Indians. Many were absolutely stone-cold afraid. You see it in the diaries. As they moved across Nebraska, where they were meeting Pawnees, Sioux, Southern Cheyennes, some of this fear would dissipate. They would see Indians and trade with them; Indians would come into camp. It was normal activity, as though the Indians were other white people. For a substantial number—it's hard to say what proportion, it's all anecdotal—some of the fear would go away. Others heard secondhand tales of Indian problems that kept the fear alive, even if they themselves weren't having any problems with Indians. Such stories could have been true, but oftentimes they were nothing more than rumors that were passed on for lots of reasons.

When I edited the Belshaw diaries, I found that George Belshaw, the brother-in-law on the trip, was so matter-of-fact about Indians that he hardly made any mention of them.[5] But his sister-in-law, Maria Parsons Belshaw, was so fearful of Indians that by the time they left Iowa, she was looking over every hill, thinking that they were going to get her. The Belshaws reached Fort Laramie just after an incident had occurred there, and they did pick up on some of the fear that was still being circulated, but they didn't have any problems with Indians themselves. Yet Maria never transformed. She continued to see Indians as an ultimate threat. So George and Maria had two very different views of the trip. It was almost as if they were on different wagon trains.

All in all, I was encouraged in doing my research to learn that a significant number of people came away from the experience with a different attitude toward Indians than they had when they left the river towns at the beginning of their trips.

DJL: Can you comment on how the emigrants behaved once they were on the frontier? Did some use the relative freedom to revert to savagery? Did the majority of them respect the rights of the Indians?

MT: I certainly encountered some outstanding cases, that were repeated over and over again, of really pathological people on the trails. One was referred to as "the Texan." He was mentioned by several people on different wagon trains. He boasted that he was going to kill as many Indians as he could. He received the condemnation of the people in his party. This was a case where someone was going to be big trouble for the wagon train if he carried out what he said he was going to do. Others were just big talkers: "I'm an Indian fighter from way back." Their main damage was to get people stirred up and worried about Indians.

There were definitely bad people, but most overlanders, especially those going to Oregon or the Mormon settlements in the Great Basin, were traveling with their families. Most people would not want to be a loose cannon in front of their family. Because they were among the very people they would spend the rest of their lives with, they would remain civil. It gets a little dicier, I think, with the small groups that were traveling to the California gold fields, many of whom were young men traveling with other young unmarried men from their home towns.[6] They may have shown more of a tendency to overboast their manliness.

For others, it was the rules that enforced civility. There was a lot more formality in the ways that some of the wagon trains were organized than is often appreciated. They weren't just a hastily thrown-together bunch of strangers. By the time overlanders had left Iowa, Kansas, or the eastern part of Nebraska, they had formalized the rules for their wagon train. You were to follow these rules right down the line, or you were out of the wagon train—and being tossed out could leave a person in a desperate situation. They weren't worried only about violence toward Indians but about violence among the emigrants themselves.

The overland experience didn't create the most violence-prone people in the world. It was a mixture: the best and the worst of America were on the trail.

DJL: In *The Frontier Army in the Settlement of the West,* you suggest that the army played a positive role in protecting the Indians against incursions by settlers, feeding them, providing medicine, and doing early ethnology to understand them better. Do you think that on balance the existence of a standing army along the trails led to more peace or to increased conflict?

MT: Most soldiers who were in the dragoons in the 1840s saw their primary duty on the trail as being to protect emigrants. It was their first and foremost responsibility. But the army was very small in that period, and the troops were stretched out over 2,000 miles, so they couldn't really protect the overlanders all that much. The emigrants looked forward to getting to Fort Laramie and Fort Kearny not so much because the troops were there, but because there were supplies there. They couldn't count on an army escort.

In addition to protecting emigrants, the army had the job of protecting Indians. You see this clearly in the army records and to some extent in the overlanders' records. The army ran white interlopers off land where they wanted to settle or where they were abusing the Indians' resources. Unfortunately, the army was understaffed, and the directions given to it about protecting the Indians were ambiguous. The army's greatest weakness in terms of protecting Indians, however, was that officers had no clear rights to arrest civilians. They did so occasionally, but it often led to legal trouble for the officers who did it. It's not the trail that provides the best examples of this. It's in the more settled areas. On the trail there were fewer white people to complain, but in the settled areas there were white timber cutters, hunters, or illegal liquor dealers who would sue the army for arresting them.

When conflict did occur, it often wasn't the regular army itself that engaged in military combat against Indians. For example, at Sand Creek, it was a Colorado militia. The army can be faulted for certain attacks on Indians; Washita and Blue Water Creek, for example, were attacks by the army that are hard to justify and that led to increased conflict.[7]

But I think that the army did about as much as it could. It got stuck between two impossible jobs and was not given enough resources to handle either one. General Sherman, who was frustrated by the attacks on the army by both the Christian reformers and those who wanted to wipe out the Indians, commented: "The army takes these fisticuffs from both sides."[8] There was no way for the army to extract itself from this dilemma. Nevertheless, I give the army very high marks for specific cases where it went in and took a stand to protect the Indians—when I say "army" I mean one or two officers, not the whole army. It was done because it was morally right to do and it also helped Indians over the short term.

The army had a major role in the development of the West. It was engaged in many things: exploration, transportation, communication, farming, contracting to local citizens, providing disaster relief, and so on. And it was the only federal agency out there for a long time that could enforce the law. There were no marshals, no local sheriffs. Until you got to the goldfields or to the Willamette Valley, the army was the only one with any authority in the broad expanse of the West, especially prior to the Civil War.

DJL: Isn't it true that, while the threat to emigrants by Indians was overblown, the Indians were always a potential hazard and emigrants could not afford to let down their guard? For example, while Unruh says that the biggest threat to the emigrants was not loss of life but theft of livestock,[9] wasn't this often devastating for emigrants, especially in the Great Basin?

MT: You are right. Whenever you deal with strangers, you are dealing with an element of the unknown, and that unknown can be threatening. That was an ultimate problem on the trails that could not be resolved. An overlander couldn't look into the hearts of people approaching his camp, whether they were Indian or white. They could be peaceful or they could be brigands. As they moved west each day, the emigrants encountered new groups of Indians who were not necessarily as friendly as those that they had met earlier. The Indians faced a similar problem. Indians could not approach a wagon train at a fast pace. It was essential that they approach it slowly, and they had to make what they considered motions of peace. Unfortunately, the people in the wagon train didn't necessarily understand their gestures.

In most cases there was no conflict. But encounters did on occasion involve acts of violence, and obviously emigrants experienced bad events, like the loss of a loved one or livestock. It was the death knell to lose livestock. It left them vulnerable. They had to buy other livestock or rely on others to loan animals to them. They could afford to lose some things, if it was just pilfering going on, but they couldn't lose livestock, food, or water supplies, particularly once they were in the Great Basin.

There also were misunderstandings. If three Indians came up to a wagon train, they probably had no prior plan to run off livestock or kill somebody. If they wanted to kill somebody, they would have found a lot easier way to do it than riding up to a wagon train. And many times, when Indians would seemingly threaten one or two men who had wandered away from a wagon train, it turned out to be a joke. The Indians would posture, making a kind of threat, but they would be laughing at the same time. Some emigrants picked up on this, that such Indians weren't really dangerous. Others would ask, "What are they up to? Why are they laughing?" That could be pretty threatening. I was surprised to see a number of such cases where, from the way the white men described it, you get the feeling that the Indians were just having a good laugh about it—a little bit of bullying, with no intention of doing anything worse. But it always was difficult to know the intentions of the other.

DJL: When violence did occur on the frontier, an important problem was that both Indians and settlers, when seeking revenge, did so indiscriminately against all members of the enemy group, without determining the actual guilty parties.

MT: I think that is a really big issue. It was true not only on the trails but also for later settlers who lived in the West. The idea that revenge is not carried out against the actual culprit who committed the act against you but that it can be generic against any of his "tribe" is totally unfair from our current view. And it was the source of a whole lot of problems because it was often the innocent who paid, while the guilty party escaped prosecution.

The town of Julesburg was in the northeastern corner of Colorado, on the trail to Denver and Pike's Peak. During the Civil War quite a few people were coming through that area on the trail. Toward the end of the Civil War, Julesburg was burned by the Cheyennes and Sioux twice within less than a year.[10] But, in my view, the people who were victimized there were pretty innocent.

DJL: Wasn't it revenge for Sand Creek?

MT: Yes, revenge for Sand Creek and other incidents that were happening in the western part of Nebraska and eastern Colorado. Most of the people who were killed, injured, or driven off were not the leaders in mistreating the Indians. I don't know how such reprisal could have been avoided, but it was a source of more problems for the Indians themselves because then there had to be a response from the army or from some other federal authority. It mushroomed out of control.

DJL: The whites engaged in inappropriate reprisal too. Sand Creek is an example of the whites attacking an innocent group.

MT: That was a frontier mob, Colorado militia, most of them coming out of the bars in Denver. It wasn't the United States Army, but mostly frontiersmen seeking revenge. They were going after Indian noncombatants that were easy to get. At Sand Creek, most of the Cheyenne and Arapaho men were away hunting in western Kansas, and the Colorado militia knew that ahead of time.

DJL: Historian Marc Simmons makes the following point: "Maybe on the Oregon Trail in particular the Indians were not as dangerous as is generally believed. . . . On the Santa Fe Trail there is no question that from the very beginning the Indians were extremely dangerous."[11] Can you compare emigrant/Indian relations on the Oregon-California Trails to those on the southern trails?

MT: While I have not studied it closely, I have given it some thought, and I believe that there might be at least three big differences. The first difference is the time span. For the southern trails, the story starts in 1821 when William Becknell's trip opened up the Santa Fe trade to Missouri.[12] So there were twenty years of white/Indian contact on the Santa Fe Trail before the first identifiable group of emigrants—the Bidwell-Bartleson party of 1841—went west on the Platte River Trail. And that probably made a difference because, as I have said, the longer the northern trails were used and the more white/Indian contact happened, the more friction there was.

The second thing that I think might prove to be different is that the tribes in the Southwest had a longer history of contact with white people—with Spain, Mexico, and eventually the Texicans—compared to the tribes along the Platte River Trail. The northern tribes' contact with whites certainly went back to the late 1700s, but it wasn't as formal or as divisive as in the Southwest and Texas. There were some areas where Spain and Mexico were successful with these tribes; but for the most part, it was a much more divisive relationship over a longer period. That bred problems that were well entrenched by the time the entrepreneurial traders on the Santa Fe Trail and the people heading for the California gold rush in the 1850s started using the southern trails.

A third big difference between the two trails, as discussed earlier, is that for the northern trail, particularly in the 1840s, most of the people going to Oregon or to the Mormon Great Basin were going as families—men, women, and children of all ages. In the culture of the Indians along the Platte River Trail and in the northwest territories, the bringing of families was almost a sign of peace by its very nature. Any group traveling with women and children was most likely on some kind of peace mission or hunting mission. They were not there for conflict. But those traveling the Santa Fe Trail from 1821 forward were mostly merchants and mostly male, not families. In the 1850s, on the southern emigrant trail, it was mostly male miners. And although the Indians did not automatically assume that each of those miners and each group passing through Arizona and New Mexico was a danger, the Indians had a more reticent view of these groups than they would have had of groups of families traveling through.

I think that one of the biggest needs in trail history right now, at least in dealing with the Indian/emigrant relations, is a study of the southern trails, beginning in 1821 with the Santa Fe Trail and including all the variant southern trails across Oklahoma, Texas, New Mexico, and Arizona. Such a study would examine as many primary sources as possible; and while there aren't as many such sources for the southern trails as there are for the northern trails, there are enough for that kind of research. Ideally ethnohistorical techniques would be applied, so it would require someone who has some ethnological background for the southern tribes, since you can't always apply the same ethnography as for the northern plains tribes. Such a study of the southern trails would allow a follow-up comparative study of all the trails taken together. But we are not at a point yet in the basic research for a big synthesis to be written.

DJL: Concerning research sources, do any firsthand accounts exist by participating Indians who had lived along the northern trails in the mid-1800s, similar to the interviews that Eve Ball and Grenville Goodwin conducted with older Apaches?[13] What surviving Indian oral traditions give voice to Indian/emigrant relations on overland trails? Are the stories of tribal descendants as reliable as the diaries, journals, and letters written at the time of the actual events? How did you determine which sources are trustworthy?

MT: I am a real devotee of Eve Ball's work on the Apaches. I grew up reading those books when they first appeared. They are excellent because they not only keep the storytelling within the Apache cultural view but do it in a way that a non-Indian can read it as traditional history. Her books *Indeh* and *In the Days of Victorio* both do that. Jason Betzinez, who was very young at the time of the Geronimo wars, also did an interview with Wilbur Nye back in the 1930s.[14] It's a very short book, but very good for the period.

The problem with a lot of the oral histories that have been written is that they are not totally oral histories. They are based upon interviews, but they basically are written by non-Indians. That raises the issue of the authenticity of an Indian account that is written for an Anglo audience in a conventional way and that goes through an interpreter. Maybe Cheyennes or Apaches wouldn't tell the story that way in their own language for their own audience.

DJL: The books by author Frank Linderman are possible examples.[15]

MT: Yes. There are a number of such books for the central and northern plains tribes. In my book, I used some that did speak to this period. John Stands In Timber's *Cheyenne Memories* is actually a very good book.[16] George Hyde did the book based on the letters of George Bent, and it has a lot of the Cheyenne history.[17] I also used Sarah Winnemucca's book.[18] Probably the best book lately has been the one by Susan Bordeaux Bettelyoun.[19] These were a series of interviews done a long time ago. They sat at the Nebraska State Historical Society until recently, when they were put together in a meaningful way.

Each of those people did talk about the trail period, but it wasn't a focus of their story. That is really sad, because they did see a lot of the transition period, particularly the more troubled later 1850s and 1860s. But for whatever reason, many of the stories that we consider to be from the better Indian sources were written by whites, and most talk about the later periods, which I think reflects the interests of the interviewers of the later time. They were often interviewed in the 1920s or 1930s, and the interviewers would ask, "What do you know about Custer's Last Stand?" It's almost as if the trail history era is ancient history, and there is no connect between the events of the 1870s and 1880s and those of the 1840s, 1850s, and 1860s.

Concerning oral traditions, I do want to mention the book by Joseph Marshall.[20] He is a Lakota man who provided two stories of Indian-white contact on the Platte River part of the trail, concerning acts of kindness that the Sioux performed, not because of profit but because white people were in a bad way. He said that these are traditions within the tribe. Maybe those kinds of stories can't be absolutely proven, but I think there is legitimacy to what he says, and I think the two examples he gave really tell about what the trend was.

I also used the University of South Dakota Oral History Collection—it's a massive collection that was done in the 1960s and very early 1970s, consisting of interviews with Indian people across the northern plains all the way to the Pacific Northwest. Quite a few tribal people, most notably Sioux, were interviewed. But there was virtually no mention of the trail period. It has material on Little Big Horn and Wounded Knee, but it's mostly twentieth-century material because that's what most of the interviewees were living through.

In terms of authenticity, over 2,000 published and unpublished accounts by whites can easily be identified for the northern trails, but there are just bits and pieces of Indian accounts. How do you deal with this? First, you go to the sources that you can identify and try to glean things, and then you go to ethnohistory. You have to understand the cultures of the tribes and try to explain how their cultural values and motivations may have caused them to react to a situation in a particular way. Ethnohistory can try to put it in the context of the time and try to understand the Indians as real and realistic people, rather than, for example, foolish little children getting pushed aside and making bad bargains. Ethnohistory is not an answer for everything, and it can lead to its own problems, for example, by reading too much into accounts. But, in my opinion, that's the way it has to be done, for the northern trails and the southern trails alike.

DJL: Some tribes, like the Kiowas, had calendar records. Chip Colwell-Chanthaphonh cites the Papago calendar stick in his book on the Camp Grant Massacre.[21]

MT: "Winter counts" prepared by plains tribes during the nineteenth century are also helpful primary sources, but they must be further explained by surviving oral traditions.[22] There are many ways to get at Indian sources, but they are limited. Anyone who thinks that it's possible to get vast new evidence about the overland trails by simply going out today and talking to a group of Indians is really naïve. It's not going to happen. Another problem with interviewing Native people today is that oftentimes they have learned their tribal history by reading the same sources that white people have read. From them, it's coming across as tribal tradition, while we are coming across as historians or ethnographers. And yet both stories are coming from white sources.

DJL: Marc Simmons has also challenged the claim by some scholars of the frontier that captivity narratives were sensationalized and exaggerated and that female captives who were carried into captivity did not suffer. He states that "the evidence that the narratives are essentially correct is overwhelming" and that "many captives were ruined mentally and physically by the experience."[23] Can you speak to captivities along the Oregon, California, and Mormon Trails?

MT: Taking captives was indeed a normal practice among the plains tribes and was a major component of the intertribal raiding process. But comparatively speaking, fewer emigrants were taken captive on the northern trails than on the southern. Most of them seem to come during the Civil War era, when there was an unofficial war between the United States and some of the tribes.

It is true that some captives were tortured and some were put to death, particularly adult men who had very little chance of being adopted into the tribe. And certainly there were women and children who were killed immediately after their capture. But most captive-taking was to gain new members for the tribe. Such captives were given a very harsh breaking-in period, lasting for several months and even up to a year, to see who was going to survive the transformation. Afterward, tribal members often adopted the captive. Once the adoption took place, the captive became a member of the tribe, with all the rights and prerogatives. The tendency was to capture children, since they were the most malleable, the ones most likely to adjust culturally. Not adult men.

Women were problematic; some were killed, but some become members of the tribe through adoption.

I don't think that the best examples of captivity narratives are from the northern trails. The best cases are from Texas and involve the Comanches.[24] The Comanches were the biggest group affecting the trails through the southern plains. They were an expanding population and needed to bring more captives into their society. They had been raiding Mexico since colonial times and bringing back lots of captives. Most of those captives eventually made it as members of the tribe. You can see that in the names of Comanche people today, many of whom are Hispanic. So Anglos just became another component of that. I wrote an article some years ago for *Chronicles of Oklahoma* on the Comanche captives.[25] It is overwhelming how successful the acculturation process into the tribe was. But it could be brutal too.

DJL: Wasn't that the case with the Apaches and their Mexican captives as well?

MT: Yes. In fact, I think there are a lot of parallels between the Apache groups and Comanches on the taking of captives.

Now, I must add that every captivity story is different. Some of the stories were brutal, heart wrenching, making you feel that there was no good bone in the body of the captors who committed such evil acts. But you also find stories of people who were captured and adopted into the tribes and who lived very successful lives. They resisted the option to go back to their white families—their families were Comanche. They had no desire to return. Many of them who were captured very young had forgotten the white world, but others who were only a few years removed from their Anglo parents would still not go back. They had defined their existence within the Comanche world. They found it comforting, warm, and fulfilling.

DJL: Margot Mifflin is convinced that Olive Oatman did not want to leave her Mohave society and return to the white society.[26]

MT: Some people have argued that, in Victorian America, it would be societal death for a woman to return to the white world after having lived with Indians. I think this was an element, particularly for those who had been captured for a very short time, so that acculturation didn't have time to take effect.

DJL: After being held captive for three months by Algonqian Indians, Mary Rowlandson assures her readers in her narrative that she is still a good Puritan woman.[27] In fact, she writes her narrative not only to retell the details of her captivity and rescue but to let her readers know that the Indians didn't touch her sexually.

MT: In *Indians and Emigrants*, in the chapter on captives, I talk more about the *perceptions* of captivity rather than what happens to captives later. Most of what I was doing there was dealing with the emigrants' perception that every Indian that came into their camp was looking to take white children or women captive, either by buying them or by sneaking in and grabbing them. Many women were filled with these notions before they even got into the West. There are funny tales of women who were just petrified of Indians. They felt that the Indians' eyes were locked on them. Someone in the wagon train might comment in his journal that old Mrs. Bailey, who was sixty-five years old, thought that the Indians wanted to take her as a captive—sort of poking fun at the whole situation.

There is a story of a woman with a small child. An older Indian man and woman were in her camp. The Indian woman wanted to pick up the child and put it on her horse. The mother wouldn't let it happen; she felt that these two Indians were there to steal the child. But if they were coming to steal the baby, why would they do it in such a public fashion? They would have been risking their lives to do it. You could just as easily read the situation as that the Indian woman simply wanted to take that child on a horseback ride through the camp.

I try to put myself in the shoes of people of the time since, even though it was very uncommon on the northern trails in comparison with the southern trails, captive-taking *was* done. If I were that white mother, I wouldn't hand over my baby either.

DJL: The Utter disaster apparently was an example of captivity on the northern trails.[28] But the events were so sensational as to be almost unbelievable, with a very vicious attack by Indians, unconscionable desertions by members of the party, and cannibalism.

MT: The Utter disaster is like a Hollywood story. If you are going to make a movie of a massacre, this is the one you should use. If I were just coming across the story for the first time, without having read Donald Shannon's book or other writings about it, I would have been incredulous about it too. Interestingly, there are suggestions that some of the people involved may not have been Indian but may have been white bad men. That's hard to tell. It's certainly not out of the realm of possibility.

DJL: While the stereotype of a tall, bronzed Indian with an eagle feather warbonnet has dominated many westerns and dime novels, isn't today's popular image of the Indian who lives in close association and harmony with nature equally false? In your opinion, what authors are contributing to a more realistic portrait of the contemporary Native American and the present-day Indian scene?

MT: There are a lot of wannabe Indians out there. Some people feel a personal attachment to the notion of the Indians of the past living in nature and close to God. And we've had a thirty-year cycle of people pretending to be mystics, preaching ancient Indian rituals, who turn out to be frauds.

What constitutes traditionalism among Indians? Who is a "traditional" person and who isn't? It is difficult to say, but I usually explain it in the following nonperfect way. You know a traditional person when you are around him or her for a long time because culturally he or she does things that are traditional. But the word "traditional" is misleading because *when* is tradition? Is it 1750, or 1850, or 1950? Indian societies have always evolved. They never have remained the same. A certain behavior that we see today as very traditional might have been something foreign to the generation of the 1750s.

I think today a lot of good work is being done on the American Indians, some by Indian authors and some by non-Indian authors. There is a whole debate out there about whether non-Indians can even do Indian topics. It's always worthy of consideration to read those points. It challenges your own way of doing things. Obviously I myself feel that non-Indian people can do Indian history. It takes a lot of transcendence of your own cultural ways and your own background. I teach in a Native American studies program where we have Native and non-Native faculty; it's a very good group of people who have integrated well with each other. I think that we all bring a lot to the table and that we are all open-minded about the pitfalls of studying Native American cultures and history.

DJL: Incorporating actual events interwoven with invented ones, Oakley Hall's novels such as *Warlock*, *Apaches*, and *Separations* concern the history of the Southwest during the 1880s. According to Hall, "the pursuit of truth, not of facts, is the business of fiction."[29] In contrast to dime novels, can't literary western novels and movies give us a good understanding of the West and of the motivations of the settlers, the army, and the Indians?

MT: In my frontier history classes, I always talk about the "real West" and the "imagined West." We deal with both sides. By the "real West" I refer to whatever knowledge we have about what really happened. But I tell students that it is wrong to reject the so-called imagined West that comes out of literature and movies. For one thing, these represent the way that most of us have perceived our history. And what literature and movies can do is give the feel for the past. Historians don't always capture that because they feel more compelled to make their story conform with what they can prove or find in the evidence. Sometimes they can bring a strong feeling, but sometimes they can't, depending on the topic. But novels and movies can. Of course, there are bad movies and novels out there but also many good ones. If you want to study western history, you have to have some feeling for the past or you are missing an essential aspect. It's soulless just to focus on the exact details, on what can be proven.

I have always had a divided opinion about John Ford's movies. Every year I tell myself I won't watch Ford's trilogy on the frontier army.[30] They are not accurate movies. The Indians are treated pretty badly in all three. Ford uses stereotypes or caricatures in his creation of the character: the Irish sergeant, the drunken commander. In *Fort Apache*, Henry Fonda is the Custer image. While I have all kinds of reasons to pick those three movies apart, they are interestingly done and they really give me a strong emotional feeling for the times that I don't think any other movie does. But when I show them in history classes, I need to give some explanation along with them. Don't look at these as typical Indians, for instance. When Ford filmed *Cheyenne Autumn*, he said that he did it to make up for all the grief that he caused in his other Indian movies in the past. But even *Cheyenne Autumn* did not provide the best perceptions of Indians.

Concerning literary works, I often assign Mari Sandoz's *Old Jules*.[31] It's not a novel but is based upon her life with her father. He was a cantankerous old man, not a cultural icon, not a wonderful father. He was god-awful to his family. Such stories also need to be told. Some of the events may be questioned as to whether they were actual truth or represent literary license. But if you want a sense of being out on the Nebraska panhandle at the time, read that book.

DJL: Do you have a final comment?

MT: I hope that anyone who wants to get a better understanding of this subject will go back to the chapters of my book that explain what the Indians sought out of the relationship with the emigrants. They didn't just trade for goods; the Indians also provided essential services for the overlanders. They provided food and livestock, helped them across rivers, and a whole host of other things. Sometimes what each side got out of the relationship was very tangible and self-serving, but sometimes it was simply hospitality. Those are amazing stories to see. Even though they are anecdotal, they help us in the twenty-first century to understand that these were people in difficult circumstances, who didn't fully understand each other and who couldn't look into the crystal ball of the future, but who acted humanely in so many ways. And that is very different from the stereotype that we all have grown up with.

Graphic of Sutter's Fort in 1847. Courtesy of the California State Library.

The earliest known photograph of John Sutter, circa 1850. Courtesy of the California State Library.

CHAPTER 6

Destruction and Survival of the California Indians

An Interview with Albert Hurtado

THE POPULATION OF THE CALIFORNIA INDIANS prior to the advent of the Spanish has been estimated to be on the order of 300,000. These Native peoples were organized into a large number of tribelets, living mostly in small villages (*rancherías*) and speaking a large variety of dialects of six major language groups. Most were hunter-gatherers and relatively peaceful. The Colorado River Indians (Yumas and Mohaves) were the exception, forming large tribes that farmed in the river bottoms and engaged in extensive warfare.

The Spanish founded a series of Franciscan missions along the coast of California, beginning with San Diego in the south in 1769 and culminating in 1823 with the twenty-first mission in Sonoma in the north. On the whole, the Indians were not coerced but came to these missions peacefully for a variety of reasons. A primary reason was that, in the face of resource depletion following Spanish colonization, they sought to participate in the agricultural economy established at the missions. Coercion was used, however, to prevent the Indians from leaving the missions once they had become baptized; in effect, the mission Indians were a semicaptive labor force. The Indians were segregated by sex and expected to abandon their culture and adopt Spanish practices of marriage, family, and religion.

Overcrowding and the introduction of European diseases such as smallpox, measles, and syphilis led to a very high death rate in the missions, but deaths also occurred due to violence. A key example was the Santa Ynez revolt. In 1824 a Spanish presidio soldier at Santa Ynez flogged a neophyte, setting off a revolt that spread to the La Purísima and Santa Barbara Missions and lasted several months. During the revolt, padres were taken hostage, even though the Indians maintained that their quarrel was with the soldiers. The Indians burned the Santa Ynez Mission and barricaded themselves into La Purísima Mission; the Santa Barbara Indians looted their mission and then fled to the San Joaquin Valley, where they tried to involve the valley Yokuts in the revolt.

Sixteen Indians died, and many were wounded. Ultimately the Indians were pardoned.

The missions were secularized in 1833, and most of the large landholdings were converted to Hispanic ranchos. These were the domains of important Californios, such as Mariano Vallejo, but a number of non-Hispanic landowners were also involved. The most famous of these was John Sutter (1804–80). In 1834 Sutter emigrated from Switzerland to America. From a base in Missouri, he journeyed to Santa Fe as a trader. While there, he presumably met mountain men who had been to California. He followed the Oregon Trail to the Willamette Valley in 1838 and then went to California by ship via Hawaii. In California, Sutter settled in what is now Sacramento, establishing over time a large agricultural empire based on Indian labor and protected by a private militia, whose soldiers were local Indians. He was notorious for incurring unpaid debts. When gold was found at his sawmill in Coloma, miners invaded the area, and his empire quickly fell apart. After many legal battles over his land claims, he retired to Pennsylvania, where he died in 1880.

It has been estimated that by the late 1840s, prior to the American takeover, the Indian population had decreased from 300,000 to 150,000; this was due to a combination of disease, destruction of traditional resources and hence starvation, and to a lesser extent violence. The onset of the California gold rush brought rapid destruction to the remaining Indians, especially those of the interior who had not been part of the mission system. Disease again played a role, as did the wide-scale destruction of the Indians' resource base due to mining in the mountains and farming and ranching in the valleys. Violence was endemic, as miners, ranchers, and settlers killed Indians in response to depredations such as theft of cattle but occasionally even for sport. This occurred especially in northern California, where the federal government had the least control over the civilian population. While some of these small-scale encounters were reported in the California press, many went unreported.

In addition, a number of large-scale massacres occurred. The Clear Lake Massacre, also called the Bloody Island Massacre, occurred on May 15, 1850, on an island called Bo-no-po-ti at the north end of Clear Lake. A group of Pomo Indians had been effectively enslaved and treated quite cruelly by two emigrants, Andrew Kelsey and Charles Stone, in a ranching operation at Clear Lake. To make matters worse, Kelsey and his cohorts took a workforce of Indians to the placer mines but didn't feed them adequately and left them behind in the wake of a malaria epidemic. Only a few of the Indians survived. The Pomos revolted and killed Kelsey and Stone. In retaliation, the United States

Army under General Nathaniel Lyon massacred over two hundred Pomos on Bo-no-po-ti.

The Burnt Ranch Massacre occurred in 1853 near the mouth of the Smith River on the northwest coast of California. In retaliation for the murder of some miners, white citizens from Crescent City attacked the Tolowa Indians who were attending a dance at the Yonktakut *ranchería.* While existing accounts are not specific, whites burned out and slaughtered a great number of Indians.

In February 1860, apparently in retaliation for Indian depredations (especially cattle theft) in the Humboldt County area, a group of ranchers from the Eel River attacked a peaceful gathering of Wiyot Indians on Indian Island in Humboldt Bay, just opposite the town of Eureka. Approximately one hundred Indians, including women and children, were killed. Simultaneous attacks on Indians apparently occurred on a beach south of Eureka and in the Eel River area.

Due to these combined causes, the Indian population in California has been estimated to have reduced from 150,000 prior to the gold rush to 30,000 by 1860.

ALBERT HURTADO is Travis Professor of Modern American History at the University of Oklahoma, where he teaches the American West and Native American history. He is an authority on the California Indians and on the effect of Spanish, Mexican, and American settlement on their populations and cultures. His books include *Indian Survival on the California Frontier* (1988), which won the Billington Prize of the Organization of American Historians; *Intimate Frontiers: Sex, Gender, and Culture in Old California* (1999), which won the Neuerburg Award of the Historical Association of Southern California; and *John Sutter: A Life on the North American Frontier* (2006), which won the 2007 Caughey Prize of the Western History Association. We interviewed Hurtado in his office in Norman, Oklahoma, on July 16, 2008, in a discussion that ranged over all three books.

DJL (Deborah and Jon Lawrence): *Indian Survival on the California Frontier* speaks of the enormous population loss of California Indians—from 300,000 prior to the Spanish, to 150,000 at the beginning of the California gold rush, to 30,000 in 1860. You point out that disease, starvation, and violence—probably in that order—accounted for thousands of Indian deaths. What studies are these figures based on? Is it possible to be more quantitative about the number of deaths in each category?

AH (Albert Hurtado): The basic figures and the basic ideas behind the population decline of the California Indians are due to Sherburne F. Cook, who was initially a biologist.[1] He became a friend of Alfred Kroeber, the great anthropologist, who asked him to work on Indian population.[2] Cook then became a historical demographer, and he started a revolution in the way we think about not only California Indians but Native American history generally.

It is probably not possible to be more precise about these numbers. First of all, you have to begin with a population estimate rather than a census. You have to decide which of the estimates you are going to accept—and they have been all over the map. I still think Cook gives reasonable figures. It was initially considered to be somewhat revolutionary when he came up with a number as

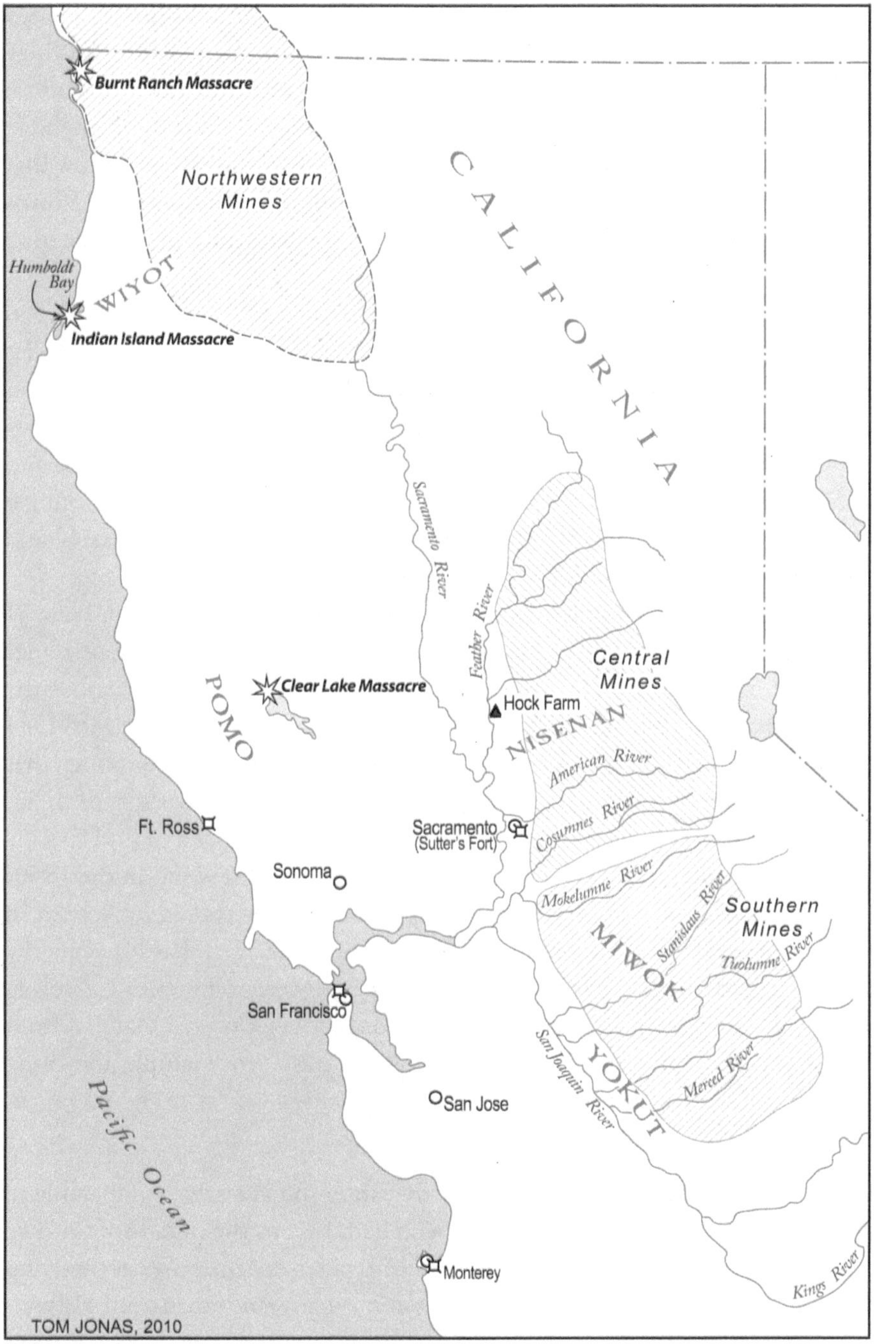

California in the mid-1800s, showing mining districts, locations of significant massacres, and the territories of several Indian tribes. Adapted from Hurtado, *Indian Survival on the California Frontier.*

large as 300,000 Indians in California prior to the Spanish. Others estimated more than a million, while Kroeber thought it was maybe 130,000. So there is no agreement on the starting number for the precontact Indian population. But even if you take the most conservative figure, which I don't think anybody accepts anymore, the censuses that came after the American takeover show that you are still dealing with a massive population decline. The argument turns out to be about the slope of the graph rather than whether a large decline took place.

It also is hard to get at precise figures on homicide. A lot was published in the local newspapers—for example, the *Daily Alta* often published articles about killings that had taken place in northern California—but these articles are often vague in terms of the numbers of casualties.[3] There are no official figures that you can go to. You can delve into the records of the state militia and a group of papers called the California Indian War Papers, where you can get detailed information about some of the massacres of Indians.[4] But that would give an incomplete accounting, even for the activities of the state militia.

The same kind of problem exists concerning the indenture of Indians.[5] I had hoped, vainly as it turned out, that since such indenture was done under the color of California state law and since the law is rather specific about the records that had to be kept, there would be a way to use those records. Or I thought that maybe I could trace back from the tax record—the money that was collected that was supposed to go into a certain fund—that sort of thing. I thought that I could go to the court records in each county and find specific statistical information. Well, I tried all of that, but it didn't work. In the 1850s a lot of these records either were not kept the way they should have been in the first place or were simply lost. It was rather scandalous that for years the county records were in a terrible state of disarray. Most counties in California did a very poor job of maintaining their records, so a lot of that material from the early period was lost. While some things still exist—for example, they were pretty good about keeping track of property records—most of the minor records, the court records, are gone.

DJL: Do any firsthand accounts by participating Indians exist, comparable to Mooney's interviews with the Kiowas who had lived in the mid-1800s or Eve Ball's and Grenville Goodwin's interviews with older Apaches?[6] What surviving Indian oral traditions give voice to the relations between Indians and Hispanics or Anglo-Americans?

AH: In California a number of books have been published that are mostly about Indian stories before contact. For example, there is *Californian Indian Nights* by Edward Winslow Gifford, a Berkeley anthropologist, and Gwendoline Harris Block, an editor of anthropology texts. And Theodora Kroeber, who was the second wife of Alfred Kroeber and the author of *Ishi,* also published on these topics.[7] But while there are a number of collections of California Indian stories—myths, creation stories, that sort of thing—there are comparatively few accounts by Indians of what happened to them after contact. One of the best, by Hans Jørgen Uldall and William Shipley, was taken down by a linguist.[8] It was published as a work in linguistics, where you have the Indian language on one side and you have it translated into English on the other side. While there is comparatively little published on their accounts of history, I think more such material exists. Kroeber and other anthropologists did a lot of interviewing. His published books on the Karoks and the Yuroks have considerable information in them, but I also think that a lot of his unpublished work remains to be gone through and published.

DJL: You offer a rather bleak view of Spanish and Californio treatment of the Indians. Were some Indians well served by the mission system and its American aftermath, and if so how?

AH: The ones who survived were well served to the extent that they had some new skills. Agricultural skills, skills as vaqueros, the skill of making braided leather such as riatas, which are rawhide lariats, would all have been very important at that time in California. So they had a way to make a living. They also knew Spanish. Some of them received land under Mexican law when the missions were secularized and their resources were redistributed. Those skills and resources gave them several ways to survive. But another thing would have been equally important: they could be recognized not as Indians per se but as Mexicans. Therefore they wouldn't be in the line of fire as would those who were identified as Indians. If they could identify themselves as Mexicans, then they were less likely to be picked up under the provisions of the state government's law for the protection of the Indians, which was basically a forced indenture law.

So there were some advantages, but it was a harsh winnowing because the death rates in the missions were very high. This was evidently due largely to the effects of the concentration of Indians at mission establishments, coupled with the introduction of new diseases, especially smallpox and syphilis. And again here I'm relying on Cook, who based his estimates of population during the mission period and his statements about disease on the writings of the missionaries themselves. It's not like this is a secret. The Indians had a lot of syphilis. The missionaries lamented that they were not able to control the sexual behavior of Indians, which was for them, of course, a spiritual matter as well as a medical matter.

DJL: One of the outstanding facts brought out by your work is it that in nineteenth-century California Indian women died at much higher rates than Indian men. It is not so clear to us why this was the case.

AH: Syphilis seems to have been more deadly among women in this population than it was among men. And it was a cause of high rates of mortality during childhood. Of course, the syphilis could be passed from the mother, so children could be born with it. Most children with syphilis did not survive childhood; but if they did, they had the disease when they became sexually active. So syphilis seems to have been a major contributor to the death rate, partly because it helped to depress both the birth rates and the survival rates of children who survived birth. The death rate was higher among women, so there were fewer women of child-bearing age. It became a vicious spiral that sucked the Indian population downward.

DJL: You suggested one other reason why the population of women was smaller during the era of Sutter and Bidwell: the populations of the ranchos where the Indians were concentrated consisted mostly of men because that's what they needed in the field.[9]

AH: Yes, that's a change that occurs among non-Hispanic employers, if I can lump for the moment rancheros and missionaries as being Hispanic. Anglos—and now I'm calling Sutter an Anglo, which of course he wasn't—were not particularly interested in maintaining an Indian community or even families. Whatever their faults may have been, missionaries were at least interested in that. Sutter and those like him wanted so many hands in the field, and they wanted mostly male hands. They put women in the field when they needed them, during periods when there was a high demand for labor, during harvest, and times like that. But otherwise they mainly wanted men. So bringing men into settlements like Sutter's Fort or into the other ranches meant that women were left behind and exposed to whoever came along, whether it was an Indian group like the one from Mission San José that sought to sell the women and children to Mexican rancheros on the coast or whether it was some Anglo group.[10] It was a hard time for women.

DJL: A small number of big massacres occurred in California, such as the Clear Lake Massacre of May 1850, where from sixty to one hundred Pomo men, women, and children were indiscriminately killed by infantry in revenge for the murder of Kelsey and Stone, who had been severely abusing their Indian laborers for some time.[11] Yet these large massacres appear to have been one end of a continuum of a much larger number of smaller violent incidents. For example, Native peoples were killed in the goldfields in retaliation for theft of livestock, and those killed were often not the guilty parties. Is it possible to get a sense of how many such smaller massacres occurred and what their total impact was?

AH: While the same problem with documenting numbers that we discussed earlier also exists here, in some areas of California the killing of Indians clearly was widespread. There were particular massacres of small *rancherías* that wiped them out entirely. These were primarily in the northern quarter of California. That's where the killings were most pervasive, where they lasted the longest, where they were most isolated from any sort of state or federal control. The federal government tried to exert some control over these local massacres, some of which were done by state militia groups and some of which were simply done by men who decided to go out and kill Indians.

For example, local citizens went in and killed all of the Chimariko people upriver from the Hupas in a place called Burnt Ranch; that was one of the worst massacres up there.[12] There were many such incidents; some of them were reported, but some of them weren't. The federal government tried to think of ways to use the troops to prevent this, but almost always without success.

DJL: It strikes us that the murder of Kelsey and Stone that led to the Clear Lake Massacre represented kind of a last straw for those Indians who had been subject to considerable abuse. It reminds us of the 1824 Santa Ynez revolt, which was a response to abuses of neophytes by presidio soldiers.[13] The California Indians appear to have been exceptionally patient with abuse, but only up to a breaking point. They were nothing like the Cheyennes or Kiowas, who would never have tolerated such treatment.

AH: As far as patience is concerned, if you are born into a situation it is different than if you are brought into it as an adult. By the time of the Santa Ynez Mission revolt, two or three generations had been raised in the missions, at least in part. So the mission was not something new. It was their community. At the same time, they were connected sometimes by blood and by linguistic affiliation with Indians out in the valley, who seemed to offer them a refuge.

They had pretty good relations with the missionaries, but the presidio soldiers could be brutal, and it was the soldiers they rebelled against at first. But once they rebelled against the soldiers, their options sometimes narrowed very quickly. Either they had to go back to the fold or they had to say: "Gather a few things together because we are getting out of here. We are heading for the valley." Or "Let's barricade ourselves in Santa Ynez and hope for the best." They had just a few options once violence broke out, and there was not a lot that they could do.

I also think that critics of the mission system have thoroughly discounted the message of Christianity. By that time, for almost two thousand years, people all over the world had found this to be an attractive, compelling message. The California Indians had to a certain extent become Christians voluntarily, but whether they had been converted voluntarily, through the compulsion of circumstance, or at the point of a sword, they had remained with the Christian church. There is no reason to think that California Indians would have been any less attracted to Christianity than other groups throughout history, even though the church and Christianity came packaged with aspects of colonialism and Spanish conquest that were negative for Native peoples.

You talk about Indians being patient. Well, patience was a Christian virtue, obedience was a Christian virtue, and they lived by those rules. But not completely, because there was a great deal of syncretism. They did not completely abandon everything else that they knew. This is one of the common themes of Christianity among Indians in the Americas. Most European Christians think that either you are or you are not a Christian. They don't see that it is possible to be both a Christian and something else too. As far as Indians were concerned, it was quite possible. The Pueblo Indians of the Southwest are a primary example. But the same kind of syncretism went on in California. It doesn't mean they were not Christians. Steve Hackel's book *Children of Coyote* does a good job of explaining this.

On the other hand, with Stone and Kelsey, I don't think that it was so much that the Indians were patient as it was that those men were well armed and they would kill without compunction. If they wanted to torture somebody, they would torture him. The Indians had good reason to fear for their lives. Stone and Kelsey were well armed, so the Indians waited for their moment. It was fear more than patience. I think what happened was that once they were taken up to the placer mines, where so many of them died, they figured: "What have we got to lose? We are going to die one way or another." It was then that they acted.

DJL: This suggests the point that while the Cheyennes and Kiowas had guns, the Pomos at Clear Lake didn't.

AH: That's right, but there also were substantial cultural differences. You are talking about Plains Indians, warrior societies, where fighting and success in war and stealing your neighboring tribe's ponies or counting coup were really good. And you had to do it before you could get married. Those societies were organized in a very particular way.

The California Indians have been given a bad rap because they don't measure up to the Sioux, who would never have let this sort of thing happen to them. But look at the reaction of Europeans of medieval times when some baron came and killed their lord and brutalized the population. They didn't do anything very different than California Indians; they tried to accommodate themselves as quickly as possible in order to stop the pain. California Indians reacted in ways that were quite human and recognizable. "How do we make the best of this bad situation?"

DJL: We would like to turn next to your recent biography of John Sutter. In order to build his empire, Sutter had to establish control over the local Miwok and Nisenan tribes. Ultimately he was so successful that he was able to use them as laborers, as purchasers, and as a defensive army. To accomplish this he used both positive inducements (trade goods, intertribal security, and participation in a power structure) and punishment (flogging, decapitation, war). Nevertheless, it is quite amazing that he was able to establish this control so quickly, and starting from such a small number of initial non-Indian collaborators (ten or fifteen). Is it possible to trace in detail how he went about it, especially in the early stages before his dominion was established?

AH: I have puzzled over that. If the Indians had just struck him down at the beginning, it would have solved a lot of their problems. For one, I suspect, but cannot prove, that Sutter knew exactly where he was going and what he was doing. He knew about the people he was going to meet. He knew what to tell them. He already understood the divisions among Indian people and the divisions between the Indians of the interior and Mexicans and Indians on the coast. He knew he was going into a borderland. I think he knew this because people had told him. He had talked to mountain men and fur traders . . .

DJL: In Santa Fe?

AH: Yes, in Santa Fe, but also in Missouri. Missouri was a jumping-off place to go down to Santa Fe and on to California. And he talked to people who had been involved in the fur trade in northern California. A series of horse-rustling operations up north had been going on for years. I think Sutter knew all about that. But he never says so. He gives only the vaguest hints. He did not convincingly explain why he wanted to go into the interior when he had other opportunities out on the coast. I think it was because he had a pretty good sense of what was there, so he knew what to tell that first group of Indians that he encountered just south of today's Sacramento. It was probably a mixed group of mostly Miwoks.

I misread this situation when I wrote *Indian Survival.* Having to deal with all of these different Indian groups with unfamiliar names, I decided that wherever Sutter was standing, he was in the territory of the Indian group that was indicated on the map that people like the anthropologist Alfred Kroeber had drawn.[14] "When he was standing there," I reasoned, "he was in Miwok territory. If he went a little farther north, then he was in Nisenan territory. And those are the people he was dealing with." But going back to the topic and looking at even more evidence when I was working on the Sutter biography, I obtained a better sense of what he did. He went to the Sacramento Valley. He hooked up with the Miwoks, who were former mission Indians, and he took them—or they took him—up to present-day Sacramento, where they drove out the Nisenans. By his accounts, the Nisenans fled in front of him. But who were the Nisenans fleeing from? Maybe they were fleeing from Sutter, but probably not. They were most likely fleeing from the Miwoks.

DJL: Are you saying that he got together with the Miwoks and said, "Let's go get the Nisenans"?

AH: Right! And he pushed them out. The area where Sutter established the fort was initially Nisenan country. Everything north of the Cosumnes River was probably traditional Nisenan country. Sutter drove them north of the American River. To accomplish this, he brought Miwoks up from the Cosumnes River drainage and he put them around the fort. Those were his shock troops. It was certainly not only Sutter and eight or ten compatriots who accomplished this.

DJL: What were the Miwoks getting from it? Why couldn't they have done it without Sutter?

AH: They probably would have done it if they could have done so without Sutter. But Sutter gave them access to trade goods and firearms. He made them part of his Indian army. He took them up there and basically gave them access to Nisenan resources. He left the Cosumnes *rancherías* empty. Eventually, when he made peace with the Nisenans, Sutter moved them south behind him, down to the Cosumnes River, where they reoccupied the old Miwok villages.

Sutter rearranged the pieces on the board, and then everybody was beholden to him. He gave the Nisenans these new semiautonomous places to live, while elevating the Miwoks and giving them a key position in the southern Sacramento Valley, which they had never had before.

Sutter was a clever man, a smart man. And while it is hard to demonstrate, Sutter had personal assets that are very difficult to appreciate without actually meeting the man to see what he was like. He impressed people, at least on a first meeting. True, by the third meeting he owed you money. But at the first meeting, you were going to be impressed. He dressed well. He spoke well. He looked impressive. And this somehow translated across linguistic and cultural boundaries. He was likable. He would kill Indians if he needed to, but he preferred to use presents and promises. If diplomacy failed, Sutter used violence. But that was not his first option. Still, when he had to be ruthless, he could be as ruthless as all get out.

Sutter is a tremendously interesting character. I heard somewhere that when you write a biography of someone, you are inviting them into your house for a couple of years. In fact, that's right. And with Sutter, I have to say . . . he was great company. He was immensely interesting all the time because I never quite knew what he was going to do. And after he had done something, I had to figure out why he did it. It was not always clear, and it was usually not for the reason that he gave in later years when he was talking to Bancroft.[15]

DJL: At the conclusion of your book, you write that John Bidwell really liked and respected Sutter and that nobody was more intimately acquainted with him. But John Laufkotter, Sutter's former friend from Missouri, who also really knew Sutter, spent his later years attempting to debunk the Sutter legend.[16]

AH: But they were describing the same person. Bidwell is surprising because he was such a straight arrow, a prohibitionist. His wife, Annie, was right out of the same mold.[17] And yet, when Sutter died in Pennsylvania, she was mindful of Sutter's importance to John's career in early California. Laufkotter, on the other hand, was bitter because Sutter had disappointed him in Missouri and New Mexico in the 1830s. He never got over it.

DJL: Under Vallejo, Sutter, Bidwell, and others, the Indians served on the ranchos as a labor force for agriculture that served the international economy.[18] This trend continued briefly during the early gold rush. To what extent were

Indian men drafted into the California European workforce, outside the goldfields, after the gold rush? Did any Indians attain success as laborers in the free-market economy?

AH: Not much outside of the agricultural and mining world. They quickly got pushed out of the mines, but agriculture remained the one sector of the economy where they could still be reasonably certain of finding work. One of my students, William Bauer, is about to publish a book on the Indians of Round Valley. It is a study of Indian labor in the later period, after 1865 until World War II. The basic story is that Indians incorporated labor into their community. Labor and even migrant labor became an expression of their identity and community. On the one hand they had the reservation, which gave them stability and a place that they were attached to. But instead of a seasonal round where they would collect acorns or go hunting and fishing, they would have a seasonal round where they would go to ranches and pick hops or some other agricultural crop.

DJL: Did they work the railroads?

AH: They did some railroad work, but not much. There are other groups who came in and worked the railroads: the Irish and the Chinese. It's an interesting story. The Chinese and the California Indians did not get along well.[19] One of the reasons the Indians didn't like the Chinese was that they were the only people on the planet who would work cheaper than the California Indians.

DJL: During the gold rush, emigrants brought their prejudices about Indians with them. However, the diaries and letters of overlanders suggest that the journey west often was transformative. To what extent do you feel that the journey to California encouraged at least some emigrants to see beyond cultural and racial distinctions, and to what extent did anti-Indian sentiment prevail among the settlers?

AH: I have a pretty dreary outlook on this. I think that very few people are looking for new cultural experiences. Most people cling to what they know. When they are confronted with something that is different, most people most of the time feel that it is not only different but bad. This is one of the themes of *Intimate Frontiers*.

DJL: Well, take Louise Clappe as an example.[20] She represents seeing things anew. She started with an image of Indians as noble savages, obtained from reading James Fenimore Cooper; but when she saw them for herself once she was in California, she appreciated the difference.

AH: Right. California Indians did not measure up to her romantic expectations. It was hard for her to escape her culture. She got divorced and wound up living as a schoolteacher, which was one of the few areas of work that was available to her as a woman in the mid-nineteenth century. I see her as an intelligent observer who was good at describing mining life. However, I should add that there is some question as to the extent that *The Shirley Letters* were hers; those letters may have been heavily edited. It is difficult to follow their provenance.

DJL: In *Intimate Frontiers,* you examine Clappe's experience in the mining camps as part of your discussion of the ways in which sex and gender shape the cross-cultural relations among California's Mexican, Indian, and Anglo-American residents in the mid-nineteenth century. How did sexual violence work in this context?

AH: The basic idea behind *Intimate Frontiers* is that every culture has its own rules about sex and gender. Genders are constructed identities. Every culture makes women into something and men into something and values certain kinds of behavior for each. Likewise, proper sexual behavior is constructed by every culture. Often when cultures come into contact, one or the other group will say, "Well, these people are immoral." But they are not immoral. It's just that their rules are different.

I thought that California offered a laboratory to study what happens when you have three distinctive cultures that come together with different ideas about gender and sexuality. One of the things that happens is that there is usually some accommodation in the direction of the more powerful group. For example, the formal sex and gender ideology of Spanish California was that which was imposed by the Catholic Church and the missions. Presumably everybody was supposed to follow those rules. But at the same time, the Native American people remembered other rules; and when they had the opportunity, they followed those rules. All of this caused a great deal of trouble.

But to make matters worse, soldiers and muleteers and other secular Hispanics had not only the Catholic point of view but also a macho point of view, consisting of ideas that revolve around masculine honor and family honor. They were more Mediterranean in outlook, rather than strictly Catholic. They valued the seduction of women. Almost always when rapes occurred between Spanish men and Indian women, the Spanish man regarded it as a kind of seduction. Of course, the Indians regarded it differently. You also had the problem of imbalanced sex ratios. There were many Hispanic men but comparatively few Hispanic women, at least in the early days. So all of this had to be negotiated and worked out. There was some intermarriage that seems to have been constructive and long lasting, leading to the formation of families, but there was this other behavior, whether rapes or sexual liaisons outside of marriage.

And then, of course, Anglos and Protestants came in and that made things more complicated. Their view was not so different from the Hispanic Catholic outlook, but just enough different to make it interesting. As time went on, the winners shaped the rule book more and more. So the outcomes were skewed toward known, established rules that Anglo-Americans brought with them from the East or that Hispanic Americans brought with them from Mexico.

DJL: It is just as you were saying about transformation: they really didn't want to transform; they wanted to perpetuate their old culture.

AH: Right. Some men took Indian wives, but this was not because they were seeing beyond their own culture but because no other women were available. Often they gave them up as soon as white women became available.

DJL: In *Intimate Frontiers,* you discuss the way in which Bret Harte's sentimental story about compassionate pioneers in "The Luck of Roaring Camp" stands in stark contrast to his earlier journalistic account of the slaughter by local white citizens of a large number of Wiyot Indians living peacefully near Humboldt Bay in 1860—the Indian Island Massacre.[21] Can you comment on how he could entertain two such contradictory attitudes toward the miners?

AH: I wish that I had the opportunity to meet Bret Harte and ask him that very question. I can only surmise. He was a Victorian man, after all, and he had Victorian sensibilities in a lot of ways. To write about something like the Indian Island Massacre as fiction would have been pretty hard. It was horrific and probably would not have been very well received as fiction. He was trying to sell his stories, and he wanted readership. I don't mean that self-interest was the primary story here, but I think it would have been just very difficult to write this event as fiction and expect it to be well received. In his "Luck of Roaring Camp" I think he was trying to make a larger point about the shared humanity of Indians and miners. And that was the way he chose to do it. It would be hard to make that point if you had the miners slaughtering all of the Indians.

DJL: We are interested in your opinion as to whether historical fiction can play a significant role in preserving the "truth" about the past.

AH: It is hard to generalize about that. I read a lot of historical fiction. As a rule, I don't read it to get at a better sense of the truth in history. Fiction writers are not constrained by the rules that I am constrained by. I think that most authors who write historical fiction use history as a backdrop and then they put their characters in front of that backdrop. The history is a dramatic device, and the author is free to make whatever points he or she wants to make. I think that is all fair game. That's why they call it fiction.

A good example of what novelists can do is *Blood Meridian* by Cormac McCarthy, which is right in the middle of my interests.[22] I think it's a great novel. It takes historical events that we know occurred and then adds a great deal to them. His portrayal of the southwestern desert landscape and the characters who inhabited it is brutal, but I think pretty much right on the mark.

DJL: The level of savagery and violence in the book is incredible. And the savagery is not confined to the Anglos—Hispanics and Indians are indicted as well. As such, it goes beyond political correctness.

AH: It's horrifying. A lot of the people who went west weren't very nice. There was a reason why they were on the move. Sutter was a gentleman by comparison to many of them, and they recognized him as such. But a lot of the people that he worked with, that he relied on, were cold-blooded killers any day of the week that they needed to be.

DJL: Like Kelsey.

AH: You wouldn't want him to move in next door—no way! In the popular imagination, we tend to see settlers as "the family." Mom and Dad are doing a good thing by breaking the land and establishing the family farm. The day-to-day reality of the human parade that was marching through Indian country was quite different from that. Sure, there were some salt-of-the-earth upstanding farmers, but some of these characters were just on the move and attached to nothing, to no one. They had led brutalized existences probably all of their lives, which is what McCarthy was getting at in *Blood Meridian.* It's a great book.

DJL: Tell us about your current project.

AH: What I'm working on now is a biography of Herbert E. Bolton.[23] A major theme is how historians live in a particular social, cultural, and political world. Bolton wrote in a world that was not altogether welcoming to him or to his ideas. He was making heroes out of Catholic priests when the Ku Klux Klan was at its height. In 1901 to 1909 he was writing in Texas, where few people had much sympathy for Spain or Mexico. In California, while there was more interest and sympathy for the California missions, there was a counter-influence from the Anglo-American gold rush crowd. He relied on the Native Sons of the Golden West for fellowships for his students and for himself.[24] There was always a contingent that was quite unhappy that money was being spent looking into this Spanish and Indian stuff.

And then there was political intrigue in the university itself, which involved a man by the name of Frederick J. Teggart. He was on the history faculty and curator of the Bancroft Library. When Bolton got there, he forced Teggart out of the curator position. Teggart stayed on the faculty, and they fought ever after that. There also is a lot of interesting detail about the nature of the world that Bolton was living in, and the alliances that he had to form that crossed ethnic boundaries. He was very good friends with Roman Catholic priests and bishops, but he was also close to some important Jewish people. (He himself was a lapsed Methodist.) And there is the story of his dealings with the California state legislature and the governors. So the book concerns the politics of history.

The point I'm trying to make is that even though we would deny it, few of us are really free agents when we write history. There is a real world that is impinging on us in a variety of ways. You spoke above about political correctness. There is certainly some truth to that: some things can get you into trouble. Certain terms, words, attitudes, points of view, and issues are inherently controversial. This was true in Bolton's time also, except that the issues and prejudices were different. Before World War II, for example, the Protestant-Catholic split was far more important than it is today. So the biography offers an interesting counterpoint to some of our current debates over political correctness.

CHAPTER 7

The Sioux Wars

An Interview with Robert Utley

THE SIOUX WARS WERE A SERIES of conflicts between the United States and the Sioux during the latter half of the nineteenth century. An early event in these wars was the Grattan Massacre, which occurred on August 19, 1854, east of Fort Laramie in Nebraska Territory. Second Lieutenant John Lawrence Grattan (1830–54) of the U.S. 6th Infantry Regiment was ordered to bring in High Forehead, who had killed a Mormon settler's cow that had wandered into the Sioux Camp of Brulé leader Conquering Bear. Refusing to give up High Forehead, Conquering Bear was shot in the back and killed. This started an armed conflict in which Grattan and thirty of his soldiers were killed.

In retaliation for the Grattan Massacre, the Battle of Blue Water Creek (also known as the Battle of Ash Hollow) occurred on September 3, 1855, when 600 U.S. soldiers under the command of Colonel William S. Harney attacked and destroyed a village of 250 Brulé Sioux along the Platte River in Nebraska, killing roughly 85 people, including many women and children.

The Santee Sioux uprising was an armed conflict between the United States and several bands of Santee Sioux. During the 1850s the Santee Sioux had been confined to a small reservation bordering the Minnesota River, surrounded by German and Scandinavian immigrant farmers. Unscrupulous traders prevented the Sioux from receiving their promised annuity payments. The conflict began on August 17, 1862, along the Minnesota River in southwest Minnesota when, in an outburst of frustration, the Sioux killed several hundred white settlers. The uprising concluded with the mass execution of thirty-eight Sioux in Mankato, Minnesota.

The Fetterman Massacre occurred on December 21, 1866, when a large band of Cheyennes and Sioux, including Crazy Horse, attacked a wood train near Fort Phil Kearny on the Bozeman Trail. The warriors decoyed Captain William Fetterman's soldiers from the confines of the fort into an ambush in which Fetterman and his command of eighty men were wiped out.

Red Cloud's War of 1866–68 was a series of battles, including the Fetterman

Lieutenant George Armstrong Custer, 7th Cavalry. Courtesy of the Little Bighorn Battlefield National Monument.

Wooden Leg's drawing of the seizing of a soldier's gun at the Battle of the Little Bighorn. Courtesy of the Little Bighorn Battlefield National Monument.

Massacre, over the use of the Bozeman Trail by miners traveling to the Montana mines and over whether the army could establish forts to defend the trail from the Indians. The Treaty of Fort Laramie (also called the Sioux Treaty of 1868) ended Red Cloud's War on terms favorable to the Sioux. The United States agreed to abandon the forts in the Powder River country, which was then designated "unceded" territory closed to all whites, where the Indians were granted hunting rights. All of South Dakota west of the Missouri River, including the Black Hills, was set aside as the Great Sioux Reservation.

The Sioux War of 1876–77 followed incursions by miners into the Black Hills, which were part of the Great Sioux Reservation. After the U.S. government failed to persuade the Sioux to agree to sell the Black Hills, it issued an ultimatum to the tribes that they must leave the unceded territory and report to the reservation. When the Indians did not respond, General George Crook was sent to bring them in. Crook's troops had two engagements with the Indians in the Powder River country. The first occurred on March 17, 1876, when troops under Colonel Joseph Reynolds attacked a village of Northern Cheyennes on the Powder River in southeastern Montana. The troops initially captured the village, destroyed the lodges and their contents, and captured the

Indians' pony herds; but after a five-hour struggle, the Indians recaptured the initiative and ultimately retrieved their ponies. This defeat and the freezing weather drove Crook's troops back to Fort Fetterman. In the spring Crook began a new offensive, designed to attack the Indians from the south, while General Alfred Terry and Colonel John Gibbon attacked from the east and north. On June 16, 1876, inspired by a vision experienced by Sitting Bull, Sioux warriors attacked Crook's troops on Rosebud Creek. After fierce fighting, Crook retreated to his supply base and consequently was unavailable when Custer engaged the Sioux at Little Bighorn.

The Battle of the Little Bighorn ("Custer's Last Stand") began on June 15, 1876, when Lieutenant Colonel George Armstrong Custer approached a combined Sioux-Cheyenne village on the west side of the Little Bighorn River in southern Montana. Custer sent Major Marcus Reno and his men across the Little Bighorn River to attack the Sioux encampment from the south. Reno floundered, recrossed the river, and fled to the top of the ridge to the east. In the meantime, Custer attempted to attack the village from the north by following the ridge and then crossing the river from the bottom of Medicine Tail Coulee. Indians who were freed up for the engagement after Reno's escape pushed Custer back up to the top of Battle Ridge, where his command was ultimately wiped out. The Indians continued to attack Reno's troops until the next day, when they were rescued by troops under General Terry.

Following the Battle of the Little Bighorn, a number of battles with the Sioux and Cheyennes continued into 1877. The Battle of Slim Buttes (September 9, 1876) involved an attack on an Indian village in South Dakota north of the Black Hills by troops under General Crook. In the Dull Knife Battle (November 25, 1876), troops under Colonel Ranald Mackenzie attacked a village of Northern Cheyennes under Morning Star (also called Dull Knife) on the Red Fork of the Powder River in Wyoming. During the Battle of Wolf Mountains on the Tongue River in Montana (January 8, 1877), troops under General Nelson Miles engaged in a battle with Sioux and Cheyenne troops under the leadership of Crazy Horse. These battles and others showed the Indians that they were not safe from attacks by the federal troops, even in the winter, and helped convince them to return to the reservation.

The Battle of Wounded Knee (December 28, 1890) was the last armed battle between the Sioux and U.S. troops. After more than ten years of living on the reservation, many Sioux took up the Ghost Dance religion. This religious movement, which was widespread among western tribes, had begun in 1889 when the Paiute prophet Wovoka had a vision: if the Indians were virtuous

The Paiute prophet Wovoka (Jack Wilson) in 1911. His visions and teachings led to the Ghost Dance, which brought solace to Indians throughout the West but led to tragedy at Wounded Knee. Courtesy of the Nevada Historical Society, Reno.

and peaceful and practiced the Ghost Dance, a paradise would be made for them, with no whites and with their dead ancestors resurrected. In adopting Wovoka's pacifistic teaching, the Sioux altered the message to a more militant version, which was extremely antagonistic to the whites. A number of hostile Sioux groups carried out their version of the Ghost Dance outside the reservation boundaries, at a site called the Stronghold. This led to an army campaign to have them forgo the dance and return to the reservation. The Wounded Knee tragedy occurred when a Miniconjou group under the leadership of Big Foot, whose ardor for the dance had already cooled, attempted to go to the Pine Ridge Reservation to help mediate peace. On December 29, 1890, Seventh Cavalry troops under Colonel James Forsyth engaged in a point-blank battle with the Miniconjous, who were resisting the troops' efforts to get them to surrender their weapons. At least 150 Indians, including women and children, were killed, as well as 25 soldiers.

Until his retirement, ROBERT UTLEY was chief historian and assistant director of the National Park Service. He is a founding member and former president of the Western History Association. The winner of many awards, he is widely considered a dean of historians of the frontier West. His books *Frontiersmen in Blue* and *Frontier Regulars* are classic treatments of the history of the U.S. Army and the American Indians in the period from the Mexican War to the end of the frontier. *The Indian Frontier of the American West, 1846–1890* gives an important interpretive overview of the same period. His work also includes books on the Lincoln County War, the mountain men, and the Texas Rangers.

We interviewed Utley at his home in Georgetown, Texas, on September 22, 2008. Our interview focused on the wars with the Sioux. In addition to the books mentioned above, we discussed material from his biographies of Custer (*Custer: Cavalier in Buckskin*) and Sitting Bull (*The Lance and the Shield*) as well as his treatment of Wounded Knee (*The Last Days of the Sioux Nation*).

DJL (Deborah and Jon Lawrence): The Grattan Massacre and its aftermath, the Battle of Blue Water Creek, constitute one of the earliest engagements in the Sioux Wars.[1] While many battles in the Indian Wars, such as Sand Creek or Camp Grant, involved punishment of Indians who were innocent of depredations committed by other tribal members, we get the impression from reading *Frontiersmen in Blue* that Harney was knowledgeable about the actual perpetrators of violence after the Grattan Massacre.[2]

RU (Robert Utley): At Blue Water, Harney attacked a village. Women and children were killed. He won that battle. He believed that they were the ones who were responsible for Grattan's annihilation, but it can be argued that, to Harney, these were simply the closest Indians. More generally, I do not believe the army knew very much about who they were after. Among a bunch of Indians, how could they tell who were the ones they were after and who were the ones they were not after? Keep in mind that we are not talking about today's values. We are talking about the attitudes and values of the Regular Army in the 1850s.

DJL: The Santee Sioux Minnesota uprising was perhaps the bloodiest massacre by Indians of noncombatant whites in the nineteenth century.[3] What was behind this massacre? While *Frontiersmen in Blue* makes it clear that the annuity system was corrupted by unscrupulous whites, were these Indians starving or was this a case where they hadn't adjusted yet to the reality of their defeat, confinement on reservations, and encirclement by white settlers?

RU: First, I wouldn't agree with applying the term "massacre" to this case, even though you are probably right in your basic assumption that more noncombatants fell casualty to that uprising than any I can think of—a large number of the farmers who were surrounding and encroaching on Santee territory.

I think, though, that what happened in 1862 was the trigger that ignited a whole decade of building resentment, a resentment of having lost their lands to the encroaching farmers and then having been confined to two very narrow reservations on either side of the Minnesota River. Contributing to the resentment was the very serious political corruption of the whole Minnesota establishment. The trading establishment was at the center of it. (I note that General Sibley was one of the prime traders.)[4] There was total corruption on the reservations. But the corruption went beyond the traders. It reached as far as Washington, where Minnesota had a delegation in Congress. While the supply of rations to the Indians never completely died, it was frequently postponed. The long delay in the issue of annuities just prior to the outbreak really stirred up a lot of resentment. It was like a match being thrown into a haystack when the Indian trader Andrew Myrick said, "Let them eat grass."[5] This is about as insulting as you can get. In addition, during this decade there had been serious agitation within the tribe itself to respond to what was happening to them, with hostility, if necessary. I think that all of this is what did it.

DJL: While you show that it was typically younger Indian men, who were poorly controlled by older leaders and who were motivated by desire for prestige, that initiated much of the conflict with the whites, isn't it also true that younger army officers—Grattan, Bascom, Fetterman—created much of the conflict and with similar motivation?[6]

RU: I don't think that is a good comparison. We are dealing with a deeply ingrained Indian culture in which young men received prestige, honors, advancement, stature, and leadership by counting coups. Now this didn't mean seeking out battle with the military. It meant raids—preferably against another tribe. Indeed, it was the back-and-forth raiding between the Crows and the Sioux that really guided the main direction of the unfolding Sioux Wars.

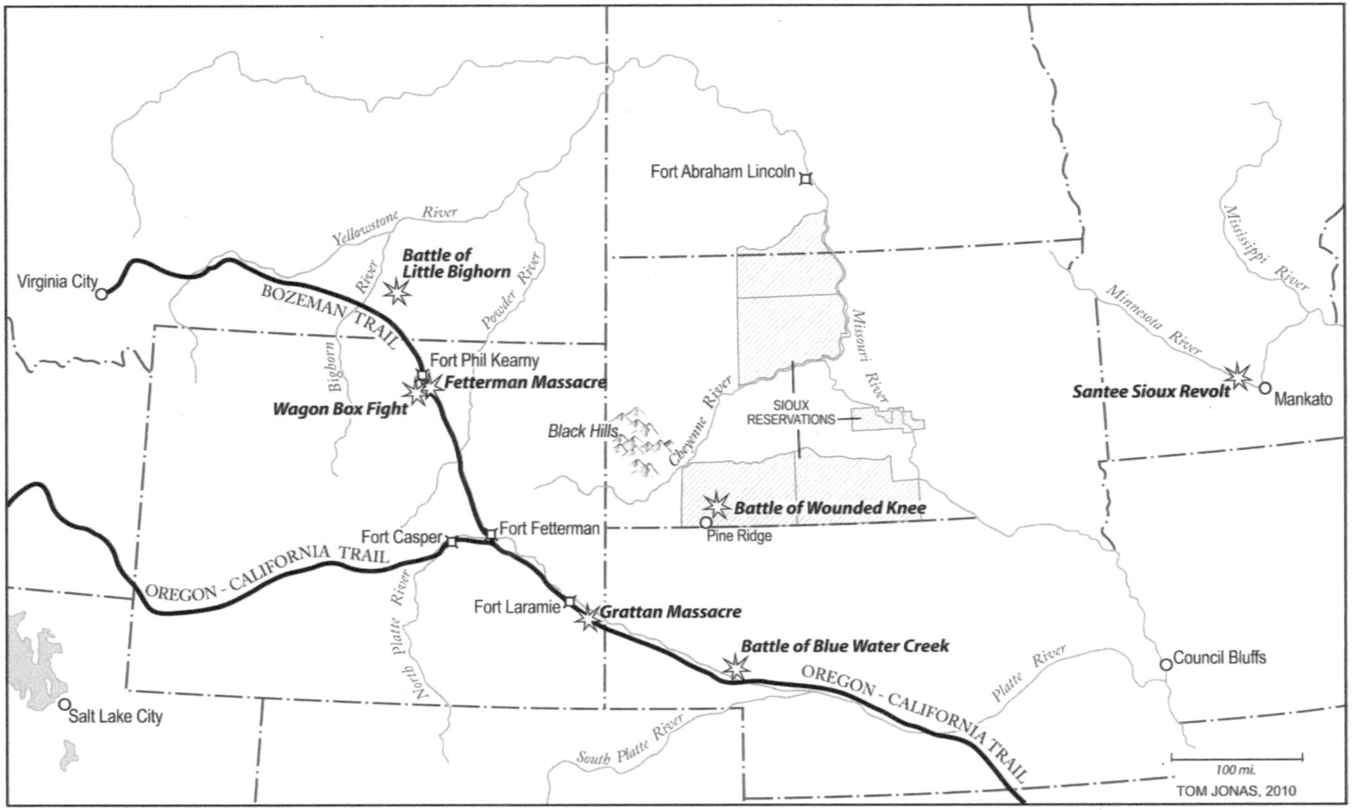

The northern plains, showing key sites in the Sioux Wars, including battle and massacre sites and the Oregon Trail and Bozeman Trail. The current boundaries of the Sioux reservations in South Dakota are also shown; the original reservation, granted to the Sioux in the Treaty of 1868, included all of South Dakota west of the Missouri River. Based on information in Utley, *The Indian Frontier.*

So it was a cultural thing that determined the advancement of the war leaders of the Sioux. As for the young officers that you mention, you can say that they were ambitious, but you can't say that they were ambitious for promotion because that was determined strictly by seniority and had nothing to do with how distinguished their record had been. I think that is crucial to understand. Grattan and Bascom were just young, inexperienced officers who had no judgment whatever. They were inexperienced and they thought the Indians were all bad. An older, more experienced officer with judgment and understanding of Cochise and the Chiricahuas would have handled the Bascom affair entirely differently. If Grattan had been more mature, he would surely have handled that situation more diplomatically and attempted to avoid bloodshed. He was looking for a fight when he went down there.

DJL: Fetterman also appeared to be looking for a fight. Officers such as Fetterman and Custer are typically characterized as arrogant and overzealous, as exemplified by Fetterman's infamous declaration that with eighty men he could ride through the entire Sioux nation. How accurate is this characterization of Fetterman and Custer?

RU: I think it may be overstating the case to call it "arrogance." Lots of officers were arrogant without being competent. Lately there has been a reassessment of the whole Fetterman battle and the role of Crazy Horse, which may entirely rewrite that story. I can't give you the details. I've just picked things up here and there. Part of the new interpretation is that Fetterman did not disobey [Henry B.] Carrington's orders. While he was a rash young officer, his belief that he could ride through the whole Sioux nation exemplifies a very common military belief—that the Indians could easily be rolled over by experienced, organized soldiers, as indeed was frequently the case. The Indians were totally disorganized, and the military was organized into formations with officers in command and so forth. But Fetterman simply blundered into a big trap. How much he can be blamed remains, I think, for further study. The extent to which Crazy Horse did what we have always believed that he did also has come under question.[7]

As was also true for Custer, Fetterman was just out of the Civil War, just out of the volunteer service. He had a distinguished service record in combat against the Confederates. What is more natural than that he figured that a bunch of naked Indians were going to be an easy pushover after he had fought and shed blood fighting the Confederates?

DJL: This brings us to Custer. Was he arrogant?

RU: While I think that you are right about Custer being arrogant, I don't believe that was his defining characteristic. Custer was one of the greatest generals in the Civil War. He was a major general at age twenty-four. It is pretty much the consensus of historians who have studied the Union cavalry during the Civil War that Custer was the number two Union cavalry officer after Sheridan. But when Sheridan took on larger responsibilities, including infantry and artillery, I would say that Custer became number one. He gloried in war. He made himself deliberately conspicuous to his men and to the enemy with a personal battle flag, with his band right behind him all of the time, and with dedicated young men who wanted to get the job over and go home. He could order a charge and he had them all right behind him. The Confederates saw that and at least in one battle they broke and ran simply because they recognized it was Custer's brigade.

After the war, Custer went out West and found out that it was a different kind of duty than before. The enemy didn't stand up and fight like the Confederates did. The men that he was commanding were pretty much the dregs of eastern civilization. He could no longer be the glorious, bright hero that he was during the Civil War. And my thesis in the biography that I wrote of Custer is that he recognized that and transformed his image entirely.[8] He put on buckskin and became known as the great plainsman, the great hunter, who entertained visiting dignitaries from back East by taking them on buffalo hunts and so forth.

The Washita rescued Custer as Indian fighter momentarily.[9] The Washita was a victory. It brought glory to him. Of course, I am often asked about all the women and children who were killed at the Washita. Well, they were killed because they were there. Black Kettle's village at the Washita was not all that innocent. It was the trail of a raiding party of Cheyennes leading directly from Kansas to the Washita Village that brought Custer there. In any case, Custer's reputation was revived by that. He became an author to keep his name burnished: plainsman, hunter, author, Indian fighter. After time, the glory of the Washita receded. When he went up on the Yellowstone Expedition, he revived his reputation again. He was regarded back East as a premier Indian fighter, which he really wasn't unless the famed Custer's luck was favoring him, as it did at the Washita and on the Yellowstone. It deserted him, of course, at the Little Bighorn.

I should add that Custer was either idolized or abominated, then as now. He was a rank partisan when dispensing favors and quasi-punishments—for example, in his treatment of Frederick Benteen.[10] He gathered his family around him. Note also that, with all the frontier regiments, they were scattered among a number of posts. The regimental commander was not the determining influence in shaping the regiment; he was the company commander. The Little Bighorn was the first time the entire Seventh Cavalry had been together.

DJL: In the late 1860s Red Cloud was a brilliant military leader during the battles in the Powder River country over the Bozeman Trail. Why was he, unlike Sitting Bull and Crazy Horse, so quick to turn to reservation life following his victories? What is your assessment of Red Cloud?

RU: I think Red Cloud did not play as significant a role in Red Cloud's War as we have believed.[11] He was characterized as the leader by the whites and by the military, and in their minds he became the central figure. Until he would come in to sign that treaty, the war wasn't over. But in actuality, there were other chiefs who played at least as significant a role in the fighting over the Bozeman Trail. Furthermore, chiefs did not necessarily lead the military offensives of the Indians. It was every man for himself. Ultimately, the war ended because the view arose in the white perception that they were sustaining losses that were too great, especially since the Union Pacific Railroad had reached a point where travelers could get to the Montana mines more easily than by traveling on the Bozeman Trail.

Red Cloud's War was important in leading to the Treaty of 1868. But Red Cloud didn't come in and sign until he was good and ready, after all of the others had signed. And let me take exception with your statement that he was quick to embrace the reservation. He wasn't. What he wanted, and the only thing he wanted at the beginning, was to continue to trade at Fort Laramie. Now, you can ask: how much of this business about reservations, and all of the legal technicalities written into the Treaty of 1868, did he or any of the other Indians understand? What he did understand was that they weren't just going to leave him alone in the Powder River country and allow him to trade at Fort Laramie. He was supposed to settle on the Great Sioux Reservation, which at that point was all of South Dakota west of the Missouri River. They finally dragged him to the Red Cloud Agency, which in actuality was not on the Great Sioux Reservation at all. The government decreed that all of those Indians had to be moved not only onto the Great Sioux Reservation but also down on the Missouri River, where it was a lot cheaper to feed them. Red Cloud wouldn't go there, so they finally settled for putting him and Spotted Tail on the Pine Ridge Agency and the Rosebud Agency.

I credit Red Cloud with being the greatest statesman that the Sioux had, because for the rest of his life he was able to walk a narrow line, keeping the government reasonably satisfied without alienating his own people. That takes statesmanship. If you recall, Sitting Bull was the unyielding patriot. Red Cloud was the diplomatic statesman. I think in those reservation years, you could say that Red Cloud was a greater leader than Sitting Bull, who was resisting everything.

DJL: In reading your books, it becomes clear that bureaucracy, in Washington and in the West, played a key role in the response to the Indians. Political and bureaucratic infighting—involving the army, the Indian Bureau, the House and Senate, and so forth—reduced the effectiveness of the nation's response to the Indian problem. What are some notable examples from the Sioux Wars?

RU: I can cite you examples from all over the West, but I can't cite you a good example from the Sioux Wars because what led to the campaign of 1876 was cooperation among the Indian Bureau, the Interior Department, and the War Department. And this was all under the influence of President Grant.

As background, once Sitting Bull took refuge west of the Missouri River, he and Crazy Horse decided that they would go on the defensive. They didn't like the white people coming up the Missouri River, and at first they did go on the offensive, raiding the forts along the Missouri River. Those weren't big battles—I would call them skirmishes. But after Red Cloud's War, they decided that their stance would now be defensive. They weren't going to make any more offensive raids against those Missouri River forts. However, they would defend themselves if their Powder River hunting grounds were in danger. And, of course, that is what brought on the 1876 war.

The army, under Philip H. Sheridan and William T. Sherman, wanted an excuse to go after the Sioux in the so-called unceded territory, the area west of the reservation that was allowed as a hunting ground for the Indians under the Treaty of 1868. They wanted a clear field for the construction of the Northern Pacific Railroad. And in the fall of 1875 the Allison Commission tried to buy the Black Hills, or at least the mining rights to the Black Hills, from the Sioux, but this got nowhere.[12] The president had a real political dilemma. An existing treaty said that the army had to bar prospectors from the Black Hills, but the miners were going to go into the Black Hills no matter what. They were demanding that the army quit trying to keep them out of the Black Hills. So what could he do? The solution was devised by an Indian inspector, E. C. Watkins, who was an old wartime buddy of [William] Belknap.[13]

Now, while it was true that in earlier years these nonreservation Indians had been raiding white settlements—Bozeman, Montana, and up and down the Union Pacific—as I just said, in recent years they hadn't. Rather, recently they had been terrorizing peaceful Indian tribes up on the Missouri River—Mandans and Hidatsas and so forth. Watkins came back from an investigation of the Sioux country, and he said that these Indians were causing all kinds of problems for the peaceful tribes. He said that all of those nonreservation Indians should be rounded up and made to go to the reservation, despite the Treaty of 1868. This gave the army what it wanted. They brought Sheridan back to Washington, and a meeting was held that included Secretary of War Belknap and the commissioner of Indian affairs as well as President Grant. They left Sherman out of it. The decision of the president was that an ultimatum would be sent to all of the tribes: all of the Indians in the unceded territory were to report to an agency by February 1, 1876. If they didn't, the army was going to come and make them do it.

I don't think that any of these Indians understood the word "ultimatum" and what it meant to the white mind. When the runners came out during the winter, the Indians said: "Sure. We'll come into the agency. We go into the agency periodically and draw rations before returning to the wilds. As soon as the winter is over and it is easier to travel, we will come in and talk with you." As I said, I don't think that they knew that they had been issued an ultimatum. I don't think that they understood what was in store for them until the Battle of Powder River. By this time Sheridan had organized Terry, Crook, and Gibbon to converge on these tribes. When Crook found them on the Powder River in March of 1876 and attacked, in their mind this was a declaration of war. They didn't know why. But that kicked them from the defensive mode into offensive mode. And that led to Little Bighorn.[14]

DJL: Despite the fact that so much has been written about the Battle of the Little Bighorn, a definitive account of the battle has eluded historians. Has any recent research shed light on the mysteries surrounding the battle?

RU: Mike Donahue, who teaches fine arts here in the Georgetown area . . .[15]

DJL: Yes, he is a volunteer at the Little Bighorn monument. We heard his talk at the battlefield this summer. We thought it was superb. It was very balanced; he gave both military and Indian perspectives.

RU: Mike has been there now for eighteen or nineteen summers, and during this whole time he has devoted intensive study to every aspect of the battle, including getting on a horse and finding how long it takes to ride from one place to another. In the early 1990s they did some archaeological work there. If you remember, the layout of the land as you come up the entry way to the monument is such that on your right is an elevation and on top of that is the National Cemetery and the old stone house. The ridge projecting north from the old stone house was subjected to archaeology, and they found tons of material. At least to my mind, and contrary to all previous interpretations, this new evidence leaves very little doubt that, by the time he got to the north end of Battle Ridge, Custer led what was left of his command down over the National Cemetery and that ridge. According to Mike, he actually reached the river in an attempt to cross. Now to my mind—of course, you can argue these things forever—he was looking for a place to cross the river and get into the village. His command and control had collapsed by the time he got here, but he may still have believed that he could have gotten into the lower end of the village.

Custer's experience at Washita and the experience of other officers was that when you surprised and attacked an Indian village—especially if you did it from more than one direction—you set off a stampede. The first concern of the Indians was the safety of their families, and so they spread out to save them. If Custer could have gotten into that village below where Reno was supposed to be fighting at the upper end, it would have created such turmoil.[16] In reality, he didn't have enough men. But I do believe that the archaeology in the early 1990s raised the very interesting possibility that Custer reached the river north of Battle Ridge and then was driven back up into what is now the National Cemetery. So that is real new evidence.

DJL: Are you implying that Custer could have won?

RU: Yes, I think that if things were done differently, Custer could have won. His idea was to attack in two directions. As I said, the theory was that if he could surprise the village, even from one direction, he could create a stampede. And the fact is, that village had no warning of Custer's approach until fifteen minutes before Reno came advancing down the valley. When Reno reached the village, the defense scared him, and he dismounted into a skirmish line, which then pulled back into the timber. When Bloody Knife had his brains blown out all over Reno, Reno panicked and went back across the river to the bluff.[17]

In the meantime, Custer had seen the village from up on the heights. He had seen Reno advancing against the upper end of the village. He saw Medicine Tail Coulee down below. I think that's where he first intended to cross. It was the premature withdrawal of Reno that released all of the warriors who had raced down there to confront Reno, allowing them to come back where they discovered Custer on Medicine Tail Coulee. They counterattacked in such numbers that Custer was pushed back onto Battle Ridge.

Had Reno held those Indians at the upper end of the village long enough for Custer to get into their village from out of Medicine Tail Coulee, I think there would have been a different outcome. I should add that Reno had taken very few casualties, even on the skirmish line. In the timber he took almost none. Given all this, while Custer may not have won, I don't think he would have been wiped out. I think that, with these two columns confronting the Indians, and with their women and children at risk, there was going to be a stampede. They would have scattered.

DJL: Returning to archaeological research, we have read in one of Jerome Greene's books about archaeology that occurred at the battlefield after the 1983 fire.[18] They used volunteers with metal detectors to help uncover artifacts.

RU: There are several books that discuss that project. I feel they claim too much about the implications of what they found. They did learn that the Indians were better armed than had been previously thought. Other than that, I don't believe they found much but little vignettes. Based on some bones, bullets, buttons, and a marker, they would theorize and speculate as to what happened in one particular place. It was subjected to so much hype. In one instance, it was asserted that they found the shell casing of the bullet that killed Custer.

I publicly opposed the archaeology that occurred back in the 1980s. I even wrote an article in *Montana Magazine* about it.[19] The operation was against National Park Service policy. I helped write that policy myself, so I knew.

DJL: In what way was the work in violation of policy?

RU: It was not only against policy—it was against the law. According to policy, the only time you put a shovel in the ground is under section 106 of the National Historic Preservation Act, to make sure you are not going to impact any archaeological remains. Once you disturb anything underground, that is all you are ever going to learn from that particular site. Since the 1980s imaging techniques have evolved that allow us to see underground. But what was dug up in the 1980s was disturbed, and archaeologists are never going to be able to learn anything new from that material.

Under section 106 of the National Historic Preservation Act, which I also played a large part in drafting, any federal undertaking that affects properties on the National Register of Historic Places must be subjected to a certain formal process that was devised to guard against damage to historic properties, both national and local. If you jump through all of the hoops, and come up with a determination that there will be no significant effect on the property, then you can proceed. There is an Advisory Council on Historic Preservation that rules over application of section 106. I was deputy director for three years.

But they went into that project without any clearance from the higher level. They went into it without any compliance with policy. They went into it without any compliance with the law. Then the Park Service, with mud on its face, brought in a very competent archaeologist, to give credibility to what they were doing. They got through the first summer. The second summer, when the volunteers from all over the country started gathering again, the Advisory Council blew the whistle on them. Well, it was hard to shut down a project that all of these volunteers had jumped into so enthusiastically. So it erupted in Congress. They leaned on the Advisory Council, which came up with a memorandum of agreement that would allow them to go forward. This was in 1984 or 1985; my article appeared in *Montana Magazine* in 1986.

DJL: At Little Bighorn, the only surviving eyewitnesses were Indians, with conflicting recollections. What problems did this present in your research? What is your opinion of Indian testimony?

RU: Indian testimony by participants tends to be almost impossible to use because they told basically what their experience was individually, and they did it from different perspectives, so that all of it clashes. When you try to put together a story based on that, you are in real trouble.

Nevertheless, I do think Indian evidence is important, but I think that very few people really know how to handle it. Finding a good, solid base on which to build, using such testimony, is where the secret lies. In my biography of Sitting Bull, I used White Bull's experiences as recorded by Stanley Vestal.[20] They were crucial to my understanding of how the battle unfolded at the time that I wrote that book. Of course, there are other possible interpretations than what I gave. But White Bull was critical, and accepting him allowed a number of the other accounts to be folded into the story, in conjunction with White Bull's testimony.

The testimony by Curley, the Crow scout, that appears in print is very difficult to understand—probably because the wrong questions were being asked and also due to bad interpretations of what he was saying.[21] In recent years it has become appreciated that Curley may indeed have made it all the way to

Calhoun Hill before he left. Curley's stories have been rescued and put in the proper context, and they have helped. Yes, I regard Indian evidence as quite important.

DJL: *The Lance and the Shield* is a masterpiece of the use of such Indian recollections, collated with various written documents of the era to create a convincing biography of Sitting Bull. Does a similar biography of Crazy Horse exist, or is the required documentation insufficient to the task?

RU: It has been done. For years Mari Sandoz has been considered the standard authority on Crazy Horse because her book was so readable.[22] But I consider it to be a work of fiction. I know for a fact that she invented much of her material. So just cancel her out. In recent years an Englishman named Kingsley Bray has been working this subject, writing several articles for the periodical *Nebraska History*.[23] Some years ago, he put all of this into a biography, which appeared last year. It is a long book, probably too long to be broadly marketable. Bray does with his footnotes what I did with mine in the Sitting Bull biography. He won the Spur Award from Western Writers of America. I think that this is the latest work on the subject.

But I'm still not sure Bray's Crazy Horse is the real Crazy Horse. How much of what we think we know and how much of what the sources, both white and Indian, say is really Crazy Horse? It has been said that no picture of Crazy Horse exists, but recently a picture has turned up of an unidentified Indian at the Spotted Tail Agency in 1873 that could very well be Crazy Horse. There is a bullet wound under the eye.[24] Was Crazy Horse at the agency at the time? He could well have been. And as I indicated earlier, there is now a very serious question as to whether he is the one who led the decoy party at the Fetterman Massacre.

DJL: What is your opinion of the use of testimony about historic events by modern Indians, recounting tribal traditions, and so on?

RU: Forget it! They have no tribal memory. They have what Momma and Grandma have passed down over the years, and while everybody believes that the oral tradition is preserved exactly as it is passed down, it isn't. In George Hyde's books, written back in the 1930s when a lot of the participating Indians were still around, Hyde said that he found that they had no tribal memory of what happened back then.[25] They had lost it.

When I was writing the biography of Sitting Bull, I wanted to talk to some of Sitting Bull's descendants. I wrote to some of them, but I never got a response. What I have heard about the experience of other people is that Indians will talk, but you have to make sure that they get well paid for talking and then they are apt to tell you what you would like to hear. So I regard modern Indian testimony as worthless. It's a waste of time. And I say so in the introduction to my book.

DJL: Marc Simmons argues that modern Native Americans' conception of themselves is mediated by literature written by sympathetic whites, such as Dee Brown.[26]

RU: It is my opinion that Dee Brown wrote one of the worst books on Indian warfare ever to appear in print, and I've said so. At the same time, I believe that Dee Brown's book did more to shape the opinion of Americans, including Indians, about Indian history than any other factor since 1970, when his book appeared. Dee Brown made millions of dollars from that book. They still use it in classrooms. It's bad history. But I think Dee Brown is one of the most significant figures of the late twentieth century in shaping today's opinion, not just of white Americans, but of the Indians themselves.

The kind of thinking represented by Dee Brown has affected the way the Little Bighorn battle is presented to the public at the monument. Up to the late 1950s the army was the primary focus. The Indians were just cardboard cutouts, a foil for the military. That treatment dates back to the turn of the century and reflects the influence of the Seventh Cavalry on the development of the park. In the late 1960s the pendulum began to swing. By the late 1980s, when they had Indian superintendents, the pendulum had swung clear to the other side, to the extent that they had some Indian interpreters there who, in my opinion, were way off the wall. So much so that I entered a protest with the regional director. He brought in several experts to assess the situation, and they came up with exactly the conclusion that I had—that these guys were really doing bad interpretation. "The army is out for nothing but to kill Indian women and children"—that sort of thing. Then the pendulum began to swing back. I know they now have a lot of Indian interpretation, and they have Indians in uniform there, but I think that the current battlefield park historian is pretty insistent on balance. I would suspect that what you heard from Mike Donahue has achieved the proper balance. I think that is essential at controversial places, especially at Little Bighorn.

DJL: Following the Little Bighorn battle, Crook and Miles led campaigns that ultimately brought most of the remaining Sioux onto the reservation. We asked earlier, using Harney as an example, if the army knew whether the

Indians they attacked were innocent or guilty of depredations. How knowledgeable were Crook and Miles about their enemy during the 1876–77 campaigns?

RU: I don't believe that they knew much about the Indians. In the 1876 campaign, Crook and Miles only knew that they were chasing Sioux. They didn't know much more about it. Following his tremendous success earlier in Arizona, Crook so mismanaged his responsibilities in the 1876 campaign that I have to conclude that he didn't do anything right. He was simply looking for Indians, any Sioux that he could find. He had Indian spies to help him, which is how the Sioux and Cheyennes were usually found.

What you have to keep in mind is that the Indian Wars—including the Sioux Wars—did not feature much fighting. The Regular Army didn't do much fighting throughout this whole period. If the Indians got any chance at all to get away, they were not going to fight. Now this wasn't true at the Rosebud, where they did fight. But it was against the counsel of their leaders—Sitting Bull and Crazy Horse. The warriors simply broke and fought, and they pretty well won that battle. Crook had to turn around and go back to his supply camp.

Your basic question is "Did they know much about the enemy?" And the basic answer is "No."

DJL: In *Indian Wars*, you suggest that, in retrospect, the army would have been more effective had it functioned explicitly as a police force, going after the actual individuals guilty of depredations rather than whole tribes.[27]

RU: I think that the Regular Army was not organized or adapted to play the role of a police force. A lot of the trouble over the years was in distinguishing the bad guys from the good guys from the in-between guys. What they needed was an organization that included a police function. While you could not replace the normal functions of the United States Army, you could organize part of it to function more as a police force.

I invite your attention to General Crook's Arizona campaigns. Crook ran the Apaches down with an organization that included Apache Indian scouts—the same Chiricahuas that they were tracking. They were the ones who ran down those Indians. But General Sheridan didn't like the fact that the Regulars were not getting their due visibility. When Crook folded his tent and turned it over to Miles, Miles's instructions were to use the Regulars more conspicuously, which he did. But in the end the final surrender was engineered by Apache scouts.

DJL: In several of your books, you refer to the "Total War" strategy of Sherman and Sheridan: converging columns would smash Indian settlements, destroy their food supplies and horses, and then hound them until they surrendered. In fact, this appears to be what happened. Can you speak pro and con to this policy? Can a case be made that this policy was more humane, leading to less death and misery in the long run?

RU: I would speak pro. I have always believed that this was the effective strategy and that the generals were right that, in the long run, this was the only way that they could operate that would bring about success. Finding an Indian village like Custer did at the Washita or Mackenzie did in Palo Duro Canyon—this was a real long shot.[28] A battle was a rarity because the Indians would do anything they could to avoid battle, especially when they had their families with them. The alternative to fighting battles was to keep them on the run all of the time, totally insecure. The Indians would be constantly thinking, "When are the soldiers suddenly going to be here, charging into our camp?" I'm thinking primarily of the Red River War, where they really executed that strategy.[29] Colonel Miles and his infantrymen, marching through the snow singing "Marching through Georgia," kept those Indians on the run until they finally gave up and went to the agency. They were just too tired and too insecure to keep it up anymore. I think it was the only strategy that would have worked.

The Navajos blame Kit Carson for the terrible things he did in 1864.[30] To round up the Navajos, they marched through the Navajo country, marched up Canyon de Chelly, destroyed their fruit trees, destroyed their herds of sheep. It left the Navajos hungry and insecure, but there were almost no casualties. They all came in and surrendered. In my view, Kit Carson was a great friend of the Navajos. He really waged what can be considered a humanitarian war against them in 1864. He didn't kill very many. They all came in and surrendered. Well, back in the 1970s some anthropologists and Dee Brown types went out and told the Navajos what terrible things Kit Carson had done to them. They even blamed him for the Long Walk, although he had nothing to do with that.[31] They still do. They hold him accountable for all those horrid things that I just described to you.

DJL: Dee Brown also has shaped the public's perception of Wounded Knee, treating it as a massacre perpetrated by whites. Wasn't it more in the nature of a tragic incident that reflected in part the belligerence of some of the Sioux? Didn't the Lakotas' militant adaptation of Wovoka's pacifistic Ghost Dance teaching, coupled with their possession of quality weaponry, presage an outbreak of violence?[32] Or would the movement have fizzled when the prophecies did not pan out?

RU: I now believe that the Sioux ghost dancers were not as militant as I myself originally described. I believe that if agents had not tried to shut down the Ghost Dances, all would have blown over when the spring millennium date did not bring the millennium. But incompetent agents (except at Standing Rock) so bollixed the issues, especially Royer at Pine Ridge, that violence to employees was possible.[33] Calling in the army united the dancers in defense of the religious freedom they had been taught.

As for Wounded Knee, Big Foot had been a dancer but had calmed down. He was known as a peace-maker, and he slipped away from his overseer, Colonel Sumner, to go to Pine Ridge and make peace.[34] The army thought he was headed for the Stronghold, where the ghost dancers were barricaded. He wasn't, but he was intercepted by a squadron of the Seventh Cavalry and taken to Wounded Knee Creek. Colonel Forsyth came out that night to take charge, with orders from General Miles to disarm the Indians and ship them to the railroad in Nebraska. What happened the next day was an effort to disarm the Indians that blew up under provocation from the medicine man. Neither the Indians nor the army expected a fight. So yes, I regard it as a tragic accident. Both sides fired at the same time, and both sides took casualties. So both sides fought. The artillery posted on the hill leveled the village. I have ample testimony to the efforts the officers made to avoid hitting noncombatants. But in the smoke and dust of battle, with all the fleeing Indians dressed alike, no one could make a distinction. Whether it was a massacre depends on how you define massacre, and I'll not get into that dispute now.

DJL: What are you working on now?

RU: Geronimo. Geronimo is the name that everyone remembers above all others as the great American Indian chief. Not even Sitting Bull is as well known as Geronimo. But there were much greater Apache leaders—Mangas Coloradas, Cochise, Victorio, even old Nana. Geronimo wasn't even a chief.

Geronimo doesn't get into the white records until pretty late, as late as the 1870s. This is a real challenge for me because there aren't as many sources as there were for Sitting Bull. His fame is based entirely on the Sierra Madre campaign of 1882 to 1886.[35] And an outstanding feature of that campaign was that there was almost no fighting involved. I mentioned earlier that Crook put Apache scouts on the Chiricahuas' trail. This required Geronimo to elude pursuit. And he did it in a masterly way, up through the Sierra Madre. Now and then, some of those Apache scouts would locate him or one of the other rancherías and attack. But there were few casualties, no prisoners, no captives either. Crook kept his scouts on the trail, hounding Geronimo. Finally Crook was ordered by General Sheridan to demand unconditional surrender, breaking a promise he had already made to these Apaches. Crook wouldn't do that, so he resigned. Miles took over and used the Regulars. They really went through some tough times, chasing those Indians all over Mexico. They had scouts with them, but it was the high profile of the Regulars that made the newspapers and enhanced the name of Geronimo. Finally it was Lieutenant Gatewood and two Apache scouts who got in to talk to Geronimo and persuaded him to surrender.[36] So the whole campaign was based on no fighting whatsoever.

Now, while I can put together a pretty good biography of Geronimo's earlier years before he emerged as a leader, what is fascinating me now is what happened after he surrendered. Here is where I can really trace the development of a real person. He lived as a prisoner of war with the rest of his people for twenty-five years after he surrendered. They were first in Florida and then in Mount Vernon Barracks, Alabama. In 1894 they were allowed to go to Fort Sill. This required political legerdemain, because every time the War Department tried to send them back west, there was a big outcry from Oklahoma Territory delegates in the Congress, the senators from Kansas, and the delegates from New Mexico and Arizona. "They are getting too close." In reality, by this time most of those Apaches were pretty old and feeble and not much of a threat.

In the 1890s a new policy authorized an Indian company to be part of every regiment in the U.S. Army. At Mount Vernon Barracks, Lieutenant Wotherspoon (who later became chief of staff of the army) decided to recruit an Indian company from the Apache prisoners of war.[37] The able-bodied signed up. When they went to Fort Sill with the other prisoners of war, they served as a police force there. This created a big dilemma for the War Department, because after they had served their three years as soldiers and took honorable discharges just like any other soldier, they returned to being prisoners of war.

Geronimo developed a persona. Like Sitting Bull, he did craft work, which he signed and sold. He became more and more a traveling celebrity, as Sitting Bull had been one summer. There is a marvelous picture of Geronimo with a stovepipe hat riding in an old car in Theodore Roosevelt's inauguration parade in 1904. I think that the real story of Geronimo is after he surrendered.

Southern Cheyenne and Arapaho leaders at Camp Weld, Colorado Territory, in 1864, two months prior to the Sand Creek Massacre. Black Kettle is second from the left in the front row. Courtesy of the Western History Department, Denver Public Library.

CHAPTER 8

The Cheyenne Wars

An Interview with Jerome A. Greene

THE TREATY OF FORT LARAMIE OF 1851 recognized Cheyenne and Arapaho occupation of the land between the Platte River on the north and the Arkansas River on the south and from western Kansas to the Rocky Mountains. During the Colorado gold rush, whites moved into this territory. The Treaty of Fort Wise (1861), which granted a much smaller portion of land in southeastern Colorado to the tribes, was signed by several peace chiefs, including Black Kettle of the Southern Cheyennes. Many Cheyennes did not consent to the treaty, however, and continued to hunt and raid in Kansas and Colorado. John Evans, the territorial governor of Colorado, sought total adherence to the Treaty of Fort Wise by all the tribesmen. He invited them to a parley in Denver in the fall of 1863, but no Indians came. Evans interpreted the rebuff as a sign that the Cheyennes wanted war. He was joined in this view by Colonel John M. Chivington, commander of the Military District of Colorado.

In the spring of 1864 Chivington began a series of attacks on Cheyenne camps. The Indians retaliated by attacking whites in western Kansas and eastern Colorado, which restricted supplies and frightened the citizens of Denver. In the fall Black Kettle segregated his band from the hostile Cheyennes and sought the protection of troops at Fort Lyon, along the Arkansas in southeastern Colorado. In a conference near Denver, Black Kettle was led to believe that by surrendering as prisoners of war at Fort Lyon his people would be protected from attacks by the army. The peace-seeking Cheyennes and Arapahos set up camp at Sand Creek, forty miles from Fort Lyon in what is today Kiowa County in southeastern Colorado, and awaited developments.

The Third Colorado Cavalry, a unit of local Coloradans who had enlisted for one hundred days, was at that time called the "Bloodless Third" for not killing any Indians. Under the excuse that Black Kettle was formally not at peace, Chivington led these troops in an attack on the camp at Sand Creek on November 29, 1864. Although Black Kettle's band flew an American flag and a white flag to indicate that they were at peace and under military protection,

The Battle of the Washita as painted by James E. Taylor in 1878. The artist's brother, Private Richard L. S. Taylor, is depicted as the central figure in the attack. Courtesy of the Little Bighorn Battlefield National Monument.

over 150 Indian men, women, and children were slaughtered. In the aftermath, the troops mutilated the bodies and raped surviving women.

This premeditated massacre of peaceful Indians became the subject of public outrage. The army and congress investigated, but Chivington was no longer in the service and was beyond prosecution. Governor Evans, however, was removed from office.

During the next few years, hostile elements among the Cheyennes and allied tribes, including the military unit known as the Dog Soldiers, began a campaign of retaliation in Nebraska, Kansas, and Colorado. The army fought back with a relatively unsuccessful campaign in 1867 known as Hancock's War. The Medicine Lodge Treaty (October 1867) assigned land in what is today western Oklahoma to the Cheyennes. Depredations by the Indians continued, however, with particularly vicious attacks on white settlers on the Saline and Solomon Rivers in the late summer of 1868. As a result of the continuing hostility, General Philip Sheridan organized a campaign to attack hostile Cheyennes in their winter camps in Indian Territory. This led to the Battle of the Washita, which occurred on November 27, 1868, when Lieutenant Colonel George Custer led the U. S. Cavalry on a surprise dawn attack on Black Kettle's Cheyenne village on the Washita River, near present-day Cheyenne, Oklahoma. The troops killed between fifty and one hundred Indians, including women and children. During the battle, a detachment of twenty soldiers led by Major Joel Elliott separated from the rest of the troops to pursue an escaping group of Indians. They were killed by a mixed party of Cheyennes, Kiowas, and Arapahos who had been camped farther down the river and were attempting to defend the Black Kettle camp. The main body of troops under Custer retreated in the face of the counterattack organized by these Indians. Following the battle, some soldiers accused Custer of abandoning Elliott. The Battle of the Washita signaled the end of the Southern Cheyennes' independent way of life.

Cheyenne women and children captured at the Battle of the Washita, photographed in December 1868 at Fort Dodge, Kansas. Courtesy of the Little Bighorn Battlefield National Monument.

Northern Cheyenne tribes living in Wyoming and allied with the Lakotas participated in Red Cloud's War and subsequent events. They suffered the first attack of the Sioux War of 1876–77, when General Crook's troops attacked a Northern Cheyenne village at the Battle of the Powder River on March 17, 1876. Following the Battle of the Little Bighorn, they retreated into a winter camp under the leadership of Morning Star (Dull Knife) on the Red Fork of the Powder River in northern Wyoming. On November 25, 1876, Crook's troops under the command of Colonel Ranald Mackenzie attacked the camp at dawn, destroyed the village, and routed the Indians, who fled into the freezing countryside. This battle led to the Cheyennes' surrender.

Jerome A. Greene became interested in Indians and the Custer story in his youth, first visiting the Little Bighorn Battlefield in 1960 on graduation from high school in Watertown, New York. After a stint in the army, he graduated from Black Hills State College in Spearfish, South Dakota. He attended the University of South Dakota and received an M.A. in 1969 with a thesis that evolved into his first book, *Evidence and the Custer Enigma: A Reconstruction of Indian-Military History.* He served as a ranger-historian at Custer Battlefield National Monument, pursued further graduate studies at the University of Oklahoma, then taught Indian history at Haskell Indian Junior College in Kansas. In 1973 Greene joined the National Park Service in Denver, serving variously as research historian, curator, and manager until his retirement in 2007. He has authored or edited fifteen books, mostly about the western Indian campaigns, especially the Sioux War of 1876–77 and the Nez Perce War of 1877. His works include studies of the Battle of Slim Buttes and Colonel Nelson A. Miles's Yellowstone campaigns. Greene has also collected and edited military and Native American accounts of this period. His recent book *Stricken Field: A History of the Little Bighorn Battlefield* documents the history of that battlefield from the time of Custer's defeat until the present.

We interviewed Greene on November 21, 2008, at his home in Arvada, Colorado. Surrounded by his collection of memorabilia from the frontier West, we focused our interview on his work on the Cheyenne Indians. *Finding Sand Creek: History, Archeology, and the 1864 Massacre Site* (co-authored with archaeologist Douglas D. Scott) relates the history of the Sand Creek Massacre and the NPS effort, combining archaeological and historical methods, to locate the site of Black Kettle's village and the principal massacre site. *Washita: The U.S. Army and the Southern Cheyennes, 1867–1869* is a comprehensive history of the events leading to Custer's attack on Black Kettle's village along the Washita River on November 27, 1868. *Morning Star Dawn: The Powder River Expedition and the Northern Cheyennes, 1876* presents the history of Colonel Ranald S. Mackenzie's attack on the village of chiefs Morning Star and Little Wolf in November 1876.

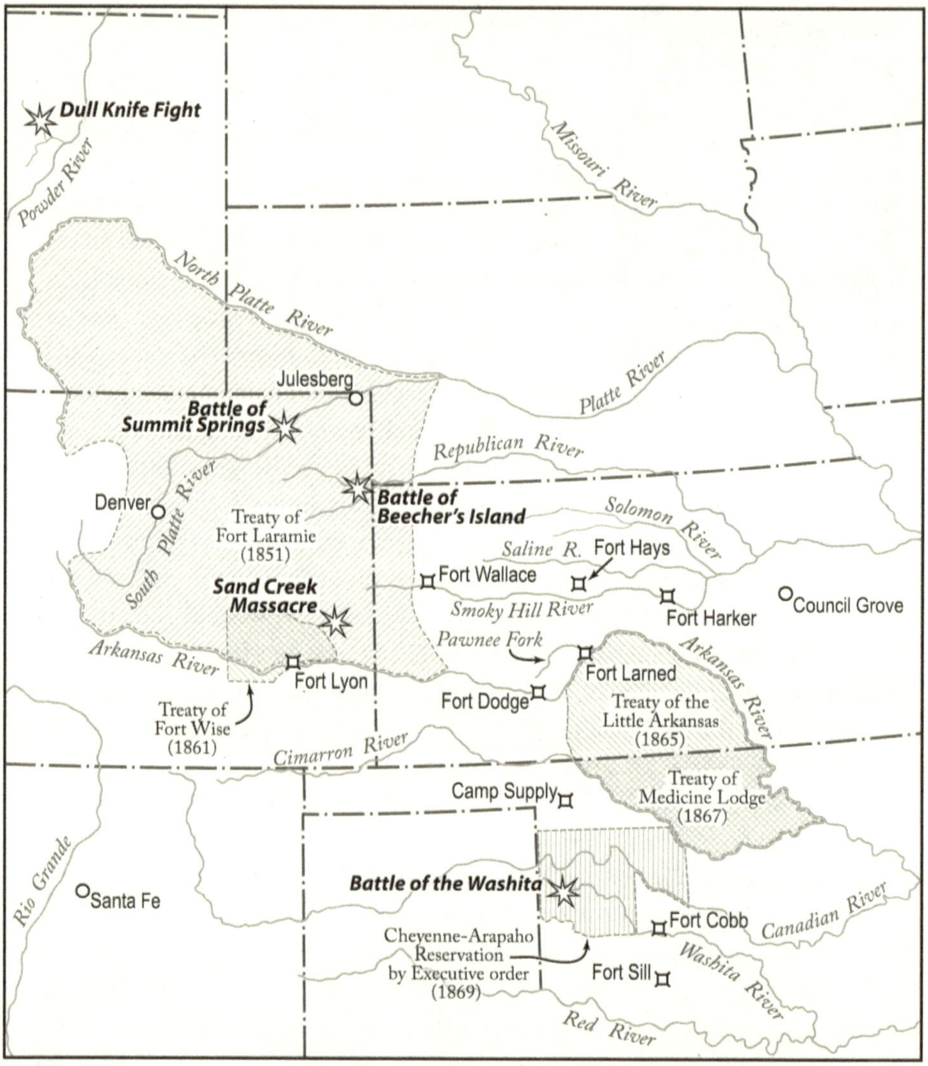

The central plains, showing key sites in the Cheyenne Wars, including battle and massacre sites. The shaded areas represent land ceded to the Cheyennes and Arapahos in various treaties (with dates). The reduction in the Indians' land base from the Fort Laramie Treaty to the final reserve in western Oklahoma is readily apparent. Based on information in Greene, *Washita.*

DJL (Deborah and Jon Lawrence): In the earlier history of the Cheyennes, as presented by George Bird Grinnell and George Bent, the tribe expelled the Kiowas and Comanches from the Black Hills.[1] Furthermore, it was customary for the Cheyennes to engage in surprise attacks on enemy villages, killing as many men as possible and taking women and children as prisoners. These approaches appear analogous to those employed later by the whites in dealing with the Cheyennes, such as at Washita. To what extent is the analogy apt and to what extent inappropriate?

JAG (Jerome A. Greene): I think it is a very apt analogy. Remember, the ambush tactic is as old as time. It is the basic attack methodology of human beings. So it is not surprising that the Indians employed this tactic. However, there are differences in motivation between the attacks on Indian villages by the U.S. troops and attacks by warriors of one tribe on another tribe. The Indians were motivated by their own cultural proclivities regarding raiding and warfare, often grounded in social and economic purposes, whereas the government troops that surprised and attacked Indian villages were motivated to destroy the warriors, their property and resources, and whatever else they could in order to punish or control the people and force them onto reservations.

DJL: In *Indians and Emigrants,* Michael Tate argues that at least during the 1840s and 1850s the interaction between the westering emigrants and the northern plains tribes was fairly benign and was based on mutually beneficial trade, cooperation, and friendship.[2] Do you agree with this proposition?

JAG: During the 1840s and 1850s that indeed was the way that the overland migrants got along with the Indians—if not with out-and-out friendship then with tolerance on both sides. I don't believe that there was a great amount of fighting. But remember that the tribes were still scattered over broad regions then, and I'm not sure that many came into direct contact with the overlanders with any great frequency during that period, except perhaps for trade purposes. Later on in the 1860s and 1870s the situation was different. The objectives of many overlanders changed in favor of settling and staying rather than passing through, and that entailed their destroying land and defoliating tracts that the Indians had roamed over and hunted for years. This created more opportunities for discord between Indians and whites as more and more emigrants decided to settle in one place, for example, in Colorado, rather than move on through to Oregon or California like many of their predecessors. That contributed strongly to the increase in conflict.

DJL: The "depredations" committed by Southern Cheyennes in 1864 prior to Sand Creek appear to have mostly involved theft of cattle or direct response to attacks on them by the territorial military. Nevertheless, the total picture in 1864 included the recent Santee Sioux uprising,[3] the resulting war on the northern plains, the existence of real efforts by the Confederates to involve the Plains Indians against the Union, continuous raiding by various tribes along the Platte and Arkansas Rivers, and some depredations in western Kansas and eastern Colorado. Without trying to justify the Coloradans' response, can we say that their paranoia was not simply understandable but to a great extent reasonable?

JAG: As I mentioned, the frequency of encounters between Indians and whites in the Colorado-Kansas area had increased by the mid-1860s. The white population was there to stay. A lot of the Indian people were opposed to the presence of the whites because they were trespassing and taking over land that had previously been guaranteed to the Cheyennes and Arapahos. I'm not sure that all of the Indians who partook in these various assaults and robberies were aware of the specifics of the treaty guarantees; probably only some of the leaders understood the broader concepts of what the treaties had called for. But in any case the tribes were facing potential loss of their lands and their traditional hunting grounds. Just the presence of white people in these areas really disrupted the availability of game and other resources. The Indians were doing what they felt they had to do in dealing with the presence of these people who had effectually invaded their domain from the east.

But these incidents did cause a lot of dismay among the whites who were there. And, of course, the government was charged with protecting American citizens who were in Colorado Territory at the time when depredations increased around the area of Denver in 1864.

DJL: Governor Evans, Colonel Chivington, and William Byers of the *Rocky Mountain News* have been accused of fanning the flames of anti-Indian hysteria and promoting an inappropriate military attack on the Southern Cheyennes in order to promote their own political and commercial ends.[4] Can you speak pro and con to this accusation?

JAG: There were indeed political pressures on prominent individuals, such as John Evans and Colonel John Chivington. I don't know a lot about Chivington, and I'm not an encyclopedia on Sand Creek either. Our charge as related to Sand Creek was to determine the *site* and *extent* of the massacre, and my whole project interest was tied up in that.[5] But from my understanding of

Chivington, he was a dishonest guy; he was not a nice person. I know it runs counter to our belief in the tenets of Christianity that a Methodist minister would do what he did, but the fact is that he was out to make a name for himself, and dealing with the military affairs of the territory was one way to do it. He had done quite a good job militarily at Glorieta Pass in New Mexico in 1862, so he came to the position of the Colorado district command with some credentials. It's not surprising that someone like that would strive to improve his record in order to press his political ambitions, which included being the delegate to Congress from the Colorado Territory. He wasn't able to accomplish that; he was defeated in the election.

With regard to Sand Creek, some say that he planned the strike against Black Kettle's village well in advance, even though he knew that Black Kettle was a noted peace chief, and that he did this to promote his own ambitions. I believe he was hoping to be appointed brigadier general. The way things turned out, that never happened.

DJL: In the Sand Creek Massacre, the troops assaulted a camp of Native Americans who had sued for peace. A common accusation is that very tough men were involved. After all, not everyone has the stomach to murder women and children. For example, George Bent asserts that the Third Colorado Cavalry had been hastily recruited from the worst class of frontier whites—toughs, gamblers, rough miners, and bad men. Do you think this was the case, or were these just ordinary men acting under extreme conditions?

JAG: I think that they were ordinary men, but when confronted with the extremities of Sand Creek, some of them followed their baser instincts. Chivington and the men of the Third Colorado—the so-called Bloodless Third—attacked a largely sleeping village of about 500 people, killed about 160, including women and children, and drove the others away. (Most of the Sand Creek villagers did survive; they made their way to the forks of the Smoky Hill River and joined with other Cheyenne bands that were wintering in that area.) After the killing was finished, some of the troops desecrated the remains of the dead Cheyennes. They did some terrible things to those bodies.

It should be pointed out that even though most modern authors refer to them as the Colorado Militia, these soldiers were actually U.S. Volunteers. And that means that the unit was legitimized by the federal government as a force composed of volunteers, as in other states and territories during the Civil War. They operated under the aegis of the United States and not under the aegis of Colorado. The governor obtained authority to raise the unit from the

War Department in Washington, and it entered service as a federalized entity. The regiment was composed of people who were in Colorado Territory at the time; during the war years, they were often the only men available for the task. While some of them may have been thieves, robbers, and men of ill repute, there were others who were good people. It wasn't the entire Third Colorado who partook in the atrocities; some of them refused to participate. In fact, one officer, Captain Silas Soule, told his troops, "Get away. You are not going to take part in that," or words to that effect, and he didn't take part in the killing at the beginning of the attack or later.[6]

DJL: Do you think that a redeeming feature of the Sand Creek Massacre is that it led to a public outcry and to a more sympathetic view of the Indians' plight, ultimately helping the evolution of the more modern view that such behavior by our own troops is reprehensible?

JAG: I don't think you can make such a big leap from that day to this day. Modern morality looks at such incidents as Sand Creek in disgust, and I can understand that, but we have to look at these events in terms of the period in which they happened. Rather than looking back today and saying that it shouldn't have happened, we should understand that the people who were facing these events at the time had a very different perspective on the situation than we have now. And perhaps the way it turned out was the only way it could have happened. I do think, in the case of Chivington at Sand Creek, that he acted in the extreme.

And we shouldn't forget that there was already moral indignation against the massacre at that time. The only people who cheered about it were mostly in Colorado and in other areas of the West. Many westerners in general thought that it was a positive thing to get rid of so many Indians at one fell swoop, but elsewhere it was viewed with disgust and dismay, especially in the East, where there was a different point of view. Of course, the Indians were not at the doorsteps of those in the East as they were out here.

DJL: This reminds us of the Camp Grant Massacre in Arizona in 1871, where, although President Grant was horrified and sent a commission to investigate, the Tucsonans applauded the killing of so many Indians.

JAG: As I see it, the difference between Sand Creek and Camp Grant is that the former case entailed a bona fide military assault. As I said, it was the First and Third Colorado cavalry regiments at Sand Creek. As bad as some of the individuals who composed those troops may have been, they were still under military control, whereas at Camp Grant the atrocity was committed essentially by a civilian mob—it was not a formal military assault.

DJL: Mostly Mexican Americans, Papago Indians, and only five or six white Americans were directly involved.

JAG: In any case, it should be stressed that at the time Sand Creek occurred, it was already recognized by the federal government as a national disgrace. There were three formal investigations into it—two congressional and one military. As a result of these various inquiries, we have transcripts taken within just a few weeks or months of the event from people who were there at the massacre.

DJL: Were some of the people who testified in the proceedings the same troops who had been there and refused to participate in the atrocity?

JAG: Yes. The book *The Sand Creek Massacre: A Documentary History* contains transcripts of the interviews and the testimony of soldiers who were at Sand Creek.[7] It gives very detailed information. This was fortunate for us when we researched Sand Creek, because we were able to use the information from these inquiries to help determine the location and extent of the massacre site.

DJL: In the archaeology at Sand Creek, what, apart from determining the location of the village, was the most significant new finding?

JAG: Determination of the location of the village *was* the most important thing. That's what we [in the National Park Service] were charged by Congress to do: to locate the site and extent of the massacre. We not only located the village site where the soldiers' attack began but projected the extent of the major killing about a half-mile upstream. That's where the banks of the creek became more and more apparent. When the attack got underway, most of the people, including children, fled upstream for about half a mile and more and attempted to dig into the sand on the banks of the stream to hide and protect themselves.

One evening in May of 1999, some time after the initial determination had been made as to the location of the village, the archaeologists and historians (including myself) stood upstream about a half-mile from the projected village site. We could look out and see the high point two miles away where Chivington first saw the village. Remember, I had been studying all the accounts for more than a year. As I looked around I had something of an epiphany. The topography of where we were standing was clearly that of the area where the biggest part of the massacre occurred. All the land forms lined up perfectly.

The written record said that the people had started digging the sand pits in the sides of the creek banks, but that didn't make sense by simply reading the descriptions. What did a bank consist of for the men who were firing howitzers at those people? And how could a long-range weapon like a howitzer be used to fire on people as near as the opposite banks of a creek? But once you are there, you can see that the forces of geologic time on that landscape had created steep banks that were possibly a quarter of a mile apart and distant from the actual streambed. Those were the banks that the people dug themselves into on either side of the creek. The howitzers were brought up to the top of these banks and then opened on the Indians dug in beneath the opposite banks.

DJL: Did they find any shell casings of the howitzer rounds?

JAG: Yes. To my thinking, that was one of the keys of the entire project. In January of 1999 I met with a local landowner who had found artifacts on his property. While some of them were old pieces of farm machinery—there was a little community there years after the massacre, called New Chicago—some were pieces that could have had something to do with the massacre. I was sitting at a table in his home, looking at all of this material, when I recognized that one of the objects was a piece of a howitzer shell. It even had the striations of the fuse that had one time been screwed into it to affect the timing of the explosion of the projectile. I knew exactly what it was.

DJL: Did the landowner keep good records of where he found the shell?

JAG: Yes. It was very important to know where that piece of howitzer shell was found. It was like a Rosetta Stone for our determining the extent of the massacre. He told me (and later showed me) where it was found; he had placed a stake there. So then we knew that this was a likely place where the troops had fired on the people hiding dug in beneath the banks. And the testimony in the transcripts regarding the lay of the land and so forth backed it all up. Now this was all part of our purview in composing the historical documentation research for the Sand Creek project. Later Doug Scott and his archaeologists confirmed our judgments regarding the location and extent of the massacre, which was a great reward for all of our efforts.

DJL: How did the archaeology at Sand Creek differ from that which took place at Little Bighorn in the early 1980s, which led to accusations by Robert Utley and others of violations of park service policy and of federal law?

JAG: Regarding Sand Creek, we were charged by Congress to determine the location and extent of the massacre site. And that consisted in finding the village site, and then from the village site projecting where the core of the massacre really took place. But we have always known where the Little Bighorn battle occurred, so that was a major difference. At Little Bighorn, the archaeology performed by Doug Scott and Rich Fox and their team was undertaken because of a fire that cleared the area and created an opportunity to collect more data on the ground. They were particularly interested in learning more about Custer's movements. For Reno's actions, there were eyewitness accounts by surviving soldiers, but without archaeology the only thing we have to determine Custer's actions is Indian participant and eyewitness testimony since no member of his battalion survived. Although Indian testimony was often discounted in the past, today we recognize that Indian testimony about the battle makes a lot of sense. But archaeology provided yet another way of getting information. Finding cartridges, determining firing positions and the sequence of battle movements, that sort of thing—taken as a whole, these findings helped better determine what happened at the Little Bighorn and added to the interpretation of the site.

Bob Utley is right in saying that the park service violated its own canons by plunging into that project without going through the proper section 106 compliance. They weren't caught until the second year, when they had to submit documents for review. These were later approved so that the project could proceed. It was something of an embarrassment to the National Park Service because some thought they had ignored their own regulations and policies in order to get sensational information. That's one way to view the controversy. I feel, however, that the archaeological findings were quite significant.

DJL: Whereas at Sand Creek you had a mandate from Congress.

JAG: Yes.

DJL: We turn now to the Washita battle. The introduction to chapter 4 of your book on Washita says that shortly after Sheridan was put in charge of the Department of the Missouri, they reckoned that there had been 110 white citizens killed, 15 women raped, 1,000 livestock stolen, and large numbers of houses and barns burned by the Indians during the last month or two.[8] Cumulatively, that constitutes a massacre as bad as Sand Creek. The attack on the Cheyennes at Washita was justified by these and other serious depredations that the Cheyennes had committed in Kansas. To what extent were the Cheyennes in late 1867 and early 1868 responding to the earlier attacks on them and the injustices that took place both at Sand Creek and during Hancock's inept campaign and to what extent would they have committed these depredations anyway?[9] As you said earlier, they were being badly squeezed by the settlers, the buffalo were disappearing, and the army was attacking Indians all over the plains, from north to south. Wasn't it inevitable that their culture of raiding would sooner or later be turned on the whites rather than just on their traditional enemies?

JAG: Yes, but I think that without Sand Creek and everything that occurred over the previous few years it probably wouldn't have happened to the extent that it did. Before Sand Creek, the Cheyennes and the Arapahos were doing their own thing, and they were staying away from the whites. It was really Sand Creek that started their furious response. There is a wonderful quote that I used in a couple of my books: wherever the Indians got together, if the troops were in the vicinity, "an angel from Heaven would not convince them but what another 'Chivington Massacre' was intended."[10] They were really shaken by that affair.

Remember this too: in the wake of Sand Creek, Cheyenne society was going through a tormented period. They were struggling as a people. Sand Creek ripped into the social fabric of the Cheyenne nation, which was a small tribe to begin with—there were only about 3,000 Southern Cheyennes and 2,000 or so Northern Cheyennes. Those were small groups compared to the Lakotas, who had 35,000 or so people. Furthermore, a large number of the chiefs who had promoted peace were killed at Sand Creek.

Hancock's expedition of 1867 stirred up those waters again. The Cheyennes were very upset by Hancock's expedition to hound the Indians in the wake of their own response to Sand Creek. When Hancock's troops attacked the village at Pawnee Fork, Kansas, the people were scared to death and so vacated the village. They probably feared another Sand Creek. As I say, wherever there was the presence of troops and Indians, bingo—the thing that went off in their minds was Sand Creek. It really traumatized the Arapahos and the Cheyennes, particularly.

DJL: To repeat, given their culture of raiding and the circumstance that they were under pressure from white expansion, wasn't it natural that they raided the white settlers, treating them like an enemy tribe?

JAG: A lot of the raids were undertaken by the Dog Soldiers. Dog Soldiers were really a militaristic hybrid band that developed among the Cheyennes. They were very antiwhite and also opposed to the peace faction of the Cheyennes. The raiding on the Saline and Solomon in Kansas was driven initially by

Dog Soldiers who were on their way to attack a Pawnee conclave in the area.[11] Some white men fired at them, and that set off those raids. Other raids were initiated by traditional bands of Cheyennes: for example, the group (including members of Black Kettle's people) that went way east in order to attack the Osages near Council Grove. That inspired some attacks on whites as well. This sort of raiding, aimed initially at traditional enemies, was definitely motivated by cultural tenets instilled in them.

But there also was a cultural response in the broader sense of what happened to the Cheyenne people. As I mentioned, the presence of more and more whites who were not just passing through but were coming into the area to stay and settle on the land upset the movement of game in the area. The Indians couldn't depend on finding buffalo in the traditional places.

The whites were preempting Indian land, operating under an attitude that was tied into the notion of America's Manifest Destiny. "God provided this land. These people aren't really using it, so we are going to use it." And that's what these settlers were trying to do, in the broad sense. The Indians' response was to strike back, which was about the only response that they had. Unfortunately for them, they couldn't unite. Historically the various tribes had never been able to unite because of cultural and linguistic differences. Plus, they never had the numbers and resources.

All of this cultural and political flux promoted the widespread outbreaks in 1867 and early 1868, and these outbreaks initially led the army to strike back. The army was the instrument of the federal government on the frontier. Its purpose was to protect American citizens. That's why these campaigns, first by Sully and then by Custer, occurred.[12] Something had to be done—it had come to that. "We have to protect these citizens."

DJL: Speaking of depredations, David Lavender claims in *Bent's Fort* that, in part for revenge for Sand Creek, Charles Bent helped stake a captive spread-eagle on the ground, cut out his tongue, and built a fire on his stomach.[13] Furthermore, during the Solomon River depredations, women were gang-raped and babies were ruthlessly slaughtered. How much a part of Cheyenne culture was such behavior?

JAG: The only instance of torture that I've heard of was the one recorded by Bent's son in Lavender, and I don't know much about that offhand. The other behavior that you mentioned was part and parcel of Indian raiding. While the killing of babies was fairly common throughout American history during Indian raids, I question some of the charges of rape. During intertribal warfare, the Indians would steal people from other tribes to use as slaves. But I can't comment on torture as a dynamic of Cheyenne culture.

DJL: At the Battle of the Washita, why do you think that Custer conducted no reconnaissance before he attacked, so that he wasn't aware of the other villages downstream from Black Kettle's village? Was he reckless, arrogant, or overconfident? Why didn't Sheridan rake him over the coals for putting his troops in such a dangerous position as occurred when the Indians from the other villages began to join the battle?

JAG: I would say that he did reconnoiter. When the troops arrived at Camp Supply, they didn't know where the Indians were other than someplace to the south. On the campaign, Custer had dispatched a column under Major Elliott to try to find evidence of Indians.[14] And Elliott found the trail of raiders coming from the north that passed back to the villages along the Washita. Custer was following up on that when he approached the village on the Washita. He approached it between 11 P.M. and midnight, and he didn't just rush into the village. He halted and left his wagons farther behind so they would not signal the appearance of the troops. He sent his Osage scouts out, and they found the village on the Washita. It was pure coincidence that it was Black Kettle's village—the same Black Kettle that Chivington's troops had attacked at Sand Creek!

But you are also asking why he didn't know about the villages farther downstream. When the scouts discovered Black Kettle's village, everyone focused on that, and they didn't extend their reconnoitering beyond that one. Of course, the troops did find evidence of those other villages after daylight and in the course of the action of the attack. Custer did what he could to extricate his command. Militarily, I think he did the right thing, even though he left Elliott behind, although apparently believing that his detachment was already lost. They got out of there and kept moving. They didn't stop. Custer was fortunate that it took the Indians of the downriver tribes a while to realize what was going on. They did not really try to push a major offensive against Custer at that time because he had some villagers—women and children—as captives. And he put them out in front when they were marching away so that the Indians would not attack. That was a very smart thing to do.

I think that Custer did what he could under the circumstances. Intelligence was always a problem during the Indian campaigns, especially in the winter under conditions of snow. If those other tribes hadn't been downstream the whole thing would have been considered a brilliant attack from a military perspective. He was lucky that he didn't get drawn into a protracted engagement. He could have met his Little Bighorn about eight years earlier.

DJL: Turning now to the Northern Cheyennes, during the offensive battles of Red Cloud's War, the tribe was fighting the military.[15] Similarly, in 1876 at the Battles of Powder River and the Little Bighorn they were defending themselves against direct attacks on their villages by the military.[16] To what extent were the Northern Cheyennes guilty of any depredations against noncombatant whites?

JAG: I can't comment offhand about the guilt or innocence of the Cheyennes in attacking noncombatant whites during that period, although it is likely some intermittent attacks by Cheyennes on whites occurred. In 1876 the government was intent on wresting the Black Hills from the Lakotas and forcing the tribes—Lakotas and Cheyennes—onto the Great Sioux Reservation. Many if not most of the Northern Cheyennes had been on the reservation, while others variously occupied the unceded hunting lands east of the Big Horn Mountains authorized to them and in fact had been coexisting rather well with the military presence at Forts Laramie and Fetterman.

It is interesting that, although they were closely aligned with the Lakotas, who were the principal objective of the army at that time, the Cheyennes were the first ones struck in the 1876 campaign. In the opening campaign, the army commanders thought that they were hitting Crazy Horse's Lakota village, but they actually hit a village of Cheyennes at Powder River.[17] The Cheyennes lost their homes during the battle, although they did recover some of their ponies. They then made their way down to join up with Sitting Bull, and they received some relief from his people.[18] There was a mutual security arrangement with the Lakotas. Reynolds's attack on that village on the Powder River really cemented that security alliance.[19] The Cheyennes stayed with the Lakotas intermittently for the balance of the year.

Margot Liberty, a cultural anthropologist who lives in Wyoming, has developed a theory of what she calls "Cheyenne primacy."[20] Since they were the first ones hit, the Cheyennes came to believe that they, and not the Sioux, were the primary target of the army in the 1876 campaign. When the Lakotas moved camp, they gave the Cheyennes the lead; because they had been the first hit by the troops, they deserved this preeminent position in the column. After joining Sitting Bull, the Cheyennes along with the various camps of Lakotas moved up the Rosebud and then over toward Little Bighorn, coming down what is now called Reno Creek, with the Cheyennes at the front of the moving assemblage. At the Little Bighorn, they moved north at the head of the column, so that their village was the northernmost tribal circle set up along the west side of the river. This happened to be the village that was directly across from Medicine Tail Coulee, where Custer's force appeared and tried to cross. So it was natural that the Cheyennes again believed that they were the main target of the soldiers.

DJL: Mackenzie's attack on Morning Star's village was not his first military success in the frontier wars.[21] He appears to have been a far greater "Indian fighter" than Custer, perhaps ranking with Miles and Crook.[22] What is your appraisal of Mackenzie?

JAG: Throughout his career after West Point and into the Civil War, Mackenzie was regarded very highly by the upper echelon of the military command. Grant called him the most promising young officer in the army. There is a biography of Mackenzie titled that: *The Most Promising Young Officer: A Life of Ranald Slidell Mackenzie.*[23] Out west during the Indian campaigns after the war, Mackenzie gained much more experience as a field commander than most other officers until 1876. He led attacks on villages, which was the essential army tactic. He attacked a Kickapoo village in 1871 and then a couple of Comanche villages in 1873. His big strike down south was at Palo Duro Canyon. So he already had considerable experience when he led Crook's directed attack on the Cheyennes at the Red Fork of the Powder River. He was very capable. He did become a Regular Army brigadier general some time after that. Unfortunately, he went insane, and in the 1880s he was committed to an asylum on Staten Island. He died there in 1889. Mackenzie crested about the time of the attack on Morning Star's village. (By the way, I like to call that chief Morning Star because that's what the Cheyennes called him—Dull Knife was his Lakota name.)

DJL: Mackenzie's attack on Morning Star's village and Mills's attack at Slim Buttes were so fundamentally similar to the Battle of the Washita that they raise the same issues.[24] They followed the "Total War" strategy of Sherman and Sheridan, which entailed converging columns that would smash Indian camps, destroy their food supplies and horses, and then hound them until they surrendered. While in principle this strategy could have led to fewer deaths, in reality it consistently involved "dawn attacks on enclaves normally containing a high percentage of noncombatants" and typically during the winter, when destruction of the Indians' possessions led to unimaginable misery.[25] What is the distinction between "battle" and "massacre," and then, under that definition, should these actions be classified as battles or massacres?

JAG: I tend to categorize many of them differently. There's no question that some of them were massacres. Sand Creek was a massacre. The attack by Connor on the Shoshones at Bear River in January 1863 was a massacre.[26] The Marias River assault that Eugene Baker led up in Montana Territory in January 1870 was a massacre, no question about it.[27] More people were killed there than at Sand Creek—I think 170 or so. More people were killed at Bear River than were killed at Sand Creek, too.

"Massacre" means indiscriminate slaughter, indiscriminate killing, that is, no distinction between combatants and noncombatants—women, children, and the elderly. This entails blanket destruction of people, not just destruction of resources, and the killing of noncombatants as well as combatants. In that sense, I think Wounded Knee was a massacre—or partly so. I equivocate somewhat because it wasn't a premeditated massacre as Sand Creek certainly was. It was something that got out of hand, in my opinion. At first the troops were trying to defend themselves against Indians who fired first. But when the Indians tried to run away, many were chased down and shot and killed, women and children included. I think that makes part of it a massacre.

"Battle" is a term that I used a lot in the past. One of my books is called *Battles and Skirmishes of the Great Sioux War.* But more recently I've come to understand a battle as more of a mutual contest. The assaults at Washita and Slim Buttes were not mutual contests. I don't use the term "battle" anyplace in my book on Washita, except in reference to the park as Washita Battlefield. But I don't like that term as applied there, and I've recommended that they change the name simply to Washita National Historic Site. In any case, I don't like the term "battle" for these assaults on villages, such as at Washita or Slim Buttes, because I think that these assaults were very one-sided, unless they evolved into a significant contest or battle. On the other hand, it doesn't mean that these assaults were all massacres, either. Certainly, Washita was no massacre; nor was Slim Buttes, as the army made efforts to collect and protect the noncombatant women and children. I don't like to throw the term "battle" around any more than I do "massacre." I try to use more neutral terms, like "engagement," "encounter," and "action."

The army had a maneuver called an "offensive battle." I stumbled on that term when I was researching Washita. The definition of an offensive battle is when an army moves around to seek out an enemy and attack him wherever he is found. So if the enemy force responded in kind, that could indeed be a battle. What happened to this concept on the frontier was that when the troops sought out and found Indian encampments containing many noncombatants and then attacked, they continued using the term "offensive battle" or "battle," even when the villagers were not able to mount a defense in force. Of course, during these assaults on villages, there were a lot of individual battles where warriors and women acting on their own tried to fight off the troops. It was a matter of life and death to them. Even in the case of Sand Creek, lots of individual battles went on within the massacre itself. And in a number of cases the people did manage to fight back to an extent that they turned the assault into a real battle. The classic example is at the Little Bighorn; there is no question that the army's attack turned into a battle. You see this at the Big Hole, too, and again at Bear Paw in the Nez Perce War.[28] The troops attacked and seemed to be winning the struggle, but then the people fought back and dragged it out. Bear Paw turned into a five-day siege before Chief Joseph finally surrendered.[29]

DJL: In *Evidence and the Custer Enigma*, you assert that Sioux and Cheyennes who related how the Battle of the Little Bighorn transpired "were not always reliable informants."[30] Even George Bent, who was in a unique position to tell the Cheyenne story, appears to understate the cruelty of the depredations committed by some of the tribal members. What is your opinion of Indian testimony, both by those who participated in the battles and by Indian descendants today? Which accounts are most reliable?

JAG: I'm glad you asked that question. The quote in *Evidence* referred to reasons why some Indian testimony on the Little Bighorn might not be credible because of poor translation, the Indians' fear of reprisal for their participation, and other reasons. Yet I really believe that Indian viewpoint is vitally important in order to make sure that we are not treating the Indians as faceless individuals. We really need to get more of the Indian perspective and weave it into our narratives as best we can so that they are not so one-sided. My favorite kinds of Indian testimony are eyewitness and participant accounts.

"Immediate accounts" were those given shortly after the events occurred—a few weeks, months, or a few years. Such accounts of the Sioux War of 1876–77 were mostly forthcoming following the Indians' surrender, although there were not a great many until more of the Sioux returned from Canada and surrendered in 1880 and 1881. After that, more and more correspondents began interviewing Indians. However, their testimony is suspect, because these reporters were always trying to make it more interesting. They often fabricated material to spice up their accounts, so you have to be careful when you are looking at those early, immediate accounts.

"Reminiscent accounts" are those given by participants, but years or decades later. I find them very useful, even though they were obtained further away in time from the events. Those were collected by people like Walter Camp, Eli S. Ricker, George Bird Grinnell, Edward Curtis, and others who got to know Indian cultures and who were students who knew which questions to ask and how to frame them.[31] They transcribed the testimony at face value and didn't try to glorify or enhance the reminiscences. So I believe these accounts are the best. I'm always on the lookout for reminiscent accounts from the earlier days by those people who were there and took part or who were eyewitnesses, especially because it's important to get various perspectives, Indian as well as white, on frontier history.

DJL: What about George Bent?

JAG: George Bent walked in two societies. He was in the village at Sand Creek. I don't view his accounts as traditional Cheyenne accounts, but I certainly used them for *Sand Creek* and *Washita* (his Washita statements are hearsay). Overall, Bent is an important source of data on so much that happened during the Indian Wars. He had good information, and his remarks on Sand Creek are almost the only Cheyenne participant accounts that bear on that event. I have a problem with some of his facts regarding the village. Many of the Cheyennes today take his two diagrams as being precise, as gospel, even though there are obvious disparities between them. I see them more as schematic representations done almost forty years after the event. While I do think they contain a lot of valuable data, they didn't really help us find the village site.

DJL: What about the modern accounts, the tribal traditions, and so on?

JAG: I think we have to worry about such later accounts, the tribal lore and the oral histories given today, the accounts passed down orally between generations. I don't use them because I don't trust them. I would say the same about non-Indian oral transgenerational history too. I fear that such accounts have been influenced and potentially corrupted by movies, books, and television shows. They are not as accurate as the participant renderings that ended during the 1920s or thereabouts when most of the old warrior-participants died off. They are not held to the same prescriptions of accuracy and care, in my view.

I was more accepting of them until I got into Sand Creek and Washita. We, that is, the park service, collected modern oral histories for those two projects.

And, for example, one of the people interviewed for the Sand Creek project said that the site was located at Estes Park. Another one said it was located at Fort Collins. That made me very wary of them.

I do, however, believe that the transgenerational accounts—oral histories—are valuable in giving us a sense of how the people today feel about the historic events that happened in their past. That is really important too, and I accept them for that, and to that extent I think that they are quite useful.

John Stands In Timber, a Northern Cheyenne historian, is an exception and stands alone in my view.[32] He had been educated in white-operated Indian schools, and he came to realize the importance of writing this stuff down. He described with total accuracy the things and events that happened during his own long life, but he also described things that happened to his relatives and their associates back during the Custer fight and other engagements and that were told to him. Much of what he reported was hearsay, as much of this material necessarily is, but in that he was very precise, very meticulous, very accurate in taking information down, and he was very intent on getting it right. I certainly make an exception with him.

CHAPTER 9

Violence over the Great Basin

An Interview with Ned Blackhawk

PRIOR TO THE ADVENT OF THE EUROPEANS, the ancestors of today's Shoshonean-speaking people—the Utes, Paiutes, Bannocks, Shoshones, and Comanches—lived in small bands in the intermountain West. Their territory extended from the California desert on the west across the Great Basin to the mountains of Colorado on the east and from northern New Mexico to southern Wyoming and Idaho. The advent of the Spanish colonizers in New Mexico in the seventeenth century brought tremendous changes to all the Indians of the Southwest. The Spanish established missions and communities among the Pueblo tribes. They also interacted with surrounding tribes, such as the Apaches and Navajos, initially raiding them for slaves and later trading with them. In turn, the Apaches and Navajos acquired the new technologies of horses, metals, and firearms through trade with and raids on the Spanish settlements. They unleashed increasing violence in the form of equestrian raids to acquire material goods and captives, both on the Spanish and Pueblo settlements and on neighboring tribes such as the Utes of northern New Mexico and southern Colorado. These neighboring tribes then sought both trade with and protection by the Spanish in order to acquire the horses and technologies needed to defend themselves. As their strength increased, the Utes perpetuated a similar pattern of violence by raiding communities farther afield from New Mexico; in particular, they raided Paiute bands in the Great Basin, bringing back captives who were sold to the Spanish in New Mexico.

Sometime in the late 1600s the Comanches moved into the high plains of eastern Colorado and New Mexico and formed an alliance with the Utes. Together, these groups began to raid the Pueblo and Spanish settlements and to push Apache groups out of the high plains. This alliance lasted until roughly 1750, when the Utes sought peace with the Spanish. By this time, the Comanches had established dominance in the southern plains, from Colorado to Texas. After 1750 the Utes allied with the Spanish in their battles against the Comanches. In 1776 New Mexico governor Juan Bautista de Anza made a treaty with the Comanches. Peaceful relations lasted from the time of the treaty until after the Mexican revolution of 1821. During this period, Utes and Comanches continued to raid tribes on the periphery of the Spanish colonies, bringing slaves to New Mexico. These Indian slaves were often subsequently freed and classed as *genízaros,* a special status of citizenship in the Spanish colony. Church and civic records indicate relatively large populations of *genízaros* in several towns in New Mexico, especially Abiquiu and Tomé.

Following their dominance in the southern plains, the Comanches established a powerful trade network, with a key center on the Arkansas River in southeastern Colorado. Guns, horses, metal implements, and food were traded between disparate peoples extending from Spanish New Mexico to Indians and Europeans farther to the east and to the north.

Spanish incursions into the Great Basin began in the 1770s. The members of the Domínguez-Escalante expedition and unlicensed traders made the first contacts with the Ute and Paiute bands of the region. These groups had not acquired horses and metals and remained easy prey for Ute and other equestrian raiders well into the Mexican era. The establishment of the Old Spanish Trail between Abiquiu and Los Angeles in the 1830s led to considerable slave-raiding by Hispanic traders, Utes, and Euro-American mountain men on these tribes.

The good relations among the Comanches, Utes, and Spanish gave way in the Mexican era, essentially because the new republic did not have the resources to provide the gifts of horses, food, and trade goods necessary to maintain the peace. The Utes attacked Spanish trade forts in Colorado and settlements in northern New Mexico. The Comanches, as well as the Apaches, began an era of extremely violent raids into the provinces of today's northern Mexico, bringing back booty and captives and destroying Mexican communities in the process.

Following the Mexican War, the Colorado Utes sought an alliance with the United States and even contributed warriors to the U.S. troops during the Civil War. The Colorado gold rush brought miners and settlers into eastern Colorado in the 1860s; foreseeing the loss of their territory, the Utes successfully negotiated a treaty in 1868 that established a reservation that covered most of western Colorado. Over the next decade, as miners and settlers moved into that part of the state, pressure was applied to decrease the size of the reservation, which ultimately was reduced to a small area in southwestern Colorado.

Beginning in the late 1840s, Mormon settlement put a tremendous strain on the hunting and gathering resources of the Utes of eastern Utah. This led to a series of conflicts, including the Walker War of the early 1850s and the Blackhawk War of the late 1860s, which were ultimately resolved when the United States moved these Utes onto the Uintah and Ouray Reservation in northeastern Utah.

In the 1850s and 1860s emigration along the Oregon-California Trails through Idaho and Nevada, as well as Mormon settlement in northern Utah, led to serious conflict with the Shoshones, Bannocks, and Paiutes of this region. The emigrants and settlers decimated the fragile ecology of the region, causing the Indians to pursue survival through begging and raiding. In particularly vicious attacks along the Oregon Trail in western Idaho, Shoshone bands killed nearly twenty members of the Ward party in 1854 and a similar number in an attack on the Utter party in 1860.

The Civil War brought a large increase in the number of federal troops in the region. On January 29, 1863, General Patrick Edward Connor led a force of volunteer troops in a surprise dawn attack on a village of Shoshones who were wintering on the Bear River in southern Idaho. The soldiers killed hundreds of Indians, including women and children, and also molested women. The Bear River Massacre effectively marked the end of conflict with the Shoshones in northern Utah, Idaho, and Nevada.

Ned Blackhawk is a professor of history and American Studies at Yale University. He received his Ph.D. from the University of Washington in 1999 and was on the faculty at the University of Wisconsin, Madison, from 1999 to 2009. He is the author of a number of scholarly articles, with a particular focus on the colonial histories of Shoshonean-speaking Indians in the Great Basin. His book *Violence over the Land: Indians and Empires in the Early American West* won several awards, including the Utley Award from the Western History Association. He is also the author of *The Shoshone*, a nonfiction book for juvenile readers. Blackhawk is a member of the Te-Moak Tribe of Western Shoshone Indians of Nevada. We interviewed Blackhawk in a telephone conversation between Santa Fe and New Haven on November 17, 2009.

DJL (Deborah and Jon Lawrence): You make a powerful case that "colonialism violently reconfigured indigenous societies before their lands became the actual sites of colonialism" and that "the Utes mastered the dynamics unleashed by Spanish colonization, becoming preeminent warriors, equestrians and statesmen."[1] What was the nature of precontact violence? Without disputing the point that the level of violence increased enormously with colonialism, wasn't there a long history of various precontact ethnic/linguistic groups violently displacing others?

NB (Ned Blackhawk): This is a question that I often get, and I think it highlights what I am trying to do with my work in general. You have probably gleaned from the material of mine that you have read that I try to work against simplistic portraits of Native American communities, some of which continue to shape contemporary understanding of our history. Many people still maintain one-dimensional or timeless portraits of Native communities without recognizing the fundamental historical transformations, the revolutions really, unleashed following the arrival of the Europeans.

The question you pose primarily points to the nature of violence prior to European contact: what was the nature of that violence? Such questions about precontact violence in many ways deflect attention from postcontact violent transformations.

The overwhelming body of scholarly study on preconquest Native peoples of the American Southwest revolves around the study of material remains found within various archaeological sites. Archaeologists, dating back to the late nineteenth century, have combed over Native American sites and have unearthed literally tons of historical evidence. From those findings, they have developed elaborate theories about the settlement of certain civilizations, primarily up and down the Rio Grande. We're all familiar with the resulting narrative about the arrival and development of various Athabaskan, Ancient Puebloan, and other precontact civilizations of the region.[2] But while that investigation has revolved around the study of precontact societies, most Native communities were much more profoundly influenced by the impact of European colonization *after* 1492. The scholarly focus on pre-Columbian, precontact Native peoples often mitigates the level of disruption that accompanied European arrival.

These are the things that I am generally working up against. When people ask about the nature of precontact violence, I have to remind them, insistently and purposefully, that European colonization accelerated, intensified, and indeed revolutionized the social, military, and economic relations among Native communities both within and outside the various Spanish and European colonial orbits. How did they do that? How did the preexisting social relations become revolutionized? What influences did those revolutions have on the making of America and what legacies do they provide to contemporary American citizens, both indigenous and nonindigenous? Those are the questions that I'm interested in.

If we think about the precontact world, we quickly realize that at that time there were no European technologies of violence upon the American landscape—no guns, no metals, no horses, and particularly, if you think of it as technology, no disease dissemination. Those four variables unleashed profound economic and social forces that transformed and destroyed communities far and wide throughout the hemisphere. To dwell on this even further, we must also recognize that pedestrian, as opposed to equestrian, societies did not have the capacity or the motivation, generally speaking, to wage the kind of warfare that Native people subsequently developed throughout the postcontact period.

What was true in the West was also true across much of the American continent: Native people, dealing with the cycles of disruption unleashed by European colonialism, necessarily adapted to and became implicated in broader sets of political, economic, and military relations in which violence became an everyday form of life. So the point is not to dispute the level of violence prior

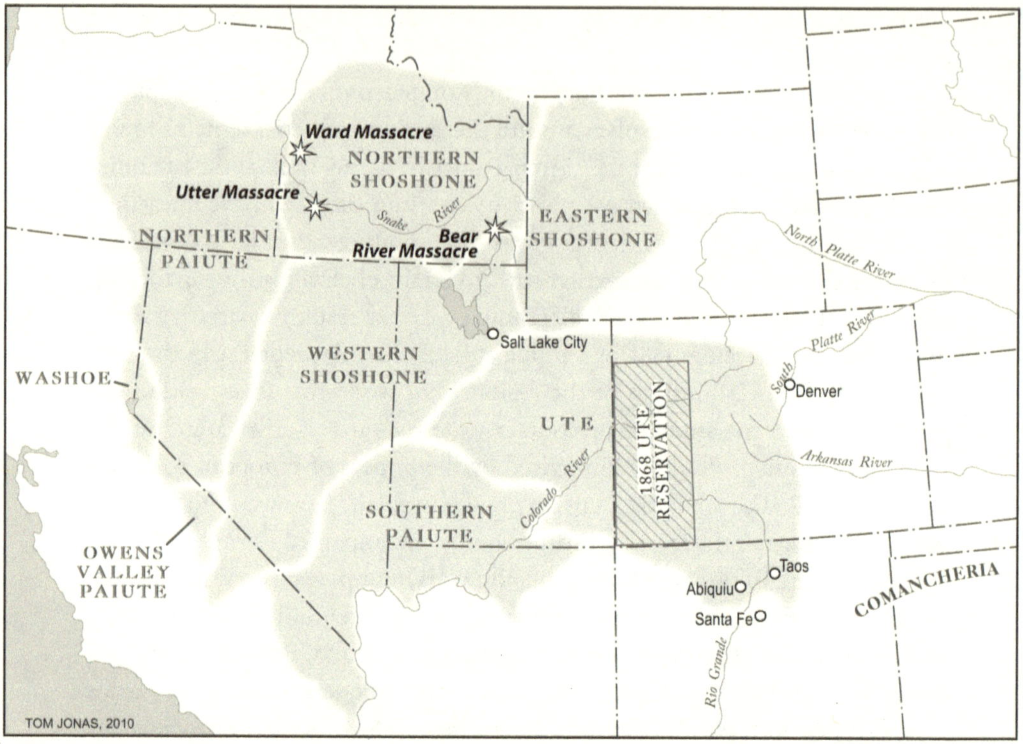

The Great Basin, showing the lands of various Shoshonean-speaking groups as they were in the early 1800s. The sites of key massacres in Idaho and the boundaries of the Ute Reservation as negotiated by the Ute chief Ouray in 1868 are also shown. The Utes were later restricted to two much smaller reservations, one in southwestern Colorado and one in northeastern Utah. Map adapted from Blackhawk, *Violence over the Land.*

to colonialism but to identify colonialism properly as a central, if not the essential, thread of early American history.

DJL: Part of your point seems to be that it doesn't matter what level of violence there was before colonialism—its onset totally created a new version that was horrendous compared to anything that had come before.

NB: That's right.

DJL: In reading your work, we were amazed to learn of the sophistication of the Utes' diplomacy, from the Spanish era well into the American era, and into the era of the establishment of the reservations.[3] We read the article that you cited by Hämäläinen about the Comanches' trade empire, which we found extremely impressive.[4] Wasn't mastery of the invaders' technologies of violence a prerequisite for this trade and diplomacy?

NB: Professor Hämäläinen has now published the long-anticipated book toward which his many articles have been building for some time. That book, *The Comanche Empire,* which has garnered an impressive number of scholarly accolades, has substantively rewritten the history of the American West. So I'm happy to talk about the ways that Utes and Comanches and other equestrian powers after the arrival of the Europeans were able to develop, gradually over time, the level of diplomatic, political, economic, and military strength that your question mentions.

This subject really points to a primary feature of the western American landscape in the postcontact period. My work and Hämäläinen's work suggest that Native communities not only adapted to European colonialism in a complicated and contingent manner but did so quite early, following the disruption of their societies that occurred prior to direct contact with or documentation by Europeans. That means that, before we can think of the Utes, Comanches, Kiowas, Wichitas, Cheyennes, Arapahos, Lakotas, and other Plains peoples as incomparable equestrian powers, as members of a multipolar diplomatic and military world in the nineteenth century, before we rush to that insight and analysis, we should think of how they got there. And that historical question brings us back to the early contact period and to the subsequent ripples of devastation and destruction that spread across the colonial hinterland. Those ripples of disruption worked across the continent and even intersected with other colonial influences, emanating from locations along the Mississippi, the Great Lakes, and eastern North America. It's extremely important to view these Native communities as historical actors and subjects living within and during a traumatic imperial and colonial period.

In the early portions of my book, and in Hämäläinen's for that matter, one sees levels of violence outside of the European frontier societies radically remaking preexisting social, political, and economic worlds. Professor Hämäläinen's book, for example, starts with the arrival of pedestrian migratory Comanche people coming into parts of what is now the American Southwest, in search of new European technologies. And they find them roughly in the late seventeenth century or the early eighteenth century, when the Comanches first begin appearing in Spanish documentary sources. Finding these technologies, what did they do with them? Essentially, they pushed the communities currently between themselves and the Spanish out of the way. From roughly 1700 to 1760 Comanches engaged in an equestrian war upon horticulturalists and semiequestrian societies up and down the Arkansas, Canadian, and various watersheds of the southern plains. They displaced Apaches from prime equestrian grounds, from an ecology where the Comanches could build herds of horses. By doing that, they put themselves into closer proximity to the Spanish empire, which had established itself in the late 1500s along the northern Rio Grande. That empire had essentially become the epicenter of radical continent-wide historical disruption that the Spanish themselves were not even aware of and that unleashed waves of violence upon the continent, waves that eventually were directed back against the colony itself by peoples like the Comanches.

The first known encounter between the Spanish and Ute communities was in approximately 1637, when Governor Rosas led a slave raid against ethnographically identifiable Utaca people.[5] Throughout the seventeenth century, the Utes dealt with the Spanish and also with other communities around them who had been coping with the arrival of the Spanish.[6] Over time, sets of violent relations characterized Ute diplomacy as well as Comanche diplomacy, trade, and ultimately life for subsequent generations—in the case of the Comanches, turning pedestrian migratory peoples into fully supreme equestrian societies capable of rapid large-scale mobilization, in ways that were inconceivable prior to European arrival.

DJL: You state that the Utes' remaking of themselves was accomplished "at the expense of others, as violence and Indian slavery became woven into the fabric of everyday life throughout the early West."[7] The violence was displaced onto Shoshone and Paiute groups farther west. What strengths did these nonequestrian groups bring to the interaction? Were they successful at defensive warfare? Did they have items of trade (other than slaves) of interest to the Utes?

NB: This is a very difficult question to answer because there are so few documentary records about the nature of the equestrian/nonequestrian encounters in the Great Basin. All we have are shards of evidence, perhaps one to two pieces per decade—as with the Spanish slave raid on the Utes that I referenced in the last question. Before and for nearly a century after the reconquest of New Mexico in 1694, the Spanish generally didn't travel within these nonequestrian communities, making it even more difficult to learn about these encounters. Indeed, it's not until the 1750s and 1760s that Paiute communities are clearly identifiable within the Spanish colonial records.

So on one level we have very fragmentary evidence and on another we have to use that evidence to make very broad analyses and conclusions that are going to be at best partial interpretations. My reaction generally is simply to sketch the few documentary shards of evidence we do have about the pre–Anglo-American settlement period when nonequestrian groups were particularly targeted by equestrian communities in much of the intermountain west or the Great Basin. And it is quite clear that over time throughout the late eighteenth century and particularly into the nineteenth century, following the establishment of the trade routes that eventually became the Old Spanish Trail between New Mexico and California, equestrian communities increased the traffic of nonequestrian peoples as slaves to New Mexico and to a much lesser extent to California.[8]

These accounts of trafficking indicate that very few items of exchange, and ultimately very few forms of escape, were available to nonequestrians once they were surrounded or targeted by an equestrian raiding party. That is not to say, however, that they were defenseless. In my book, I include accounts where Paiutes and various nonequestrian communities fled from the equestrian raiders, or burned landscapes to try to discourage the arrival of horse parties, or used communal alarms to accelerate their community's rapid removal from the region the traffickers were coming into.[9] So those fragments and shards of evidence point to trafficking and also point to the relatively limited nature of resources other than slaves that the nonequestrian communities could offer. But they don't, I believe, constitute a sense that the entire region was under siege by marauding equestrian traffickers. While that is true in the nineteenth century in certain parts of the central Utah, such as the Salt Lake/Wasatch front region, and it is true of certain water holes and springs in the southern portions of the Great Basin and eastern California, by and large, the nonequestrian communities over time came to understand the relative terror that equestrian raiders brought and found ways to survive it.

DJL: The point has been made by several authors, such as Michael Tate, that the interaction between the westering emigrants and the northern plains tribes in the 1830s and 1840s was initially fairly benign and was based on mutually beneficial trade, cooperation, and friendship.[10] As it became clear to the Native populations that their resource base was being destroyed, then the situation turned around and the violence began in earnest. Do you agree with this? Did anti-emigrant violence begin earliest in the Great Basin because the destruction of the Indians' resource base was much more rapid in that fragile ecology, more easily disrupted by the emigrants' herds of cattle and horses?

NB: This is a particularly broad question because it requires both temporal and geographic comparative analysis. The northern plains, the central plains, and the Great Basin were all very different places in the 1840s and 1850s. I have not yet read Tate's work carefully, so I won't comment on it directly. In answer to your question, I will say that it is likely true that there were places and periods in which western emigrants or Anglo-American settlers and traders and the Indian tribes established mutually beneficial relations. We can point to a whole host of examples. However, viewing the history in such a limited geographical or temporal frame wouldn't be very helpful for sketching a broader portrait of western North American Indians. For one thing, even in the places and times where these mutually beneficial relationships were established, the Indian worlds had been created beforehand by highly competitive, violent processes of the kind I've been talking about.

The subsequent diminution or dissolution of those worlds in the wake of the Anglo-American takeover was even more traumatic. One of the great contributions that Elliott West's book *The Contested Plains* made was to point out the irony of the fact that many Native communities, such as the Comanches, the Cheyennes, and others, were entering into their greatest economic and political prominence, their most successful postcontact equestrian lifestyle, at the same time when their lands were becoming heavily contested by new economic and political orders. The moment of rising equestrian military, political, and economic strength had ultimately sown the seeds of its own destruction. What Hämäläinen is saying is that, by the late portions of the Spanish era and during the Mexican era, the Comanches were establishing an equestrian and bison-centered economic world in the plains that was ultimately untenable, making the subsequent expansion of the United States that much more devastating.

But those moments, those momentary, seemingly optimistic or seemingly successful forms of adaptation, were exactly that: they were moments, chapters in a larger subject. And that larger subject has to be seen as being inherently both violent and ultimately traumatic.

DJL: A good deal of the problem on the Oregon and California trails involved "bad" men, such as roughneck frontier whites who shot Indians on sight. In the 1850s there were believed to be "White Indians" or white criminals who raided emigrant trains, sometimes together with Indians. Some of these may have been escapees from California justice. And there were ex-trappers who went bad, who rode together with Indians in raiding parties. Would the level of Great Basin violence have been significantly different without these "bad" men?

NB: It would have. Brigham Madsen points toward this in his landmark book *The Shoshoni Frontier*.[11] One of the things that really stuck out for me as I was embarking upon the work that I did is that these were lawless lands. But there is no good scholarly study of the subject, of the lawless behavior in the region, and there should be—one that is written in a manner that is not singular or episodic but structural and contingent.

When we think of the West as a lawless society, we tend to think of it as a place where men and cowboys, gunslingers, confronted each other in highly dramatic encounters along dusty streets. But prior to the establishment of any saloons or corrals, prior to the establishment of an Anglo-American or English-speaking society, many different men came into the area and fought each other. There were roving bands of not just white men but marauders of all flavors and nationalities. Peg-leg Smith and the host of mountain men who raided their way across the Old Spanish Trail often were working with various indigenous marauders.[12] These were groups that roved and lived off the land and the peoples upon it. This was true along the Oregon Trail, it was true along the California Trail, and it was true earlier during the period of the mountain men.

People have a romanticized vision of fur trappers, but many of the mountain men deployed violence and utilized it in a very gratuitous form. These were the first agents in the West of what ironically came to be called civilization. But the mountain men are very poorly contextualized in the study of the West because they were not romantic, isolated individuals breaking off from the rest of society to live a naturalistic lifestyle. They were in reality political agents who were engaged in their own political project, which was the utilization of the region's resources for their own ends. The fact that their relationships with tribes were often familial, often based on incorporation into existing kinship networks, hides the kind of brutality that they were engaged in when they were away from these tribal communities.[13]

It's a really important subject that very few people have any sense of. In part, this is because we conceive of western American history as moving from east to west, when in fact, as your question posits and as we all know, there were traders and individuals traveling from west to east, from California, and also from south to north, from New Mexico into the mountains and into the West. In my book, there's a whole portion of a chapter about the Snake River brigades, fur trappers coming from the northwest into the intermountain west. So we really need to think of this region, these peoples, and ultimately our country, as being inherently multilingual, inherently shaped by influences emanating from a whole constellation of places, inherently diverse, and often contested at the region's core.

DJL: The level of anti-emigrant violence that occurred on the Snake plains, as in the Ward and Utter disasters, is almost unbelievable.[14] The sources for information on these disasters include reminiscences of survivors and newspaper accounts dating to the period. Such sources often suffer from a high level of sensationalism. How reliable do you think these sources are?

NB: These incidents not only were covered by the survivors of the incidents and the newspapers but also were covered by various government agents and officials. You can best evaluate their reliability when you triangulate or situate these accounts within larger fields of documentary materials.

For most of western North America, fighting between emigrants and Indians was not as common as people believe. As your question indicates, however, it was very common along the Snake River plains and along the Oregon Trail. It was particularly common in the interior portions of the Territory of Oregon and the northern portions of the Territory of Utah, which is now in the state of Idaho. Madsen estimates that 90 percent of all emigrant deaths at the hands of Native Americans occurred west of South Pass, particularly between Wyoming, Forts Hall and Boise, and the Willamette Valley in Oregon, where so many migrants were heading.[15] That's kind of shocking. And it points us back to our primary subject at hand: it points us to communities involved in extensively violent relations with one another and also with intruders, foreigners, or migrants.

But it is not only shocking in the level of the violence. It is shocking in the level of economic necessity that these tribes were enduring. Along the Oregon Trail, along the California Trail, from Salt Lake to California along the Humboldt River, communities were undergoing severe economic disruption. Many of the emigrant accounts, not just of massacres but of Indian attacks on overlanders, relay harrowing forms of economic behavior that are themselves unbelievable: Native communities stealing flour and eating it raw because they were so hungry . . . Native communities begging and violently trying to seize various food resources.

What are the origins of those forms of deprivation? That's the question we need to ask ourselves. And those are the questions that will point us toward the history that we've just sketched: the history of the arrival of the European technologies of violence, the arrival of European diseases, the arrival of ecological destruction that attends the arrival of horses, the forced alteration of indigenous ecosystems due to the threat of equestrian raiders, and so forth. Those are the kinds of deep-seated economic bases out of which many of these raids developed.

DJL: You rightly argue that the Bear River Massacre, perhaps the largest mass murder of Native peoples in the American West, demands a place in the nation's historical consciousness.[16] Why do you think that the Bear River Massacre is absent from most history textbooks? At the same time, we feel that the description of the actual event in your book is conspicuously muted. The interested reader, of course, can go to Madsen and other sources to learn more of the details. Nevertheless, we are interested in your narrative strategy for this part of the book.

NB: The Bear River Massacre is understudied, despite Madsen. It seemingly has been discarded from the narrative of American history and sits at the margins of the nation's memory. In a disturbing way, Sand Creek, Wounded Knee, Washita, the Long Walk, and all the countless forms of brutality unleashed upon Native communities that have been more widely studied—these studies have created a kind of collective fatigue about the subject of indigenous massacres. Perhaps this is partly because Dee Brown did such a thorough job in his book *Bury My Heart at Wounded Knee* of bringing these subjects to light. Because of all this, Bear River, along with the Snake plains emigrant conflicts of the 1850s that we talked about earlier, just sits quiet.

But it is nevertheless surprising that prominent surveys of American Indian history continue to omit this most bloody morning in American Indian history. Apparently they have recently uncovered a Mormon biography or diary about the battle that in fact asserts a higher fatality rate than Connor's reports published in the Civil War series *War of the Rebellion.*[17] The account has the total number of bodies closer to five hundred than to three hundred. So how and why has this subject not received any substantial historical interrogation other than the work of Madsen? That's the question. It's a big one, it's a long one, and it's a complicated one. It partly points to the history of the state of Utah's often antagonistic relationship with the federal government during that period, to the Mormon church's legitimate concern about controlling the source material of its own members, to the history of the American Civil War in the West, and it points to the history of American conquest of the West in a very rapid period shortly after the war. It's really an invitation for subsequent study.

I'm glad that you've raised the question about my narrative approach because it suggests critical elements in the production of any historical analysis: motivation and intent, as well as, in some real way, time constraints. The Bear River Massacre, partly because it is so underwritten, required an enormous amount of broader contextualization. I could not understand the event in isolation. Even though the Utes weren't involved in the massacre, I could not understand the event divorced from the history of Mormon-Ute relations. I did not want to understand the event episodically; I wanted to understand it broadly. And the more I learned, the deeper my surprise became regarding the scant secondary materials. There's scant previously written work on the really dramatic, traumatic transformations that affected the region and the Native peoples of the Great Basin. Not just on the Bear River Massacre, but on the staggering levels of warfare and violence emanating from New Mexico, the traffic of nonequestrian Paiutes and Shoshones as slaves, and the collapse of the Ute reservation in the 1870s and early 1880s.[18] All of these subjects sit in many ways outside the narrative of our nation's past, and they disturb and trouble it.

So I really was intent on getting the subject laid out, establishing the deep origins within the history of the encounter with colonialism, within the history of equestrianism, and within the history of growing forms of federal political control of the region. I was interested in situating the history of that conflict in the broader context of the Colorado and Utah Indian Wars of the 1850s. I chose not to write on the military history of the battle itself, partly because I was well into a very long chapter of my book and already found myself wanting that chapter to provide an interpretive overview of the crisis that Mormon settlement occasioned for the Ute, Paiute, and Shoshone peoples of the region. The Bear River Massacre is one moment in a much larger regional transformation that I was trying to investigate, although it is obviously the most traumatic and bloody moment of that conflict.

DJL: In *The Frontier Army in the Settlement of the West,* Michael Tate suggests that the Regular (as opposed to Volunteer) Army played a positive role in protecting the Indians against incursions by settlers, in feeding them, in providing medicine, and in doing early ethnology to understand them better. We were interested to learn that Sarah Winnemucca shared this view, at least as concerned the Paiutes.[19] On the other hand, "some glory-seeking California volunteers" (as Madsen called Connor's troops) engaged in a dawn attack in freezing weather at Bear River, killing not only warriors but also many women and children, excusing such killing as collateral damage.[20] Similar attacks were made by the regular army after the war at Washita and other places. In your opinion, did the existence of a standing army in the West lead to more peace or to increased conflict? If the army had a greater presence in the Great Basin, would there have been less violence?

NB: It's hard for those of us who teach these subjects or work with them to convey the complexity of the sets of historical relations that we're talking about because you will find that the same military officer both mediated conflicts and initiated them. And you will find that American Indians, from various communities, both led army troops into battle and also suffered from attacks of the troops.

We have to understand the military in the American West as an instrument of the federal government. Some of the major tragedies of the army in the West arose because the federal government's policies for the region were uneven, they were chaotic, they changed, and they were often completely ineffective. This started already prior to the Civil War when, except for a few places where the army was well established, such as in New Mexico, along the coast of California, and at the mouth of the Columbia, the U.S. military in the American West was tiny, disorganized, and ineffective. But such chaotic policy continued after the war, when the army was larger and reorganized.

For the Native communities of the region that I examine, great tragedy arose from the government's inconsistency and ineffectiveness. When the control of the federal government was weak in the region, the tribes had to involve themselves solely with settlers, who were often bent on resisting federal initiatives. Or they had to deal with the bad white men that you referred to earlier, the lawless communities that were roving in this region outside the purview of federal authority, control, and surveillance. In addition, the communities interacted with a federal government that changed its mind, a government that entered into agreements and subsequently walked away from them. One cannot help but feel empathy for so many of these indigenous communities who suffered harrowing, harrowing challenges throughout the nineteenth-century West, only to see their communities fall victim to an ineffective federal government and its army and/or a spineless one. The Bear River Massacre and the abrogation of the Ute treaties of 1868 and the Long Walk and the Sand Creek Massacre—all the traumatic chapters of the American West—should be seen in relationship to the power and/or ineffectiveness of the federal government, and not just the overeagerness of the volunteer forces like those you mentioned.

DJL: Often Anglo-Americans justified their own savagery as part of what they viewed as an essentially just cause, and their testimony can therefore be unreliable and contradictory. What is your opinion of Indian testimony? Certainly, no history of the frontier West can be complete or true without such testimony. But if you want to get the Native American side of the story, what testimony can you rely on? Those who participated in the battles and were later recorded by reporters and anthropologists had excellent reason to veil the truth: they could be punished for admitting what they had done. And Indian descendants today testify at a big remove from the culture and actions of their ancestors—as removed as we are from our great-great grandparents, of whom we know almost nothing. How do you use that kind of material methodologically?

NB: Another big one. I think that the best strategy, as I suggested in a previous question, is to try to triangulate or situate historical materials within broader fields of information. And while it is true that there can be no history of the American frontier without incorporation of Native American voices, we must treat these Indian testimonies as historically produced texts and documents, just as we treat all historically produced testimonies. Despite how appealing or enticing it might be, we should try not to take testimonies from the twentieth century and project them back deep into the presettlement past. I would find it extremely helpful if people were to use testimony only from the period that they study and not project or transpose testimony across time.

Part of what makes this an interesting question is that it points to the lingering nostalgia that many non-Native people have for the history of the American West and the special role of Indians within that cultural history. As we all know, an enormous imaginary field of what Native American identity, culture, and life really are about has been created. It's a mythology that Indian people themselves often have a hard time confronting and counteracting. Many of us spend parts of our lives literally shaped or responding to this often very negative or simplistic imagery. I personally find it inappropriate for western mythologies to project American Indians as their antitheses. And these problems are complicated by the fact that many Indian peoples themselves are often unequal participants in the construction of some of these dynamics, meaning that we often receive cultural misinformation as other Americans do.

For example, *Black Elk Speaks,* which was edited and organized by the poet and writer John Neihardt, has become a kind of classic vision or testimony of the prereservation Lakota life.[21] Some see in that narrative a history of lost cultural autonomy, diminished religious fulfillment, and other forms of loss for a culture that many have a deep nostalgia for. Because it's in bookstores and libraries, because people teach it, and because we read it, we tend to believe it. But such testimonies themselves are products of mediation: they are organized by non-Native people, often anthropologists or writers like Neihardt, and they are written and published in English. While we can try, as we said, to triangulate them or to situate them in the field of other documentary records, we must not conceive of them as being primary source testimonies in other historical subjects. We do ourselves a tremendous disservice when we believe the narrative of the mediated indigenous voice to be the truth of a particular epoch or era of precontact American Indian history.

Raymond DeMallie, a preeminent ethnographer of Lakota culture, went back and looked at Neihardt's transcriptions of Black Elk's testimony, and he found a different narrative.[22] He found Black Elk not to be a defeated man, not hopeless but optimistic, not exclusively rooted in only Lakota cosmologies but active in a broad variety of religious activities. He found a much more complicated narrative. He published his findings in a book called *The Sixth Grandfather*, which fundamentally reoriented that narrative.

So these testimonies cannot, as we said, be used to re-create indigenous lifestyles, behaviors, and histories outside of the times in which they were produced, and if they are mediated we have to look at them as such. Perhaps we would be well served by turning to the testimony not of individual indigenous community members but of the collective community itself, looking at things like testimonies before Congress over particular political claims, rather than these broader cultural assessments that are often circulated.

DJL: A related issue is your point that certain current views of precontact violence, captive-taking, and slavery are not solidly based on evidence but often reflect ethnohistories of nineteenth- and twentieth-century Indians, who had long been subject to Spanish or American modes of violence. Can you explain your statement that James Brooks's positing of precontact slavery is based on troubling ethnographic and documentary accounts?[23]

NB: I hope it is evident, both in my work and in this interview, that I am at no point trying to diminish the often remarkable achievements that many scholars have accomplished through their investigations of the early American West. We all are engaged in common projects that ultimately depend upon one another for both insight and production. Scholarly concerns that are raised between professionally trained and professionally employed historians are exactly that: they're scholarly concerns and/or disagreements between individuals who approach certain subjects differently, as well as often for different purposes.

DJL: We consider your review of Brooks's book to be a model of collegiality, both how to say what's good about a book and how to be reasonably critical.

NB: Thank you. Going back to your question, it did strike me that it is logical to move from your earlier question about my possible underemphasis of precolonial violence to my admitted disagreements with other scholars over their portrayals of indigenous behavior—portrayals that are based on the use of what I consider to be unsuccessful evidentiary source material. First of all, as I just mentioned, I am less comfortable using nineteenth- or even twentieth-century ethnographic materials to understand the behavior of my sixteenth- or seventeenth-century subjects, who were struggling with the arrival of European diseases, technologies, warfare, and various major disruptions. The seminal ethnographic accounts of the Comanches, Utes, and Western Shoshones were produced in the aftermath of the colonial encounter, in the aftermath of the postequestrian lifestyle that many of these societies once maintained, in the aftermath of the establishment of reservations, and I feel uncomfortable upstreaming, so to speak, this more recent ethnographic material. That seems to me to be a slight violation of the historian's Hippocratic Oath, at least in the twenty-first century.

Where I disagree in particular with several eminent scholars is in their portraits of the motivation behind indigenous behavior. In the article in *Ethnohistory* that you cited, I included a rejoinder to an aspect of the work of James Brooks and Dan Flores.[24] While both of them have made extremely important contributions, they make an assertion that I would encourage them, as well as those who use their work, to revisit. They claim that indigenous communities, in times of economic or social difficulty in the precolonial world, initiated forms of human social population control in which they purposely murdered their children. Now I find that to be a difficult claim. And I feel uncomfortable that I am often the only one who is concerned when Flores and Brooks both invoke the term "infanticide" as a form of cultural explanation for indigenous behavior in the precolonial West. I am troubled by this attribution of indigenous action to vague cultural norms of behavior. Ramón Gutiérrez also unfortunately did something like this in *When Jesus Came, the Corn Mothers Went Away,* and there are slight elements of it in Brian DeLay's book *War of a Thousand Deserts.*[25] DeLay in one chapter claims that motivations for vengeance carried Comanche and other southern plains people deep into northern Mexico during the antecedents of the U.S.-Mexico War. In a book that has otherwise brilliantly rewritten the history of the Mexican-American War, there's an attribution of behavior to its indigenous subjects that seems at times to be inscrutable: they wanted revenge so they undertook massive campaigns.

Maybe that's the case or maybe it isn't. Pekka Hämäläinen makes a different case, which I find more convincing because it contextualizes such actions within deeper economic and political forms.[26] Similarly Brooks makes a claim about captivity in the precolonial American world that cites a shred of information found in Cabeza de Vaca's travel accounts across Texas in the late 1520s and early 1530s.[27] In a fleeting moment, Cabeza de Vaca recorded a comment that Native communities preferred to keep their population down by killing the young women in their society. Brooks subsequently makes this claim the basis for his paradigm for captivity across the pre-Columbian American continent. That's a methodological concern that I am perhaps dwelling upon a little too deeply here, but I am ultimately concerned that far too many people investigating the indigenous colonial encounter might inadvertently fall prey to such approaches without contextualizing them as best as they can within larger fields of social inquiry.

Concluding Comments

Familiar with life in the nineteenth-century West, Colonel Richard Dodge asserted in his book *Our Wild Indians* that he knew of a "frontier ruffian" who made "a journey of two hundred miles to have a fight with another whose fame as a 'dead shot' rivaled his own."[1] More recently, Cormac McCarthy wrote: "Some of the old time sheriffs wouldn't even carry a firearm. A lot of folks find that hard to believe, but it's a fact."[2] Western writers have long disputed the topic of whether the violence on the frontier was as commonplace as has been traditionally depicted by popular culture, including dime novels, Hollywood movies, and sensational journalism. The authors interviewed in *Violent Encounters* offer their perspective on the types of lethal conflicts that those on the frontier—Indians, soldiers, emigrants, settlers—faced. In this chapter, we provide an overview of their comments, drawing attention to the variety of responses to certain themes addressed in the interviews.

First, as evidenced in the interviews, the violence that occurred during the era of western expansion involved all ethnic groups. And no group exercised a monopoly on perpetrating violence. The interviews indicate that the U.S. military massacred Indians with particular brutality at Clear Lake and Sand Creek. Army attacks on Indian villages, with considerable killing of women and children, occurred at Blue Water Creek, Bear River, Washita, and Slim Buttes and at Morning Star's camp on the Red Fork of the Powder River. An important, albeit little-known, massacre of Piegan Blackfeet Indians by U.S. troops, not discussed in the interviews, was the cavalry's attack on a Piegan village on the Marias River in Montana in 1870; of the 170 killed, 50 were women and children.[3]

The violence perpetrated by white civilians and volunteer armies on Indian populations, such as at Camp Grant, Sand Creek, and Bear River, was often premeditated and carefully choreographed. This is especially evident in early California, where, as Albert Hurtado makes clear, the destruction of the Indian population was rapid, to a great extent purposeful, and very thorough. A number of significant massacres, not discussed in the interviews, occurred in California; many went unreported. As evidenced by historian William Secrest in *When the Great Spirit Died,* California Indians who occupied land desired by whites were systematically killed between 1850 and 1860.[4]

Much of the violence that Indians directed against whites occurred in small-scale encounters, such as the Oatman Massacre, where less than ten people were killed. Another encounter where Indians killed only a handful of people not discussed in the interviews was the Warren Wagon Train Massacre in Texas.[5] Some cases of small-scale slaughter were single incidents in larger campaigns. For example, the McComas Massacre, where only two were killed, was part of Chato's raid, where more than thirty-five whites in Sonora, Arizona, and New Mexico were killed over the course of a few weeks. During the depredations on the Solomon and Saline Rivers in western Kansas prior to Custer's Washita campaign, 110 white citizens were killed, 15 women raped, 1,000 livestock stolen, and large numbers of houses and barns burned by the Indians during a month or two. Judged by the perspective of the number of people killed at Little Big Horn, even events like the Ward and Utter massacres are considered tiny. It should be remembered, however, that the nineteenth-century frontier was sparsely populated: when the violent encounters left thirty or forty dead, it was no small thing. The one massacre of whites by Indians that left a higher body count was the Santee Sioux Revolt, in which over four hundred farmers and their family members were killed in a single day, "with a savagery rarely equaled in the history of Indian uprisings."[6]

Despite the large number of whites killed by Indians, it is worth emphasizing that the number of Indians killed by whites was even larger. Michael Tate cites John D. Unruh's assertion that during the period 1840–60, when more than 500,000 emigrants traveled the Oregon-California Trails, only 362 emigrants were killed by Indians (vastly more died from disease and accidents), while 426 Indians were killed by white emigrants, mostly in small skirmishes associated with livestock raids.[7] Chip Colwell-Chanthaphonh cites army documents showing that for every thirteen Apaches killed, only one soldier was killed by the Apaches. As Hurtado discusses, the Indian population of California fell from 150,000 at the beginning of the gold rush to 30,000 by 1860. While many of the Native communities were decimated by disease, a large fraction fell to direct violence or to starvation, a result of land dispossession and displacement by white colonizers. The scale of killing of Indians by the army at Clear Lake, Bear River, Sand Creek, Washita, and the Marias River, where a hundred or more were killed in each incident, was much larger than the scale of killing of white Americans by Indians in any given incident, with the exception of the Santee Sioux Revolt.

Indians also massacred Indians. The main case discussed in the interviews is the Papago participation in the massacre of Apaches at Camp Grant. In *Shadows at Dawn,* Karl Jacoby places this tragedy in its historical context by providing the long history of attacks and counterattacks between Papagos and Apaches, as well as between Hispanic Arizonans and Apaches, that had plagued the territory for preceding decades. As discussed in the interview with Jerome Greene, the Cheyennes expelled the Kiowas and Comanches from the Black Hills, often engaging in surprise attacks on enemy villages, killing as many men as possible and taking women and children as prisoners. Ned Blackhawk points out that, following this expulsion, the Comanches attacked Plains Apache villages in the Canadian and nearby watersheds in the process of establishing dominance in the southern plains. An interesting study of the Plains Indian wars, *Tribal Wars of the Southern Plains* by Stan Hoig, chronicles Indian-Indian conflicts, especially as white incursions forced tribes from the north and east onto the Great Plains. The Cutthroat Massacre, where an Osage party wiped out a Kiowa village, cut off the heads of the dead, and left them in cooking pots, is only one example that Hoig discusses.[8] Many other incidents of Indian/Indian violence were related by Native Americans themselves, such as the mutual attacks by Apaches and Yavapais and Navajos that were related by Western Apaches in interviews with Grenville Goodwin.[9]

Of course, white Americans massacred white Americans. An example discussed in this volume is the Mountain Meadows Massacre, where Mormons slaughtered a party from Arkansas. It should be noted, however, that this tragedy had been preceded in the 1830s by the Haun's Mill Massacre, where a Missouri militia killed noncombatant Mormons.[10] Finally, Sonora and Chihuahua and what became the American Southwest had a long history of Mexicans attacking Apaches and vice versa.[11] In fact, hatred between Apaches and Mexicans far exceeded the animosity between Apaches and Anglo-Americans in both brutality and longevity. Spanish settlements and later Mexican settlements suffered Indian raids from the north for over two and a half centuries.

All ethnic groups were victims at one time or another. Colwell-Chanthaphonh makes graphic the viciousness of the attack on the sleeping village of Aravaipa Apaches at Camp Grant. In chapter 3 Will Bagley comes to the defense of the members of Fancher party who were ruthlessly slaughtered at Mountain Meadows. He also censures the Mormon officials' falsehoods when they later accused the Arkansas emigrants of inciting the attack by virtue of alleged depredations on the local Utah populations. The violence had profound consequences for the survivors and shadows their descendants even today.[12] As Colwell-Chanthaphonh aptly puts it, for both the Aravaipas after Camp Grant and the Cheyennes after Sand Creek, "the massacres represented a loss of land and a loss of a way of life. These were really turning points for all the tribes that were involved." Greene concurs and emphasizes that the attacks on the Cheyennes at Sand Creek, at Washita, and on the Red Fork of the Powder River were devastating to that comparatively small tribe. Albert Hurtado declares that the result of the European takeover was "demographic disaster" for the California Indians but adds: "That any Indians survived is testimony that abhorrent conditions can produce courage and strength in a people, a tribute to the persistence of humankind."[13]

Violent attacks in the West often involved the taking of captives. The surviving seventeen children of the Fancher party were initially adopted into Mormon families until being rescued and transported back to relatives in Arkansas. Even the U.S. Army took captives at Washita and Bear River; these captive women and children were treated, in effect, as hostages to induce the warriors onto the reservation. According to Michael Tate, Comanches, Apaches, and other Plains Indians often adopted women and children captives into their own tribes. Hispanics in New Mexico and Arizona adopted Indian captives into their families even after the American takeover. In New Mexico, this led to a special class of citizenship—the *genízaros.*[14] Hostages were seen as valuable trade "commodities" in transcultural and intersocietal trade on the frontier. For example, in the Southwest, Utes and Comanches traded captives taken from other tribes (such as Paiutes) to the Spanish. Apache children taken at Camp Grant were traded into Mexico. Olive Oatman was traded by the Yavapais to the Mohaves and then ransomed back to the whites at Fort Yuma. If they survived, captives like Oatman were in the unique position to serve as emissaries in cross-cultural communication.

Captivity at times led to full-scale integration of the captive into the tribe. Margot Mifflin stresses the ambiguity that Olive Oatman felt as to whether she wanted to return to white civilization, after having acculturated to the Mohaves. In *Captives and Cousins,* James Brooks posits that such captivity sometimes led to kinship networks between different ethnic groups, such as the Utes and the Hispanics of New Mexico. In his review of Brooks's book, however, Ned Blackhawk emphasizes that the trauma of the process should not be underestimated. In chapter 1 Marc Simmons strives to understand the Indians' raiding and captive-taking from the perspective of the tribal cultures but stresses the cruel treatment that was often the fate of the captive women. Even ransomed captives found it difficult if not impossible to reintegrate back into their precaptivity societies. For example, Mifflin discusses how Olive Oatman's captivity had a profound effect on her life after her return to white civilization, including bouts of deep depression.

Granted, hostile relations on the frontier were not necessarily the norm. Tate emphasizes that trade, mutual assistance, and friendship often prevailed between Indians and emigrants, especially in the 1840s. These mutually beneficial relations that existed in the 1840s, however, occurred when the Plains Indian societies were at their cultural and military zenith, the number of whites in the West was small, the tribes' enemies were primarily other tribes competing for the same territory, and trade with the Anglo-Americans was of enormous benefit to the various Native communities. This tranquil pattern changed in the 1850s, when Indians found their resources being depleted by the increasing number of overlanders. Blackhawk argues that any moments of cooperation during the trail era "were exactly that: they were moments, chapters in a larger subject": the history of inevitable white takeover of the Indians' territory.

Clearly the term "massacre" is controversial: when is a violent encounter a massacre? Of the eight interviewees, only Greene makes an effort to define the term, carefully distinguishing massacres, battles, and assaults. Robert Utley does not consider the Santee Sioux Revolt a massacre, even though he agrees that very large numbers of noncombatant whites were killed over the course of the first few days of the uprising. As Greene points out, while army attacks on Indian villages were formally considered "offensive battles," they nevertheless involved dawn assaults on sleeping villages in freezing weather in which considerable numbers of women, children, and elderly people were killed. Greene also notes that while the killing of Sioux by the army at Wounded Knee was not premeditated—the Indians started the shooting—it evolved into the murder of innocents as the day progressed. While the slaughter of noncombatants in such cases might euphemistically be called "collateral damage," we consider it reasonable to include it in a more general concept of "massacre." Such a generalization includes small-scale incidents, especially when the killing of one or two people was part of a larger program of slaughter. This occurred notably in California, where there was a systematic effort by white settlers to eliminate the Native population, one or two people or one or two small *rancherías* at a time. As mentioned above, small-scale Indian depredations were often part of larger campaigns, such as Chato's raid or the Dog Soldiers' raids on the Saline and Solomon. While the Paiute and Shoshone raids on emigrants, settlers, and mail stations along the Humboldt and Snake Rivers were not coordinated, cumulatively they resulted in a great deal of killing.

A related question is whether to refer to the conquest of the Native American populations by the Europeans (Spanish, British, French, and Anglo-American) as genocide.[15] For example, did the destruction of the California Indians amount to genocide? As Hurtado asserts, "extermination" was a byword in California newspapers and in certain California government circles. While there were always groups within the American society and government who favored extermination of the Indians, it seems to us that these groups were consistently and often effectively opposed by other groups who favored accommodation. In his book *Bárbaros*, historian David Weber makes it clear that this was also true in Mexico and South America.

In addition, to view the extinction of such large numbers of people as deliberate requires dealing with the fact that greater numbers of Native Americans in the West died from diseases introduced by the Europeans than were killed in attacks. It is on this basis that Noble David Cook, in *Born to Die,* attempts to revise the so-called Black Legend, which blames all the injustices of the early conquest on the Spanish. While Cook's work focuses on the Spanish colonies prior to 1650, it is apparently true that disease was also a major cause of death of Native Americans in the eighteenth- and nineteenth-century West. Hurtado stresses that syphilis and smallpox were major causes of the high death rates in the California missions.[16] In *Indian Wars*, Robert Utley and Wilcomb Washburn point out that 15,000 Indians were wiped out in the smallpox epidemic that was brought up the Missouri River by the annual supply boat that docked at Fort Union in June 1837.[17] In *Indians and Emigrants*, Tate discusses the devastating impact on the Native American communities of the cholera and smallpox epidemics brought by those traveling the overland trails. He states that these diseases "may have killed as many as half of the Kiowa population between 1849 and 1851 and produced a similar mortality rate for the Southern Cheyennes during the same era."[18] Blackhawk views disease dissemination, along with horses, metals, and guns, as one of the technologies of violence introduced by colonialism.

Several of our authors discuss the positive role that the U.S. Army played vis-à-vis the Native populations. In chapter 5 and in *The Frontier Army in the Settlement of the West,* Tate presents evidence that an essential aspect of the army's role was to protect the Indians from incursions by emigrants and settlers as well as to provide annuities and to enforce treaties. He makes the case that the army was caught between two divergent philosophies of federal Indian policy:

one that demanded extermination of the tribes and the other that demanded a more humane treatment. Blackhawk stresses that the resulting inconsistencies in federal policy led to great tragedy for the Native communities. In chapter 4, Colwell-Chanthaphonh argues that army personnel who are currently viewed as having liberal attitudes toward the Indians were often simply carrying out orders. As a result, "the same military officer both mediated conflicts and initiated them," as Blackhawk puts it. General Crook and other officers who on occasion were strong champions of Indian rights were often among the most effective in destroying tribal communities.

An important series of questions involves the motivations of those who carried out the massacres. As Greene notes, "the ambush tactic [involving surprise attacks on enemy villages, killing as many men as possible and taking women and children as prisoners] is as old as time. It is the basic attack methodology of human beings." The level of brutality during massacres such as Camp Grant and Sand Creek, however, was horrendous, involving not just killing warriors but also killing women and children and mutilating and raping the victims as well. According to Colwell-Chanthaphonh, "the acts were so incredibly vicious, and they were so unjustified on so many levels, that those kinds of acts are really hard to understand. . . . We face the same problem when we try to understand mass murderers or serial rapists. We can study them and try to dig into their psychology, but can we truly understand people who perpetrate those kinds of acts? I'm not sure that it's entirely possible." Similar levels of viciousness were perpetrated by the Shoshones during the Ward Massacre near Fort Boise, where women were raped, scalped, and dismembered and children were burned to death.[19] According to Utley, during the Santee Sioux Revolt in 1862 in Minnesota, "families [were] burned alive in their cabins, children nailed to doors, girls raped and then hacked to pieces, [and] babies dismembered."[20]

How do we account for this kind of savagery? In some cases perhaps the men involved in such barbarities were simply "bad men." Tate points out that a common view of the Colorado Volunteers at Sand Creek is that they were "a frontier mob . . . most of them coming out of the bars in Denver. . . . mostly frontiersmen seeking revenge. They were going after Indian noncombatants that were easy to get." Greene disagrees with that assessment. He asserts that the men involved at Sand Creek were ordinary men who had been inducted into the Civil War Volunteer Army and who, in the stress of the engagement, followed their baser instincts. Colwell-Chanthaphonh also disagrees, arguing that the Tucson citizens who led the Camp Grant Massacre were not unusually tough; he points out that all the citizens of frontier Arizona had to be tough to survive in such a hostile environment. He makes a distinction "between characters who were simply tough and people who had extremist views or who reacted in extreme ways to the events of the time." On the other hand, it is clear that pathological people were involved; Tate cites the case of the man known as "the Texan," who bragged about how he would kill any Indian he encountered. According to Hurtado, the incredibly vicious mistreatment of the Pomo Indians by Kelsey and Stone led directly to the Clear Lake Massacre. Criminal elements were also involved in raids along the Oregon and California Trails, including "white Indians" who worked with local tribes in raids on emigrant parties. Blackhawk notes that this phenomenon, as well as incidents of violence by trappers and ex-trappers in the Great Basin, is a history waiting to be researched and written.

A related and widespread view is that certain Indian groups—such as the Apaches or the Comanches—were particularly vicious, engaging in such reprehensible behavior as the murder of babies, rape, torture, and mutilation of the dead. Colwell-Chanthaphonh, however, cautions that "for more than a century now, Americans have cultivated the image of the Apache as a cruel, inhuman creature who was willing to mutilate and attack Americans almost at random. It is very difficult for us to get underneath that stereotype." He goes on to state that "we need to have a deep skepticism of all historical claims, whether they come from the army, from the Anglo-American writers of the time, or from the Apache or Tohono O'odham perspectives. I think we need to be acutely skeptical about the historical validity of the truth claims embedded within these versions." In contrast, Simmons notes that, when Geronimo was asked what he regretted about his career of raiding, he replied, "It was all the children I killed." Simmons adds: "If you read some of the stories about how he killed them, it will turn your stomach. It is unbelievable. There are so many unimpeachable sources and so much collaborative evidence about what they did to children that you can't dismiss all of this as journalistic hyperbole."

It is important to point out that the treatment of the Indians by Anglo-Americans and Hispanics was often equally vicious. One example of such violence is the torture of Mangas Coloradas by a California Volunteer. A second example is the killing of babies and mutilation of the dead by the Colorado Volunteers at Sand Creek and cases of rape at Bear River. This violent treatment of Indians by whites and Hispanics includes the dark history of scalp hunting in the Southwest, where Apache scalps were exchanged for money in Chihuahua.[21] Many of the scalp hunters were former Texas Rangers. Cormac

McCarthy's novel *Blood Meridian* incorporates historical events chronicling scalp hunter John Glanton and his gang, who operated in northern Sonora, New Mexico, and Arizona.[22]

A common view espoused by Simmons, Hurtado, and Tate is that the Indian cultures were based on raiding and warfare and inherently prone to violence. Raids to steal horses and captives were a primary way for young men to prove themselves; as such they represented an important aspect of most Indian cultures in the West. Colwell-Chanthphonh makes the case that raiding and violence should be carefully distinguished. Raiding was done for economic motives, to get food, horses, ammunition, and so on. Warfare undertook violence that the tribes considered socially justified in some sense; this included revenge. Unfortunately, the two cases are not always easy to separate, with elements of revenge warfare often accompanying raids.[23]

Enormous evidence from statements by the Indians themselves—given, for example, in John Stands In Timber's *Cheyenne Memories* and in Keith Basso's *Western Apache Raiding and Warfare*—indicates that the motivation of revenge was widespread among tribal communities of the frontier West. In *War of a Thousand Deserts*, Brian DeLay argues that the Comanche violence in northern Mexico was so extreme that it can't be understood as having an economic motivation—the violence went beyond stealing horses and goods and capturing women and children for the slave trade to a level of wanton killing, burning, and destruction that worked counter to the Comanches' economic interests.[24] In chapter 9, however, Blackhawk disputes that we can know with any certainty whether revenge was the motivation for this Comanche violence, given the nature of the evidence used to attribute revenge as a primary mode of these Indians' culture. In any case, the motive of vengeance is very basically human and is not restricted to Native Americans. The Mormons at Mountain Meadows were clearly acting out of vengeance for the Haun's Mill Massacre in Missouri, the murder of Joseph Smith at Carthage, Illinois, and the murder of Parley Pratt in Arkansas. Custer's Washita campaign also can be viewed as having an element of revenge for the Saline-Solomon depredations. Of course, under many circumstances it is hard to sort out vengeance from reprisal: more-or-less rational calculations about the best way to deter and eliminate the enemy's violent behavior. For example, despite their violence, the Dog Soldiers had excellent reasons for opposing white incursions into their territory.

One of the striking features of reprisals is that the violence was typically directed against members of the larger community even when a small subset was responsible for the heinous deed calling for vengeance. This was true for all ethnic groups. In response to the murder of their tribal members by an individual emigrant, Indians would attack the next available wagon train, which typically had nothing to do with the initial murder. Likewise, emigrants would often attack an innocent party of Indians in revenge for an earlier attack on their train by a different Indian group. The attack on the Aravaipas at Camp Grant was in response to depredations that Colwell-Chanthaphonh believes were carried out by Chiricahua Apaches. The extent to which Black Kettle's band—which was known for seeking peace—was responsible for the outrages that led to the attack on the Washita is very unclear and was so at the time. According to Utley, Harney at Blue Water Creek and Crook and Miles during their Sioux campaigns had no real idea as to the identities of the Native communities that they attacked. The Mormons at Mountain Meadows slaughtered a group of Arkansas emigrants that had nothing to with the murder of the Mormon elder Parley Pratt in Arkansas. And Tate notes that the Cheyennes, in attacking Julesburg in revenge for Sand Creek, targeted people who had no connection with the earlier massacre. As Colwell-Chanthaphonh states, there were two reasons for this misdirection of reprisal. One was ignorance of the social organization of the enemy; as he points out, almost no one in the army or among the Arizona citizenry appreciated the significant differences among Apache bands such as the Chiricahuas, the Aravaipas, and the Pinals. The second reason was that in the mindset of the times "an attack on one of your own was an attack on the whole group. Reciprocally, you could attack anyone in the other group to obtain some kind of appeasement or revenge."

Blackhawk insists that the violence that occurred in the frontier West must be viewed as part of the historic process arising from colonialism. The technologies—horses, guns, and metals—introduced by the colonizing Spanish, French, and English introduced a level of violence into the West that was extreme compared to anything that had come before colonization. The technologies led to radical transformations in the Indian societies and to enormously increased levels of violence utilized by those societies. Sedentary linguistic/ethnic groups who had been engaged in farming in the Great Lakes region or in hunting-gathering in the Great Basin evolved into powerful equestrian bison-based cultures on the Great Plains and engaged in raiding and warfare over vast distances. Certain preconquest societies—the Navajos, Apaches, and Utes, for example—initially strove to obtain the new technologies to protect themselves directly from the colonizers but eventually turned the violence against neighboring Native groups. The warfare became particularly vicious in the early nineteenth century, as Indian communities from the east were pushed west of the Mississippi; the resulting competition for resources led to heightened levels of violence.

Although many Indian groups, both on the Great Plains and in the Southwest, became masters of the new technologies of violence, ultimately they were in no position to contest the westward colonizing expansion of the relatively enormous and technologically advanced civilization of the United States. According to Greene, the desperation evidenced in the battles and depredations of the Cheyennes with the American army and citizens reflects a rapid and total destruction of their resource base as American miners, farmers, and buffalo hunters moved into the region of western Kansas and eastern Colorado. As Blackhawk points out, the issue was even more tragic in the Great Basin. The destruction of the ecology by the emigrants and settlers had a terrifying impact on American Indians. According to Blackhawk, the Shoshones and Paiutes were essentially starving, as reflected in incidents in which these groups would attack wagon trains to steal flour and eat it raw on the spot.

Desperation and paranoia over depredations committed on the settler communities in Kansas, eastern Colorado, and Arizona also help to explain, to some extent, the extreme violence committed on the Indian groups at Sand Creek, Washita, and Camp Grant. According to Colwell-Chanthaphonh, "many of the Tucsonans really did feel that they were under siege, that their lives and their livelihoods were being threatened, and they really did have to do something about it. They felt compelled to try in some way to curb the raiding and the violence." Bombastic journalism also contributed to the paranoia and racism of white settlers. Even authors like Mark Twain, who at one time claimed to be an admirer of the "Noble Red Man," described the Goshutes as "treacherous, filthy and repulsive."[25] Newspaper reports were often highly sensationalized, evoking strong emotions in settlers. At times they were extremely partisan as well. The roles of the local newspapers in vindicating and supporting the Sand Creek and Camp Grant massacres are cases in point. Indeed, Colwell-Chanthaphonh emphasizes that the vitriolic journalism of John Wasson did not just validate the Camp Grant Massacre—it helped to inspire it.

As Bagley aptly states: "Reliable history requires accurate data."[26] In the interviews, the authors discuss the ways in which they deal with their sources. The oldest evidence about Indian cultures comes from archaeological digs. As a general rule, the efforts to reconstruct the cultures of precontact civilizations entail using ethnographic materials about the descendant societies; for example, observations obtained in the nineteenth and twentieth centuries about the modern Pueblo culture are projected backward in time, in the context of the archaeological remains, to infer the Anasazi culture. Blackhawk strongly objects to this type of procedure used to impute infanticide and ritual captive-taking to precontact societies. His argument stresses that the social, economic, and military revolutions brought about in the wake of European colonization so altered the cultural landscape as to make such "upstreaming" of cultural traits highly dubious.

The interviewees not only use newspaper accounts as their sources with caution but also talk about their concerns regarding the reliability of the diaries and reminiscences of emigrants and settlers. Tate points out that many of the emigrants had formed opinions about Indians based on the literature of the time, which included captivity narratives and the novels of James Fenimore Cooper. While some emigrants altered their views in response to a relatively benign experience with the Native communities while on the trail, others clung to their preconceived notions of Indian barbarism. This cultural ignorance colored the emigrants' accounts in significant ways. Blackhawk notes that the strong tendency to view the Shoshones and Paiutes as nearly subhuman beggars and thieves reflected deep ignorance of how these groups had been reduced to near starvation by the actions of the settlers and emigrants in their domain. Reminiscences were also colored by published accounts of massacres and violence written in the intervening years between the massacre and the reminiscence. This is particularly apparent for the Mountain Meadows Massacre. Bagley shows that the lies and distortions—such as John Higbee's explanation of the massacre—created by the perpetrators to deflect criticism of the massacre became standard folklore in the region, repeated in many later reminiscences.[27]

The authors interviewed in this volume also discuss the use of works by nonprofessional, local historians as source material. While some local historians have high standards for gathering and evaluating evidence, others are prone to treat local lore as substantive source material and offer fictional speculation. Utley considers Mari Sandoz's book on Crazy Horse to be a work of fiction. Nevertheless, used with caution, works by amateur historians can be extremely helpful. Simmons relied on such sources in reconstructing the McComas Massacre. Mifflin used collections made by descendants in reconstructing Olive Oatman's life and experience.

The extent of the sources used to reconstruct the histories discussed ranges from very sparse to voluminous. Concerning the Paiutes of the seventeenth and eighteenth century, Blackhawk warns that "on one level we have very fragmentary evidence and on another we have to use that evidence to make very broad analyses and conclusions that are going to be at best partial interpretations." This was essentially because the Spanish did not interact directly with these Great Basin tribes, who do not appear in the colonial era documentation. The Mountain Meadows Massacre represents the opposite problem: the historian must sift through a mountain of evidence, often contradictory and often embodying deliberate misrepresentations.

No history of the frontier West can be complete without including the testimony of Native Americans, who were typically not literate. We questioned nearly every interviewee concerning the use of oral accounts given by Native American participants in the violence. Each of our authors has dealt with this issue, and every one considers such accounts to be highly important if properly used. Colwell-Chanthaphonh, who uses Apache accounts of the Camp Grant Massacre that were recorded by Grenville Goodwin as an essential element of his book, stresses that existing treatments of the massacre that rely only on Euro-American sources are inherently biased. Given the complexity and internal inconsistencies of the source material, he argues that "the best way to try to understand events is by incorporating as many perspectives as possible, an approach of multivocality." Utley, who regards Indian testimony as extremely important but warns of its inconsistencies, makes masterful use of such accounts, combined with more conventional documentation, in reconstructing the life of Sitting Bull. Drawing a distinction between "immediate accounts," made shortly after the battles, and "reminiscent accounts," made years later by participants, Greene warns that immediate accounts are often distorted because the Indians still feared reprisal for their actions. He considers the reminiscent accounts recorded by the likes of Walter Camp, Eli S. Ricker, George Bird Grinnell, and Edward Curtis to be particularly useful because these men "got to know Indian cultures and . . . knew which questions to ask and how to frame them. They transcribed the testimony at face value and didn't try to glorify or enhance the reminiscences." Tate similarly lauds the work of John Stands In Timber, George Bent, and Sarah Winnemucca. According to Simmons, the participant accounts of Apaches need to be treated with care, because "these Apaches often were not intending to tell what happened in an accurate manner. They were trying to protect their people." He finds the accounts of the Apaches transcribed by Eve Ball and Grenville Goodwin to be particularly useful.

On the other hand, several authors warn of the serious problems associated with certain classes of accounts. Greene cautions that immediate accounts recorded by newspapers often suffered from poor translations and from the reporters' frequent use of fabricated material to spice up the accounts for their newspapers. Utley asserts that the Indian accounts of Little Big Horn can be confusing, because each participant recounted only the small portion of the battle that he witnessed. And most significantly, as both Blackhawk and Tate emphasize, the accounts by Indians were typically "mediated" by white anthropologists, reporters, writers, and amateur historians; they were translated into English and published for an English-speaking audience. As Tate puts it, the accounts were "based upon interviews, but they basically are written by non-Indians. That raises the issue of the authenticity of an Indian account that is written for an Anglo audience in a conventional way and that goes through an interpreter. Maybe Cheyennes or Apaches wouldn't tell the story that way in their own language for their own audience." Blackhawk emphasizes that "we must treat these Indian testimonies as historically produced texts and documents, just as we treat all historically produced testimonies. . . . So these testimonies cannot, as we said, be used to re-create indigenous lifestyles, behaviors, and histories outside of the times in which they were produced, and if they are mediated we have to look at them as such."

Our authors express considerable skepticism concerning the testimony of modern tribal members. Utley is adamant that the Indians "have no tribal memory." Simmons agrees, quoting an elder Apache who was asked what life was like in the old days: "I can't tell you that. I don't know how they lived—that was too long ago. You white men don't know how your grandparents lived either. There have been too many changes." Simmons also stresses that "the modern Apaches, having been influenced first through missionary teachings when they were held captive at Fort Sill and later through the American school systems, do not think like the old Apaches." Furthermore, the views of the modern Indians have been strongly affected by the books they have read on their history that were written by whites. According to Simmons, much of the modern Indian testimony "is a modern white man's view, in particular, a white man's view of what he would feel if he were an Indian. This view gets back to the Indians and gets transformed into the official traditional Indian view." Interestingly, Blackhawk implicitly agrees with this statement, stating that the evaluation of such testimony is "complicated by the fact that many Indian peoples themselves are often unequal participants in the construction of some of these dynamics, meaning that we often receive cultural misinformation as other Americans do." Greene agrees with these points. "I think we have to worry about such later accounts, the tribal lore and the oral histories given today, the accounts passed down orally between generations. . . . I don't trust them. I would say the same about non-Indian oral transgenerational history too. I fear that such accounts have been influenced and potentially corrupted by movies, books, and television shows." Greene adds, however, that "the transgenerational accounts—oral histories—are valuable in giving us a sense of how the people today feel about the historic events that happened in their past. That is really important too, and I accept them for that."

One of our efforts in *Violent Encounters* is to question the authors about their motivations for exploring particular historical events and, in addition, how they conceptualize the events. In regard to the balance of different perspectives in *Massacre on the Lordsburg Road,* Simmons notes that he wasn't consciously trying to maintain balance: "I was trying to tell as much of the story as I could find." Blackhawk consistently insists on the need to provide context for historical events and admits that in understanding the deep background of the Bear River Massacre he had little room left to describe the event itself. In talking about his recent work on Herbert Bolton, Hurtado reflects a modern view: "A major theme is how historians live in a particular social, cultural, and political world. . . . even though we would deny it, few of us are really free agents when we write history. There is a real world that is impinging on us in a variety of ways." In *Massacre at Camp Grant*, Colwell-Chanthaphonh is concerned not only with the Camp Grant Massacre but with the making of history, the ways in which history is used as a political tool, and the need for the incorporation of multiple viewpoints when reconstructing past events.

A related set of questions concerns an understanding of the role of literature in furthering historic understanding. In structuring historical data, the historian employs a model that imposes particular presuppositions (which typically include moral or aesthetic preferences) on the reader, which has the virtue of endowing the events with a coherent meaning. Literature can, and often does, inform this process. While the authors we interviewed are careful in pointing out the historical errors, both large and small, in the fiction about the frontier West, they are often quite open to the insight into historical conditions that well-written literature can give. Bagley comments that the historian, operating under the constraints of the profession, tends to discount important aspects of life that are hard to quantify through historical evidence. As an example, he praises Judith Freeman's *Red Water* for graphically showing how truly oppressive the mandate to use the Deseret alphabet would have been for many citizens of Utah. Mifflin is interested in Elmore Leonard's story "The Tonto Woman" because it adds a sexual dimension to Olive's character. Given the norms of the Mohave culture to which she acculturated, Mifflin argues that

Olive "was probably much more sexually uninhibited than other white women of the Victorian period." The implicit point is that the novelist can raise issues that are difficult to treat in a work of history. According to Hurtado, "Fiction writers are not constrained by the rules that I am constrained by." He praises Cormac McCarthy's *Blood Meridian* for adding to historical events that we know occurred to emphasize the brutality of many of the people of those times and being "pretty much right on the mark." Tate distinguishes the "real West" from the "imagined West," telling his students that they would be missing an essential aspect of history without a feeling for the past, most readily obtained from novels or movies (read or watched critically).

Working on this project has made us aware of the extent to which the American frontier, as represented in historical discourse and popular culture, is marked by violent encounters. Our concern in this volume, however, is not the cultural construction of violence. Instead, we have tried to maintain a focus on understanding the dynamics of actual violence on the American frontier that was often fomented by the complexity of different cultures sharing a region in transition. The scholars we interviewed use interdisciplinary methodologies to offer a portrait of the tensions surrounding land use, religion, race, and ethnicity that fueled violence. Some of the encounters they detail are little known today: the massacres at Bear River, Camp Grant, and Clear Lake, for example. Other massacres have not been forgotten: Sand Creek, Washita, Little Big Horn. In many cases these brutal encounters have been romanticized, however, and the savagery of what occurred has been sanitized. It is our sincere hope that these interviews help to discount any glamorous views of historical violence and that this book will be read in the spirit of dialogue with the history of American frontier violence.

Notes

Chapter 1. The McComas Massacre

1. Simmons's *Murder on the Santa Fe Trail* gives an account of the murder of Don Antonio José Chávez, a popular New Mexico trader, on the Santa Fe Trail in central Kansas. The assailants were a gang of outlaws from western Missouri.

2. On March 26–28, 1862, at the Battle of Glorieta Pass—often referred to as the "Gettysburg of the West"—Colorado Volunteers faced an invading Confederate force from Texas. Colonel John M. Chivington captured and destroyed the Texans' supply wagons, which brought the invasion to an end. The battlefield is currently part of Pecos National Monument, east of Santa Fe, New Mexico. For a description of the battle, see Josephy's *Civil War in the American West.* The Pigeon's Ranch building is one of the only surviving structures from the time of the battle.

3. See, for example, Simmons's *Millie Cooper's Ride* and *Friday, the Arapahoe Boy.*

4. See Woodin, "Whatever Happened to Charley McComas?"

5. The argument for this is given most forcefully by Tate in *Indians and Emigrants.* See chapter 5.

6. Apparently the men killed at McNees Crossing were shot with their own guns. The rest of the wagon train then retaliated by killing another group of Indians, who were probably innocent and ignorant of the murder. This led to further retaliation by the tribe of the Indians who had been killed. For an account of the incident, see Duffus, *The Santa Fe Trail,* chapter 9. Duffus's source appears to be Gregg's *Commerce of the Prairies,* 18.

7. Eve Ball (1890–1984) was a longtime resident of Ruidoso, New Mexico, on the edge of the Mescalero Apache reservation. Beginning in 1950 and over three decades, she conducted interviews with Apaches and ranchers from southern New Mexico. Her books include *In the Days of Victorio: Recollections of a Warm Springs Apache* and *Indeh: An Apache Odyssey.* The former is based on interviews with James Kaywaykla, a Warm Springs Apache who as a boy lived through the Victorio campaigns, including the defeat at Tres Castillos. The latter is based in large part on interviews with Asa Daklugie, a son of the Nednhi Apache leader Juh; Daklugie also participated as a boy in the Apaches' final struggle to stay off the reservations. Another important Apache

account is by Jason Betzinez, who took part in the campaigns of the 1880s. A cousin of Geronimo, Betzinez participated in the surrender to the U.S. Army, after which he was sent to Florida as a prisoner of war. He attended the Carlisle Indian School in Pennsylvania. Having learned English, Betzinez later wrote an autobiography, *I Fought with Geronimo.*

8. In August 1680 Indians from several New Mexican pueblos rose up in revolt against the Spanish, killing more than 400 Franciscan missionaries and colonists and driving the surviving Spanish out of northern New Mexico. See Roberts, *The Pueblo Revolt.*

9. For treatments of Apache culture, see Haley, *Apaches,* and Basso, *Western Apache Raiding and Warfare.*

10. During the 1930s, ethnographer Grenville Goodwin (1907–40) lived among the Western Apaches of Arizona, studying their history and culture. Men who had participated in late nineteenth-century warfare were still alive when he conducted his fieldwork. When Goodwin died at age thirty-three, he had already published several papers and one book, *Myths and Tales of the White Mountain Apache.* A set of his unpublished interviews with Western Apaches edited by Keith Basso, a cultural and linguistic anthropologist noted for his study of the Western Apaches, was published as *Western Apache Raiding and Warfare.* Goodwin's journals chronicle his attempt to search for a band of wild Apaches still living in the Sierra Madre in the early 1930s. His son, film producer Neil Goodwin, edited and annotated the journals and traveled to Arizona and Mexico in an attempt to explore his father's years among the Apaches. The result was *The Apache Diaries* and its sequel, *Like a Brother.*

11. Romo, "Hail to the Chief."

12. In 1905–1906 Geronimo told his story to Asa Daklugie, who translated it for S. M. Barrett, the superintendent of education in Lawton, Oklahoma. It was published as *Geronimo: His Own Story.*

13. Dorris Alexander "Dee" Brown (1908–2002) was an American novelist and popular historian. He is best known for his book *Bury My Heart at Wounded Knee.*

14. Roessel, *Navajo Stories of the Long Walk Period.*

15. The Cheyennes and their allies the Arapahos had long been enemies of the Kiowas and Comanches. In 1837 a Cheyenne war party set out to attack a Kiowa encampment; but their effort backfired, and the Cheyenne soldiers were all killed. The following year, in retaliation, a combined Cheyenne-Arapaho party attacked a Kiowa-Comanche village on Wolf Creek in Oklahoma. A number of people on both sides were killed before the Cheyennes withdrew. In 1840 the two groups of antagonists met at a treaty ground three miles below Bent's Fort and made what turned out to be a lasting peace. See Mooney, *A Calendar History of the Kiowa Indians,* 271–76; Grinnell, *The Fighting Cheyennes,* chapters 4–6; and Lavender, *Bent's Fort,* 186–89.

16. For a description of the Wagon Mound Massacre, see Utley, *Frontiersmen in Blue,* 86.

17. Instrumental in saving the Texas Longhorn from extinction, James Frank Dobie (1888–1964) was a folklorist and writer. He is best known for his books depicting rural life in Texas and the open range. *Coronado's Children* and *Apache Gold and Yaqui Silver* recount tales about lost mines and buried treasure in the Southwest.

18. See, for example, French, *Four Days from Fort Wingate,* and Purcell, *The Lost Adams Diggings.*

19. An important watering site on the Southern Emigrant Trail, Shakespeare Ghost Town is two miles south of Lordsburg, New Mexico. It served as a military mail station and as a stage stop for both the Jackass Mail and the Butterfield Mail before the Civil War and later was a mining town. For the history of Shakespeare, see Hill, *Then and Now.* In the 1930s the town was purchased by Frank and Rita Hill, who deeded it to their daughter, Janaloo Hill. Following Janaloo's death, ownership passed to her husband, Manny Hough. By late 2008 efforts to have the State of New Mexico take over operations had ceased. See Lawrence and Lawrence, "A Tour of Shakespeare with Manny Hough."

Chapter 2. The Captivity and Return of Olive Oatman

1. McGinty (*The Oatman Massacre*) uses the spelling "Roys" and notes that Oatman signed his name that way.

2. Oakley Hall (1920–2008) was the author of short stories, novellas, libretti, and over twenty mainstream novels. His best-known book, *Warlock* (which was made into a movie in 1959 starring Henry Fonda), is a fictional retelling of the myth of Tombstone. His book *Apaches* combines the Lincoln County War and the efforts to bring the Apaches Victorio and Geronimo to bay. His novel *Separations* conflates the railroad surveys of the Grand Canyon in 1889–90 with the history of Olive Oatman, the Mountain Meadows Massacre, and the San Francisco literary scene of the late 1800s. See Lawrence and Lawrence, "Interview with Oakley Hall."

3. The well-known author Elmore Leonard began his writing career with western stories and novels. The movie *The Tonto Woman* (2007), directed by Daniel Barber, is based on Leonard's story of the same title, which appeared initially in *Western Writers of America Anthology Roundup* in 1982.

4. Anthropologist Michael Tsosie taught in the American Indian Studies program at San Francisco State University. He is currently director of the Colorado River Indian Tribes Museum in Parker, Arizona. Mifflin interviewed Tsosie in March 2007 to obtain background for her book on Olive Oatman.

5. Kathryn Derounian-Stodola is a professor in the English Department at the University of Arkansas, Little Rock. She is the editor of *Women's Indian Captivity Narratives* and the author of several articles on Olive Oatman.

6. Royal B. Stratton was a charismatic clergyman from New York. He met Olive and Lorenzo Oatman when he was minister of the Methodist Episcopal Church in Yreka, California, and the Oatmans were living in southern Oregon. He agreed to ghostwrite

Olive and Lorenzo's story, which appeared in 1857 as *Captivity of the Oatman Girls;* a second edition appeared in 1857 and a third in 1858. The books gave highly sensationalized and editorialized accounts of the massacre and captivity. In part to promote the sale of the book, Stratton arranged for Olive to give lectures on her experience, beginning in 1859 in New York. Olive severed her relationship with Stratton when she married John Fairchild in 1865. Stratton later preached in Massachusetts, went insane, and died in an asylum in 1875. For more on Stratton, see Mifflin, *The Blue Tattoo.*

7. Father Edward J. Pettid, S.J., was an amateur researcher who accumulated information on the Oatman Massacre. He was the author of several articles, such as "The Oatman Story: A Frontier Tragedy." His papers and his unpublished book on the Oatmans can be found in the Special Collections of the University of Arizona Library, Tucson.

8. We have viewed the collections in the historic societies of El Monte, California; La Harpe, Illinois; Red Cloud, Nebraska; and Sherman, Texas. We can confirm that there is little in these collections beyond popular accounts of the Oatman Massacre. Most of these articles are cited in McGinty, *The Oatman Massacre.*

9. James Colin Brewster was a young dissident Mormon who, in opposition to polygamy, split from the main group of Latter-Day Saints led by Brigham Young. Based on purported visions of an angel, he claimed to translate the lost Books of Esdras. He asserted that Esdras commanded the faithful to establish a new Zion in the "Land of Bashan," which was in the Colorado River valley near Yuma, Arizona. Brewster quit the expedition to Bashan in Socorro, New Mexico, and was noted as living there in the 1850 census. Gary Vitale, professor of English at Springfield College/Benedictine University in Illinois, has written several articles on Brewster's later life. See, for example, "Whatever Happened to James Colin Brewster, the Boy Mormon Prophet?"

10. Sidney Rigdon (1793–1876), who was initially a Campbellite preacher, converted to Mormonism in 1830. He was high in the administration of the Church of Jesus Christ of Latter-Day Saints (LDS) during the 1830s. His impassioned speeches against the anti-Mormons fanned the flames that led to the Mormon War in Missouri in 1838. His opposition to polygamy caused his relations with Joseph Smith to deteriorate. Brigham Young took control of the church after Smith's death and excommunicated Rigdon in 1844. For a few years Rigdon led an independent Mormon faction in Pittsburgh, Pennsylvania.

11. Susan Parrish was the daughter of Ira W. Thompson, who was part of the Brewsterite group that followed Royce Oatman to Arizona but divided from Oatman at Tucson. The Thompsons were among the earliest settlers of El Monte, California. A few years before her death in the early 1900s, Parrish related her story to Virginia Root, who published it as *Following the Pot of Gold at the Rainbow's End in the Days of 1850.*

12. "Notice," *Times and Seasons* (Nauvoo, Ill.), December 1, 1842, 32.

13. The anthologist Alfred Kroeber (1876–1960) spent most of his career at the University of California, Berkeley, where he worked as a professor and as the director

of the University of California's Museum of Anthropology (now the Phoebe A. Hearst Museum of Anthropology). Kroeber and his students did important work collecting cultural data on western tribes of Native America. His work on California tribes appeared in the *Handbook of the Indians of California* (1925) as well as many specialized books and monographs. He is especially noted for working with Ishi, who was claimed to be the last California Yahi Indian. Kroeber's relationship with Ishi was made into the film *The Last of His Tribe* (1992), starring Jon Voight as Kroeber. As a student of Mohave culture, Kroeber took a great interest in the Oatman captivity. His article in the *California Historical Society Quarterly* (co-authored by Clifton B. Kroeber) was based on interviews with Mohaves who were alive at the time of the Oatmans' captivity.

14. Pamela Munro, the author of *Mojave Syntax,* is a professor of linguistics at the University of California, Los Angeles. She specializes in the grammar and syntax of American Indian languages.

15. Captain Lorenzo Sitgreaves of the Corps of Topographical Engineers led an exploring expedition, which included the artist Richard Kern, from Zuni Pueblo across northern Arizona, arriving at the Mohave villages in November 1851. From there the expedition traveled south to Yuma and then west to San Diego. See Weber, *Richard H. Kern,* chapter 5; see also Wallace and Hevly, *From Texas to San Diego in 1851.*

16. Lieutenant Amiel Weeks Whipple (1818–63) led the U.S. War Department Railroad Survey of the 35th parallel between Fort Smith, Arkansas, and San Diego, California, in 1853. They reached the Colorado River and the Mohave villages and traded with the Mohaves in February 1854. For a description of his trip, see Dodge, *The Road West.*

17. An intense beam of light is created by the oxidation of lime.

18. Harrison Oatman to Olive and Lorenzo Oatman, October 12, 1857, Richard Nolan private collection.

19. Pettid, "Olive Ann Oatman's Lecture Notes and the Oatman Bibliography."

20. John Brant Fairchild participated in cattle drives from Texas to California in the early 1850s; his brother was killed by Apaches on one of these drives. He met Olive Oatman near his farm in Michigan and married her in 1865. In 1872 the couple moved to Sherman, Texas, where Fairchild became a successful banker. Throughout their marriage, he was very protective of Olive. For information on Fairchild, see McGinty, *The Oatman Massacre,* and Mifflin, *The Blue Tattoo.*

21. Willa Cather (1873–1947), the author of *My Ántonia* and *Death Comes to the Archbishop,* is Nebraska's most noted novelist. She moved with her family to Red Cloud, Nebraska, at the age of ten. The town is featured in six of her twelve novels.

22. Rister, *Comanche Bondage* (the 1839 narrative of Sarah Ann Horn). Leaving Dolores, Texas, in the wake of the Alamo and Goliad disasters, the Horn family and their neighbors (including a Mrs. Hill) headed toward Matamoros and were captured by the Comanches. Horn and Hill were later ransomed and returned to Missouri.

Chapter 3. The Mountain Meadows Massacre

1. A noted Utah historian, Juanita Brooks (1898–1989) is recognized for the integrity with which she examined the Mountain Meadows Massacre. Working in defiance of the local church leadership, she produced her two best-known books, *The Mountain Meadows Massacre* (1950) and *John Doyle Lee* (1961). While she found no direct evidence for Brigham Young's involvement in the Mountain Meadows Massacre, she considered him an accessory after the fact, believing that he both set the stage for the event with his fiery rhetoric during the period of the Utah War and obstructed the subsequent investigation.

2. Bagley, *Blood of the Prophets*, pp. 357, 363. Mormon apostle George A. Smith (1817–75) was a cousin of the prophet Joseph Smith and a commander of the Nauvoo Legion in southern Utah. In John D. Lee's version of the story, Smith brought the orders to kill the Fanchers to southern Utah. On August 25 Smith and a mixed party of Mormons and Paiute Indians camped near the Fancher party at Corn Springs, south of Fillmore.

3. Eleanor McLean Pratt was the widow of the beloved LDS apostle Parley P. Pratt, who was murdered in western Arkansas in May 1857 by Eleanor's legal husband, Hector McLean. She had deserted him to join the Mormon church. Vengeance for Pratt's death was undoubtedly a motive for the murder of the Arkansas-based Fancher party.

4. Orrin Porter Rockwell (1813–78) was one of the early converts to the Church of Jesus Christ of Latter-Day Saints. He served as bodyguard to both Joseph Smith and Brigham Young. A controversial figure, he was the reputed Mormon "Destroying Angel," a notorious gunman and a religious zealot.

5. A writer at the *Salt Lake Tribune* for over fifty years, Harold Schindler (1929–98) is the author of *Orrin Porter Rockwell: Man of God, Son of Thunder* (1966) and other books on Mormon and Utah history.

6. Quoted in David M. Kennedy and Thomas A. Bailey, *The American Spirit: United States History as Seen by Contemporaries, Volume 1: To 1877,* 12th ed. (Boston: Wadswoth, Cengage Learning, 2010), p. 101. John Peter Zenger (1697–1746) owned a newspaper that printed articles attacking William Crosby, the governor of New York. He was sued for libel and defended by Alexander Hamilton, who won an acquittal based on the argument that true statements cannot be considered libel.

7. David L. Bigler, former president of the Oregon-California Trails Association, is the author of the award-winning *Forgotten Kingdom: The Mormon Theocracy in the American West, 1847–1896* as well as the editor and co-editor of a number of narratives by early Mormons, including *Innocent Blood: Essential Narratives of the Mountain Meadows Massacre* with Will Bagley.

8. George Armstrong Hicks became a Mormon while living in Nauvoo and came to Utah in 1852. In 1863 he was sent on a mission to southern Utah, where he learned of the involvement of local Mormon leaders in the Mountain Meadows Massacre. In two

letters to Brigham Young, he questioned why John D. Lee and other Mormons who had been involved in the massacre and had innocent blood on their hands were still allowed to be local authorities in the church. In a very sarcastic reply, Young suggested that Hicks had participated in the massacre (which he clearly did not) and that a "rope round the neck taken with a jerk would be very salutary" as a remedy. Hicks was later excommunicated from the church. Bigler and Bagley, *Innocent Blood,* 262–70.

James Gemmell was a Scottish immigrant who settled in Salt Lake City in 1849 and converted to the Mormon faith. He accompanied Judge John Cradlebaugh's investigation of the Mountain Meadows Massacre as a translator. In the early 1860s he moved to Montana, where he lived out his days. Gemmell's obituary included his story that he was in Brigham Young's office when Bishop Jacob Hamblin reported that the Fancher train was near Cedar City. Gemmell recounted that he heard Young say that if he was in command of the local militia he would wipe out the Arkansas train. See Bigler and Bagley, *Innocent Blood,* 289–93.

9. Since the interview took place, LDS historians have issued an account of the massacre. It stresses that the event occurred in the context of extreme Mormon paranoia due to the approach of federal troops and that the plot to kill the emigrants was hatched locally but that the efforts of higher Mormon authorities (including Brigham Young) to prevent the disaster came too late to stop the slaughter due to slow communications. These authors also discount the existence of a cover-up, asserting that church leaders only learned the details of the massacre incrementally over time. In defense of this assertion, they note that Isaac Haight and other Cedar City church leaders were removed from their callings in 1859 and that Haight and John D. Lee were excommunicated in 1870. For a full account, see Walker, Turley, and Leonard, *Massacre at Mountain Meadows.* For a brief version, see Turley, "The Mountain Meadows Massacre."

10. Commanding a troop of U.S. dragoons from California, U.S. Army Brevet Major James H. Carleton (1814–73) was the first federal officer to investigate the massacre. He visited the site in 1859, almost two years after the tragedy. In his report to Congress, he stated: "In pursuing the bloody thread which runs throughout this picture of sad realities, the question of how this crime, that for hellish atrocity has no parallel in our history, can be adequately punished often comes up and seeks in vain for an answer" (Carleton, *The Mountain Meadows Massacre,* 37).

11. William Rogers, a non-Mormon who ran a hotel in Salt Lake City, accompanied Judge Cradlebaugh's investigation as a deputy U.S. marshal. In letters to newspapers, he stated that he witnessed the confessions of participants in the massacre, who requested anonymity for fear of their lives. The letters are reprinted in Bigler and Bagley, *Innocent Blood,* 213–18.

John Cradlebaugh (1819–72) came to Utah in 1858 as a district judge. He initiated the first investigation into the Mountain Meadows Massacre, asking General Albert Sidney Johnston to provide troops to serve as a *posse comitatus* to arrest and hold the accused. He opened a grand jury inquiry into the massacre in March 1858 and accompanied the army to the site of the massacre. In an effort to appease the Mormons, territorial authorities successfully appealed to Washington to remove Cradlebaugh's authority to call out the army. The judge was shortly thereafter sent to a new post in Nevada, and the investigation was terminated. Cradlebaugh became Nevada Territory's first delegate to the U.S. Congress, giving a speech about the massacre before the House of Representatives on February 7, 1863. For details, see Bigler and Bagley, *Innocent Blood,* chapter 7.

12. An adopted son of Brigham Young, John Doyle Lee (1812–77) converted to the Mormon faith in 1848 in time to participate in the Mormon War in Missouri. In the early 1850s he was sent to help develop the Mormon colonies in southern Utah. He became a U.S. government Indian agent in Iron County, Utah, and Mountain Meadows came under his jurisdiction as the Fort Harmony militia major. Acting in these two roles, he became the central figure in the Mountain Meadows Massacre. In October 1870 Brigham Young excommunicated him from the Mormon church for his role in the affair. In an effort to escape arrest, Lee moved to a remote crossing of the Colorado River, where he established Lee's Ferry, which connected southern Utah with Mormon settlements in northeastern Arizona. Lee was arrested in November 1874 and was tried and convicted of murder. While imprisoned, he wrote "Lee's Last Confession" for a San Francisco newspaper (Bigler and Bagley, *Innocent Blood,* 338–52). Later, working with lawyer William Bishop, Lee wrote his autobiography, *Mormonism Unveiled.* He was executed by a firing squad at the meadows on March 23, 1877. For a biography, see Brooks, *John Doyle Lee.*

13. On October 27, 1838, Governor Lilburn W. Boggs of Missouri issued an order to force Mormons out of Missouri or exterminate them. Three days later, a Missouri militia unit massacred eighteen men and boys who sought refuge in a log fort at Haun's Mill, a Mormon settlement in eastern Caldwell County, Missouri. A militia member justified his act of shooting a ten-year-old Mormon boy by saying "nits make lice." The history of the conflicts of 1838 between Mormon settlers and citizen militias in western Missouri and the ultimate expulsion of the Mormons to Illinois is treated in LeSeur, *The 1838 Mormon War in Missouri,* 162.

14. William Bishop was John D. Lee's lawyer in both the first and second trial. He was also Lee's literary executor and the editor of his autobiography and confession, *Mormonism Unveiled.*

15. "New Publications: Mormonism Unveiled; or, The Life and Confessions of the Late Mormon Bishop," *New York Times,* September 17, 1877, 3.

16. "Horrible Massacre of Emigrants!!" *Los Angeles Star,* October 10, 1857, 2/2.

17. Some early writers about the massacre claimed that a group of young ruffians known as the Missouri Wildcats accompanied the Fancher train. These writers included Thomas Cropper, who was fifteen years old at the time of the massacre and was eighty-four when he dictated his autobiography, which contains significant errors and

inconsistencies. For an extract, see Bigler and Bagley, *Innocent Blood,* 400–402.

18. Captain John Williams Gunnison was in charge of the 1853 Railroad Survey of the 38th parallel. In August 1853 the expedition crossed the Rockies, following the North Branch of the Old Spanish Trail into Utah. On October 26, on the Sevier River near Sevier Lake, local Indians killed seven members of the party, including Gunnison and the artist Richard Kern. See Weber, *Richard H. Kern,* chapter 7.

19. An extract from Samuel Pitchford's diary is given in Bigler and Bagley, *Innocent Blood,* 107–108. The extract mentions efforts by Mormons to prevent the emigrants' cattle from grazing and destroying the local citizens' winter feed, requests by the Arkansas train to purchase flour, and the passage of an express rider conveying news about the emigrants from Iron County to Brigham Young.

20. Brigham Young appointed Jacob Hamblin to be president of the Southern Indian Mission to the Paiutes on August 4, 1857. Hamblin's ranch was at the upper end of the meadows, about four miles from the site of the massacre.

21. Edward Abbey's comic masterpiece *The Monkey Wrench Gang* tells the story of a group of eco-raiders, who attack mining, lumbering, road building, and dam building sites in the Utah/Arizona wilderness. Seldom Seen Smith, a key character in the novel, is a polygamist "Jack Mormon" and a river runner and wilderness guide.

22. White desperadoes, sometimes allied with or dressed as Indians, harassed wagon trains on the overland trails, often stealing livestock from one wagon train and then selling to another. Many emigrants believed these "white Indians" were acting under orders from LDS leaders. The Fancher party itself was subject to such theft. See Bagley, *Blood of the Prophets,* 47, 59–60.

23. The background to the Mountain Meadows Massacre was the so-called Utah War of 1857, during which President James Buchanan sent federal troops under the command of Albert Sydney Johnston to suppress a perceived rebellion by the citizens of Utah Territory. Apart from the Mountain Meadows Massacre, the confrontation was essentially bloodless. The war was ultimately resolved by negotiation, wherein the governorship of Utah was transferred from Brigham Young to a federal appointee, Alfred Cumming, and the army peacefully established a presence in Utah at Camp Floyd.

24. Daniel Boorstin's *The Americans: The National Experience* treats U.S. history during the period from the Revolutionary War through the Civil War.

25. Freeman's novel *Red Water* is told from the perspective of three of John D. Lee's nineteen wives: Emma, Ann, and Rachel. Juanita Brooks wrote of these women and Lee's other wives in her biographies *John Doyle Lee* and *Emma Lee.*

26. In January 2002 Allen Malmquist discovered a lead sheet buried under debris in the old "fort" at Lee's Ferry. The lead sheet, signed "J. D. Lee," asserts that he acted at Mountain Meadows "on orders of Pres Young thro Geo Smith." Bagley, *Blood of the Prophets,* 383.

27. A disaffected member of the Church of Jesus Christ of Latter-Day Saints, Mark

Hofmann was a skilled forger who murdered two people in Salt Lake City. He is currently serving a prison sentence at the Utah State Prison in Draper, Utah. His most famous Mormon forgery, the Salamander Letter, was purchased by LDS Bishop Steven F. Christensen in 1984 for $40,000. Worrall, *The Poet and the Murderer,* chronicles Hofmann's life.

28. The Drake's Plate of Brass is a forgery that purports to be the brass plaque that Francis Drake posted when he landed in northern California in 1579. The hoax, initially perpetrated in 1936 by E Clampus Vitus (informally called the Clampers), a playful fraternity of California history enthusiasts, was successful for forty years.

29. During the commemoration of the sesquicentennial of the Mountain Meadows Massacre on September 11, 2007, a powerful local developer temporarily removed a nearby sign on State Road 18 that advertised forty-nine lots for sale at "Mountain Meadows Estates." See Havnes, "Housing Lots Sprout near Mountain Meadows Site." More recently the LDS authorities have begun to support the effort to create a National Monument at Mountain Meadows; for updates, see the newsletter of the Mountain Meadows Association at www.Mtn-meadows-assoc.com.

Chapter 4. The Camp Grant Massacre

1. On November 29, 1864, Colonel John Chivington led the Third Colorado Cavalry in an attack on a peaceful village of Cheyennes and Arapahos encamped on Sand Creek in southeastern Colorado under the leadership of Black Kettle. Over 150 Indian men, women, and children were slaughtered. The Sand Creek Massacre is a subject of the interview with Jerome Greene in chapter 8. For a brief account of the massacre, see the synopsis in that chapter. For a fuller discussion, see Hoig, *The Sand Creek Massacre.*

2. As discussed in detail in chapter 8, the National Park Service began a project in 1998 to verify the location of the Sand Creek site. In their book *Finding Sand Creek,* the team's lead historian, Jerome Greene, and lead archaeologist, Douglas Scott, describe the method that the research group used to find and verify the massacre site.

3. For a treatment of Apache culture, see Haley, *Apaches.* For a discussion of the Western Apache clan system and Apache raiding and warfare, see Basso, *Western Apache Raiding and Warfare.* For a study of the wars between the Apaches and the U.S. Army, see Thrapp, *The Conquest of Apacheria.*

4. A Pinal Apache, *haské bahnzin* was born about 1828 and married into the Aravaipas. His name, which means "Men Stand in Line for Him," has been recorded in various ways, including "Eskiminzin" and "Eskininzin." He was the leader of the Aravaipa and Pinal Apaches who were massacred at Camp Grant. Later he was instrumental in the negotiations that led to the establishment of the San Carlos Reservation. He fled San Carlos when troops were called in to quell disturbances but was later captured and imprisoned. When John Clum became agent, he had *haské bahnzin* released and befriended him. *Haské bahnzin* left San Carlos in 1877 and established a farm near Aravaipa Canyon. Although he was considered a model citizen by many, he was run

off the farm by a group of armed citizens in 1887. He was exiled to Mount Vernon in Alabama in 1891, was released in 1894, and died a year later.

5. Simmons, *Massacre on the Lordsburg Road,* 24–25.

6. On Grenville Goodwin, see chapter 1, note 10. Keith Hamilton Basso, an emeritus Distinguished Professor of Anthropology at the University of New Mexico, is a cultural and linguistic anthropologist noted for his study of the Western Apaches. In addition to publishing several books on Western Apache linguistics, he edited the field notes of Grenville Goodwin under the title *Western Apache Raiding and Warfare.*

7. Led by Cochise and later Geronimo, the Chiricahua Apaches were the last band of free Indians to resist U.S. government control of the Southwest. They surrendered in 1886 and were exiled to Florida, Alabama, and Oklahoma; they later were moved to the Fort Sill military reservation in Oklahoma until 1913. For histories of the Apache campaigns, see Thrapp, *The Conquest of Apacheria,* and Roberts, *Once They Moved like the Wind.*

8. Born around 1855, Sherman Curley was a member of the *tcéjiné* band of Apaches and was present as a youth at the massacre. Grenville Goodwin interviewed him on March 12, 1932. For a transcription of Curley's account of the battle, see Colwell-Chanthaphonh, *Massacre at Camp Grant,* 25–27.

9. For a note on the Haun's Mill massacre, see chapter 3, note 13.

10. William S. Oury (1817–87), organizer of the assault on Camp Grant's Apache Indians, was a Virginian who fought in the Texas War for independence, serving in the Alamo garrison. In 1856 Oury and his wife, Inez García of Durango, Mexico, moved to Tucson, where he became a cattle rancher. He was elected sheriff of Tucson several times. Known for his violent temper, he killed two men in separate duels in Tucson. For Oury's account of the massacre, see "Article on Camp Grant Massacre."

A skillful tracker, Jesús María Elías (1829–96) was the leader of those Tucson-area Mexicans who participated in the Camp Grant Massacre. Shortly before the massacre, Apaches had attacked the Elías homestead, killing two of his brothers.

11. Born in Ohio, John Wasson (1833–1909) arrived in California in 1852. During the 1860s he was engaged in the publication of pioneer newspapers in Idaho and Nevada. In 1869 he became editor of the *Oakland Tribune.* In 1870 he founded the *Tucson Citizen,* the first permanent newspaper in Tucson. Twelve years later, he moved to Chino, California. Appointed to the Centennial Commission by President Grant, Wasson served through its final meeting in 1879, when he settled in Pomona, California.

12. In December 1871 the posse members were indicted and brought to trial in Tucson, Judge John Titus presiding. For an account of the trial, see Schellie, *Vast Domain of Blood.*

13. For *bija gush kaiyé*'s version of the massacre, see Colwell-Chanthaphonh, *Massacre at Camp Grant,* 33–37.

14. A native of Maine and a descendant of *Mayflower* pilgrims, Lieutenant Royal

Whitman (1833–1913) fought in the Civil War and went west, first to Fort Sumner, New Mexico, and then to Camp Grant. For a synopsis of Whitman's life, see Waterfall, "Vengeance at Sunrise," 118.

15. The new Tohono O'odham Nation's Cultural Center and Museum is in Topawa, approximately sixty miles southwest of Tucson. The complex includes a community cultural and educational center with artists' studios, a special collections cultural archive, and two artifact repositories.

16. Located about ten miles south of Tucson on the Tohono O'odham San Xavier Indian Reservation, San Xavier del Bac Mission was founded in 1699 by the Jesuit missionary Eusebio Francisco Kino. The mission continues to serve the Native community by which it was built. The original mission church, which was located about two miles away, was destroyed by Apaches in about 1770.

17. Robinson, "Appendix A b, No. 3."

18. Colwell-Chanthaphonh, *Massacre at Camp Grant,* 61.

19. Schellie, *Vast Domain of Blood,* 131.

20. Jacoby's *Shadows at Dawn* (2008), a scholarly book on the Camp Grant Massacre and its background, was published after this interview was conducted.

21. The Grenville Goodwin Papers, 1922–39, Arizona State Museum Archives.

22. The calendar stick or event stick was a device used by the O'odhams as a tool to aid in remembering their history. The calendar stick itself was a cactus stick with notches carved at various intervals to help the history keeper remember events.

Ruth Underhill (1883–1984) enrolled in the Ph.D. program in anthropology at Columbia University. She studied with Franz Boas, Ruth Benedict, and Gladys Reichard and made a series of field research trips among the Tohono O'odhams. Underhill's detailed study of traditional O'odham tribal structure and life style is *Social Organization of the Papago Indians.* Underhill's *A Papago Calendar Record* is a record of events in Papago history between 1839 and 1932 as related by José Santos of San Xavier del Bac, the keeper of the calendar stick. This is one of the primary sources of Papago history from a Papago (O'odham) perspective.

23. On Eve Ball, see chapter 1, note 7.

24. In 1948 Richard van Valkenburgh published an oral tradition of the Camp Grant Massacre related to him by an Apache man identified as "Old Lahn." For Lahn's account of the battle, see Colwell-Chanthaphonh, *Massacre at Camp Grant,* 22–25.

25. The 1997 archaeological investigation at Sand Creek is discussed in the interview with Jerome Greene in chapter 8. For a description of the archaeological artifacts and analysis of the field investigations at the Sand Creek Massacre site, see Greene, and Scott, *Finding Sand Creek.*

26. Elliott Arnold (1912–80) was an American newspaper writer, novelist, and screenwriter. He is probably best known for *Blood Brother,* which was made into the film *Broken Arrow* (1950). His novel *The Camp Grant Massacre* hews closely to the historical record.

27. John Philip Clum (1851–1932), known as the "White Chief of the Apaches," was an Indian agent at the San Carlos Indian Reservation in the Arizona Territory from 1873 to 1877. He was the first mayor of Tombstone and the founder of the *Tombstone Epitaph*.

28. Roberts, *Once They Moved like the Wind,* 152–69.

29. The *New Mexico Historical Review* published John Clum's two-part essay "Es-kin-in-zin" in 1928 and 1929.

30. George Stoneman, Jr. (1822–94) was a career U.S. Army officer, a Union cavalry general in the Civil War, and the governor of California between 1883 and 1887. At the time of the Camp Grant Massacre, Stoneman was commander of the Department of Arizona. Although responsible for Arizona's safety, he continued to maintain his headquarters in California.

31. For a discussion of Whitman's correspondence with Stoneman and Stoneman's response, see Haley, *Apaches,* 256–61.

32. George Crook (1828–90) was a career U.S. Army officer. After the Civil War, he returned to the Pacific Northwest and waged a two-year campaign against the Paiutes. Because of this success, President Grant put Crook in charge of the Arizona Territory, where he waged a successful campaign from 1871 until 1875 to force the Western Apaches onto reservations. In 1875 he was appointed commander of the Department of the Platte and was involved in operations against the Sioux and Cheyennes prior and after the Battle of the Little Bighorn. In 1882 Crook returned to Arizona when the Chiricahua Apaches fled their reservation under their leader Geronimo. For four years Crook attempted to force his adversary to surrender. In 1886 he was relieved of his command and replaced by General Nelson A. Miles, who was in charge of the troops when Geronimo finally surrendered. In his campaigns in Arizona, Crook successfully used Apache scouts to locate and fight the Apache enemy. During the 1879 trial of Standing Bear, he spoke on behalf of Native American rights. He vigorously opposed the exile to Florida of the Apaches who had served him as scouts and spent his final years speaking out against the unjust treatment of his former Indian adversaries.

33. John Gregory Bourke (1843–96) was a captain in the U.S. Army. From 1870 to 1886 he served as an aide to General George Crook in the Apache Wars. Bourke was an avid journalist and had a lifelong habit of recording his opinions, military and personal accounts, and ethnographic impressions. His 1891 book *On the Border with Crook* remains a classic of Western Americana.

Lieutenant Britton Davis (1860–1930) served in the post–Civil War U.S. Army. Specializing in managing Indian scouts, he was the officer in charge of the Apaches who lived at San Carlos Reservation in southeastern Arizona. He was subordinate to General George Crook and helped Charles Gatewood track Geronimo and convince him to surrender. For his firsthand account of the Geronimo campaign, see *The Truth about Geronimo.*

Chapter 5. Indians, Emigrants, and the Army on the Overland Trails

1. The 1841 Bidwell-Bartleson party was the first organized group of emigrants to reach northern California by way of the Humboldt River. For information about their journey, see Nunis, *The Bidwell-Bartleson Party.*

2. Tate, *Indians and Emigrants,* 145, 59.

3. Two guidebooks used by the emigrants were Lansford W. Hastings's *The Emigrants' Guide to Oregon and California* (1845) and Joseph E. Ware's *The Emigrants' Guide to California* (1849).

4. For an interesting discussion of James Fenimore Cooper's portrayal of Indians, see Slotkin, *Regeneration through Violence.* For an examination of how repressed feelings in the American national psyche regarding race led to the development of the "good Indian" in frontier romance novels, see Barnett, *The Ignoble Savage.*

5. Tate also wrote the introduction to Belshaw diaries: *Crossing the Plains to Oregon in 1853.*

6. For an examination of the gold rushers' journey across the plains and mountains to the mining camps of northern California, see Holliday, *The World Rushed In.*

7. The Sand Creek Massacre and the Battle of the Washita are the subjects of the interview with Jerome Greene in chapter 8. For a brief account of these battles, see the synopsis in that chapter; for an extended account, see Hoig, *The Sand Creek Massacre,* and Greene, *Washita.* The Battle of Blue Water Creek is discussed in the interview with Robert Utley in chapter 7. For a brief account, see the synopsis of the Sioux Wars in that chapter; for an extended account, see Paul, *Blue Water Creek and the First Sioux War, 1854–1856.*

8. The actual quotation (Tate, *The Frontier Army in the Settlement of the West,* 259): "There are two classes of people, one demanding the utter extinction of the Indians, and the other full of love for their conversion to civilization and Christianity. Unfortunately, the army stands between and gets the cuffs from both sides."

9. A descendant of Mennonite pioneers, John D. Unruh (1937–76) is the author of *The Plains Across: The Overland Emigrants and the Trans-Mississippi West, 1840–1860,* a comprehensive study of western trails.

10. After the massacre at Sand Creek in 1864, the surviving Cheyennes fled north to the Smoky Hill and Republican Rivers. Their retribution began in January 1865. Sioux, Cheyennes, and Arapahos concealed themselves in some sand hills a short distance from Julesburg, Colorado, and Fort Rankin, which was a mile from the town. A decoy party lured the soldiers from the fort; in the ensuing battle fourteen soldiers and four civilians were killed. The citizens of Julesburg fled to the fort, and the Indians pillaged the town. In February the Indians again returned to Julesburg and burned and looted the town while the citizens and soldiers watched helplessly from the fort. These attacks were part of a series of raids along the South Platte during which ranches and stage stations were burned, fifty people were killed, and fifteen hundred head of cattle

were stolen. For an account of these raids, see Utley, *Frontiersmen in Blue,* 301–303.

11. The quotation is from the interview with Marc Simmons in chapter 1.

12. In September 1821 William Becknell (1788–1856) left Franklin, Missouri, for Santa Fe, New Mexico, with a pack train of trade goods. The trip was so profitable that he returned the following year. Soon other American traders followed Becknell's route, which became known as the Santa Fe Trail.

13. On Eve Ball, see chapter 1, note 7. On Grenville Goodwin, see chapter 1, note 10.

14. On Jason Betzinez, see chapter 1, note 7. Wilbur Sturtevant Nye (1898–1970) was a frontier historian. His works include *Bad Medicine and Good* (1962) and *Plains Indian Raiders* (1968).

15. Frank Bird Linderman (1869–1938) was a Montana politician and writer. He served in the Montana state legislature and was Montana's assistant secretary of state from 1905 to 1907. He was devoted to Montana's Indians, learning and writing about their culture. His books include *Plenty Coups: Chief of the Crows* and *Pretty Shield: Medicine Woman of the Crows.*

16. John Stands In Timber (1884–1967) was a Northern Cheyenne whose grandfather was killed at the Battle of the Little Bighorn. During his adult years he actively sought out the oral history of his people. In 1956 he met Margot Liberty, an Indian Affairs Bureau teacher, who helped him tape-record and compile his reminiscences. Stands In Timber's *Cheyenne Memories* is an oral history of the Cheyenne Indians from legendary times to the early reservation years.

17. Considered the "dean of American Indian historians," George Hyde (1882–1968) ran a bookshop, checked the manuscripts of other historians for accuracy, and authored his own histories. Among his works are *Red Cloud's Folk* (1937), *The Pawnee Indians* (1951), and *A Sioux Chronicle* (1956). When Hyde was working as a research assistant for George Bird Grinnell, he met George Bent. Bent and Hyde began corresponding in 1905 and continued almost until Bent's death in 1918. Their letters led to the book *Life of George Bent, Written from His Letters,* which describes life with the Cheyennes, Arapahos, Comanches, and other tribes of the Arkansas and Platte valleys. It also includes information on events such as the Sand Creek Massacre and the raid on Julesburg.

George Bent (1843–1918) was the son of the trader William Bent and his wife, Owl Woman, a Southern Cheyenne. He was born and raised at Bent's Fort in southern Colorado. He received his education in Westport and St. Louis and served in the Confederate Army at the beginning of the Civil War. In 1863 Bent returned to live with his mother's people, the Southern Cheyennes. He was present at the Sand Creek Massacre and lived with the Cheyennes almost continuously after the tragedy.

18. Sarah Winnemucca Hopkins (ca. 1844–91) was the daughter of the prominent Northern Paiute leader Winnemucca. She knew English, Spanish, and several Native American languages and served as an interpreter for the military and various Indian

agencies. After the Bannock War in 1878, the entire Winnemucca band was relocated to the Yakima Reservation in Washington. At the request of her people, she went to Washington, D.C., in 1880 to appeal for their rights. In 1883 and 1884 she gave over three hundred lectures in the eastern United States. Her book *Life among the Piutes: Their Wrongs and Claims* (1883) is an autobiographical account of the Paiutes during their first forty years of contact with explorers and settlers. It is the first book written in English and copyrighted by a Native American woman. For more information on Winnemucca, see Zanjani, *Sarah Winnemucca.*

19. Susan Bordeaux Bettelyoun (1857–1945) was the daughter of a French-American fur trader and a Brulé Lakota woman. Raised at her father's post near Fort Laramie, Wyoming, she saw firsthand the devastating changes that the Lakotas underwent. In the 1930s, when she lived at the Old Soldiers Home at Hot Springs, South Dakota, she met Josephine Waggoner, a mixed-blood Hunkpapa Lakota. Waggoner recorded Bettelyoun's reminiscences, entitled *With My Own Eyes: A Lakota Woman Tells Her People's History.*

20. A member of the Rosebud Sioux tribe, Joseph Marshall III is a Lakota teacher, historian, actor, and craftsman. He is the author of several books, including *On Behalf of the Wolf and the First Peoples.* He has appeared in several episodes of *The Real West* as well as in the miniseries *Return to Lonesome Dove.*

21. For a description of the Papago calendar stick, see the interview with Chip Colwell-Chanthaphonh in chapter 4 and note 22 in that chapter.

22. A "winter count" was a calendar used by the Plains Indians. Pictures painted on a large tanned hide symbolized outstanding events that happened during the given year. For example, a picture for "The Year the Stars Fell" represented 1833, when the Leonid meteor shower occurred. As with the Papago calendar stick, some knowledgeable tribal member was required to interpret the story of the year corresponding to each drawing. See Greene and Thornton, *The Year the Stars Fell.*

23. The quotation is from the interview with Marc Simmons in chapter 1.

24. The experiences of nine children who were abducted by Comanches or Apaches in Texas between 1865 and 1871 are recounted in Zesch, *The Captured.*

25. Tate, "Comanche Captives."

26. See the interview with Margot Mifflin in chapter 2.

27. A resident of Lanacaster, Massachusetts, Mary White Rowlandson (1637–1711) was a Puritan minister's wife who was taken captive by a group of Nipmuck and Narragansett Indians in 1676, near the end of King Philip's War. Her narrative of the eleven weeks and five days she spent living with her Indian captors, *The Sovereignty and Goodness of God,* is the first full-length, fact-based captivity narrative to appear as a separate book.

28. The worst emigrant disaster on the Oregon Trail occurred in September 1860, when the Elijah P. Utter party, composed of eight wagons and forty-four men, women, and children, was attacked by Shoshone Indians in southwestern Idaho. Eighteen emi-

grants were killed and four children were abducted during the attacks. Of the members of the party who managed to escape, several were later captured or starved to death as they awaited rescue. Almost two months later a rescue party found ten survivors nearly a hundred miles from the place where the party was first attacked. Like Mary Rowlandson's *A Narrative of the Captivity,* survivor Emeline Fuller's narrative *Left by the Indians* focuses on the psychological loss and the role of religion in the victims' suffering. For a compelling account of the tragedy, see Shannon, *The Utter Disaster on the Oregon Trail.*

29. Hall, *Warlock,* v (prefatory note). On Oakley Hall, see chapter 2, note 2.

30. For an examination of John Ford's historical portrayal of the frontier army in his trilogy *Fort Apache* (1948), *She Wore a Yellow Ribbon* (1949), and *Rio Grande* (1950), see Prater, "John Ford's Cavalry Trilogy: Myth or Reality?"

31. Mari Sandoz (1896–1966) was one of Nebraska's foremost writers about pioneer life and the Plains Indians. First published in 1935, *Old Jules* is considered to be her masterpiece. This portrait of her father is a careful balance of tribute and exposé.

Chapter 6. Destruction and Survival of the California Indians

1. A pioneer in population studies of the Native peoples of North America and Mesoamerica, Sherburne Friend Cook (1896–1974) was a professor in the Department of Physiology at the University of California, Berkeley, and the author of *The Population of the California Indians, 1769–1970.* According to Hurtado, "When Cook was on the faculty at the University of California in the 1920s, he wrote pioneering articles that showed that chicken feed contained a lot of heavy metal that could be passed on to human consumers. The reaction of the University of California was to take away his lab. Apparently the chicken feed producers and the chicken farmers had considerable power in California at that time. While Cook remained on the faculty, he had no particular departmental affiliation, so he became interested in other questions, including California Indians. He became a friend of Alfred Kroeber, who asked him to work on Indian population. He did that for the thirty years until he died."

2. On Kroeber, see chapter 2, note 13.

3. A number of such articles can be found in Heizer, *The Destruction of California Indians.*

4. The Indian War Papers, 1850–80, include the muster rolls of the local militia groups that were formed to eliminate the "Indian menace," as well as field reports, claims, correspondence, and other items. An inventory of the Indian war files can be found online in the Inventory of the Military Department, Adjutant General, Indian War Papers, Online Archive of California, on the website www.oac.cdlib.org.

5. In 1850 the California legislature enacted Chapter 133, An Act for the Government and Protection of the Indians. While this law provided some protection to California Indians, it also included features allowing for the indenture of Indian children and the effective indenture of Indians found loitering or found guilty of minor crimes.

The text of the act can be found in Heizer, *The Destruction of California Indians*, chapter 6. See also Hurtado, *Indian Survival on the California Frontier*, 5, 129, 198.

6. James Mooney (1861–1921) was an early ethnographer of American Indians, especially those of the southeastern United States. His investigations of the history, heraldry, and culture of the Cherokees and Kiowas included deciphering the Kiowa calendar. On Eve Ball, see chapter 1, note 7; on Grenville Goodwin, see chapter 1, note 10.

7. Anthropologist Theodora Kracaw Kroeber Quinn (1897–1979) is perhaps best known for her accounts of Ishi, the last member of the Yahi tribe of California.

8. Uldall and Shipley, *Nisenan Texts and Dictionary*.

9. John Bidwell (1819–1900) led one of the first emigrant groups to California, the so-called Bidwell-Bartleson party of 1841. A key employee of John Sutter during the early 1840s, he later went into mining and ranching, purchasing the 26,000-acre Rancho Chico in 1845. The founder of Chico, California, Bidwell ran for governor of California in 1875 on the Anti-Monopoly ticket, presided over the Prohibition Party state convention in 1888, and was the Prohibition candidate for governor in 1880.

10. In 1840 a group of Indians from Mission San José arrived at Sutter's Fort. Despite their claim of peaceful intentions, they attacked a Nisenan *ranchería* whose men were absent, off working for Sutter. They killed elderly people and infants and captured women and children with the intent of selling them as slaves to Hispanic rancheros on the coast. Sutter quickly retaliated, capturing the Indians and executing a number of them. See Hurtado, *Indian Survival on the California Frontier*, 61, and also Hurtado, *John Sutter*, 74.

11. For a discussion of the Clear Lake Massacre, see Hurtado, *Indian Survival on the California Frontier*, p. 104; Secrest, *When the Great Spirit Died*, 23–35; and Heizer, *Collected Documents of the Causes and Events in the Bloody Island Massacre of 1850*.

12. For a reconstruction of the Burnt Ranch Massacre, see Gould, "Indian and White Versions of 'The Burnt Ranch Massacre.'"

13. For a discussion of the Santa Ynez revolt, see Hurtado, *Indian Survival on the California Frontier*, 37.

14. An example of this map can be found in Heizer and Elsasser, *The Natural World of the California Indians*, 5.

15. Hubert Howe Bancroft (1832–1918) was an American historian and ethnologist. He published thirty-nine volumes on the history of western North America. The personal narratives taken down by Bancroft's scribes provide historical material related to nineteenth-century California. Among the prominent pioneers and settlers he interviewed were John Bidwell and John Sutter.

16. See John Laufkotter's *John A. Sutter and His Grants*, reprinted in Kenneth N. Owens, *John A. Sutter, Sr., and His Grants*.

17. Annie Kennedy Bidwell (1839–1918) was a California pioneer with her hus-

band, John. She is known for her contributions to education and women's suffrage.

18. Born in Monterey, California, Don Mariano Guadalupe Vallejo (1807–90) was a California military commander and politician during the era of Mexican control of California. He had vast landholdings, which were worked by local Indians, in the Sonoma area. During the Bear Flag Revolt, John C. Frémont had Vallejo incarcerated in Sutter's Fort. See Rosenus, *General Vallejo and the Advent of the Americans.*

19. For a discussion of the Indian mistreatment of the Chinese, see Heizer, *The Destruction of California Indians,* 287–92.

20. Louise Amelia Knapp Smith Clappe (1819–1906) wrote under the pen name "Dame Shirley." In 1849 she moved to California with her physician husband, Fayette Clappe. While living in the mining camps, Clappe became a chronicler of the California gold rush. The *Pioneer,* a California-based literary magazine, published each of Clappe's letters in separate issues collectively titled "California in 1851 and 1852: A Trip into the Mines." Published in 1922 as a book under the title *The Shirley Letters,* Clappe's writing provides a woman's unique perspective on gold-rush California.

21. Bret Harte (1836–1902) came to California in 1853, working initially in the mining camps and later as a journalist. As assistant editor of the *Northern Californian,* a Humboldt Bay newspaper, he strongly condemned the Indian Island Massacre. This action cost him his job. In 1868 he became editor of the *Overland Monthly.* He is best remembered for his accounts of pioneering life in California. Harte's short story "The Luck of Roaring Camp" appeared in the *Overland Monthly*'s second issue and brought him nationwide fame. His sentimental tales about the miners and settlers stood in stark contrast to the behavior that he had observed at Indian Island.

For a synopsis of the Indian Island Massacre, see Hurtado, *Intimate Frontiers,* 136; for background on violence in Humboldt County, see Secrest, *When the Great Spirit Died,* chapter 18; for relevant documents, see Heizer, *The Destruction of California Indians,* 253–63.

22. American novelist Cormac McCarthy (1933–) is widely regarded as an heir to William Faulkner for his biblical prose and rural settings. McCarthy's fifth book, *Blood Meridian* (1985), focuses on a teenaged runaway's experiences with the Glanton gang, a historical group of scalp hunters who massacred Indians on the borderlands of the United States and Mexico in 1849 and 1850.

23. American historian Herbert Eugene Bolton (1870–1953) was one of the most prominent authorities on the history of the Mexican/American borderlands. He spent most of his career at the University of California, Berkeley.

24. Founded in 1875, the Native Sons of the Golden West (NSGW) is a charitable and fraternal organization to promote the history of the early days of California. Although the organization now has Asian American and African American members, the Native Sons initially stood in open opposition to Chinese, Mexican, and Japanese immigration.

Chapter 7. The Sioux Wars

1. For a treatment of the Grattan Massacre, see Utley, *Frontiersmen in Blue,* 113–16. On the Battle of Blue Water Creek, see Paul, *Blue Water Creek and the First Sioux War, 1854–1856.*

2. William Selby Harney (1800–1889) was a U.S. Army cavalry officer during the Mexican-American War and the Indian Wars. In 1855 he commanded the U.S. troops at the Battle of Blue Water Creek. He also commanded American troops in Bleeding Kansas in 1857 and was the original commander of the Utah Expedition against the Mormons in 1857–58. Harney Peak, the highest point in the Black Hills, is named for him. For an account of Harney at Blue Water Creek, see Utley, *Frontiersmen in Blue,* 115–19.

3. For an overview of the Santee Sioux uprising, see ibid., chapter 13.

4. Fur trader, politician, and brigadier general of volunteers Henry Hastings Sibley (1811–91) was the first governor of Minnesota. During the Sioux uprising of 1862, he was colonel of the state militia. In 1863 he led a second successful expedition again the Sioux in Dakota Territory. For an examination of Sibley's role in the Minnesota outbreak and the Dakota campaign, see ibid., 266–73.

5. Andrew Myrick (1832–62) was a trader who operated a store in southwest Minnesota. When Indians appealed to Myrick to give them food on credit, he said, "So far as I am concerned, if they are hungry, let them eat grass or their own dung." During the Sioux uprising, Myrick's mutilated corpse was found outside his store—grass had been stuffed in his mouth. Utley, *The Indian Frontier of the American West, 1846–1890,* 76 (quotation) and 80.

6. On Grattan, see note 1 above. Lieutenant George Nicholas Bascom (1836–62) was responsible for what is now called the Bascom Affair. In 1861 Indians raided the ranch of John Ward at Sonoita Creek, Arizona, stealing livestock and kidnapping Ward's stepson. Bascom and his soldiers were ordered to recover the boy. Determining incorrectly that Cochise's Apaches were guilty, Bascom met with Cochise and attempted to imprison him and his family during the meeting. Cochise subsequently escaped and with a large party of Apaches attacked a group of Americans. They captured three hostages, offering them to Bascom in exchange for his family, but Bascom refused. Cochise killed the American prisoners and left their remains to be discovered by Bascom. Several days later, Bascom hanged Cochise's brother and nephews. Cochise took revenge in the form of numerous raids and murders, beginning the 25-year-long Apache Wars.

William Judd Fetterman (1833–66) was an officer in the U.S. Army during the Civil War and Red Cloud's War. He allegedly boasted that with eighty soldiers he could ride through the Sioux nation. In December 1866 a large band of Cheyennes and Sioux attacked a wood train near Fort Phil Kearny. Fetterman pursued the Indians into an ambush, and he and his command of eighty men were wiped out.

7. For a detailed description of Crazy Horse's participation in the Fetterman Massacre, see Bray, *Crazy Horse,* 97–102. See also Utley, *The Indian Frontier,* 103–105.

8. See Utley, *Custer: Cavalier in Buckskin.*

9. The Battle of the Washita is a topic in the interview with Jerome Greene in chapter 8. For a brief account of this battle, see the synopsis in that chapter; for an extended account, see Greene, *Washita.*

10. Frederick Benteen (1834–98) served in the Union Army during the Civil War. After the war, he commanded Troop H of the 7th Cavalry. He had an intense dislike of George Armstrong Custer and accused him of abandoning Major Joel H. Elliott at the Battle of the Washita. At the Battle of the Little Bighorn, Custer deployed Benteen on a scouting expedition. On his return, Benteen came to the defense of Major Marcus Reno's troops but was criticized for dawdling and not arriving soon enough to help Custer. See Utley, *Custer: Cavalier in Buckskin.*

11. Red Cloud's War of 1866–68 is treated in chapters 7 and 9 of Utley, *Frontier Regulars,* and in chapter 4 of Utley, *The Indian Frontier.*

12. The Allison Commission (led by U.S. senator William B. Allison) arrived in Sioux country in the fall of 1875. Although the commission attempted to get the Sioux to sell the Black Hills to the government, the Sioux refused. See Utley, *Frontier Regulars,* 245–46.

13. In his report on Sioux country, Inspector E. C. Watkins stated that hundreds of Sioux and Cheyennes under Indian leaders Sitting Bull and Crazy Horse were openly hostile against the white settlers and peaceful tribes. It was his judgment that the government "should send troops against them in the winter, the sooner the better, and whip them into subjection" (Utley, *Frontier Regulars,* 247).

14. For these battles conducted by General Crook, see Utley, *Frontier Regulars,* chapter 14, and Greene, *Battles and Skirmishes of the Great Sioux War,* chapters 1 and 3.

15. Michael Donahue, chair of the Art Department of Temple College in Temple, Texas, has spent nineteen summers at Little Bighorn Battlefield. He is the author of *Drawing Battle Lines: The Map Testimony of Custer's Last Fight,* a compilation of primary maps of the Battle of the Little Bighorn.

16. An extended discussion of the battle is given in Utley, *Custer: Cavalier in Buckskin,* chapter 8.

17. Bloody Knife (1840–76) was an Indian scout with the U.S. Seventh Cavalry Regiment. Assigned to Major Reno at the Battle of the Little Bighorn, he was killed by a gunshot to his head.

18. For an overview of the Indian and army relics discovered on the battlefield, see Greene, *Evidence and the Custer Enigma.*

19. Utley, "On Digging Up Custer Battlefield."

20. The subject of T*he Lance and the Shield,* the Hunkpapa Sioux leader Sitting Bull was one of the the greatest Indians of the nineteenth century. He played a major role in the Sioux Wars of 1876–77 and fled to Canada in its aftermath but ultimately

returned to the United States and resided on a Sioux reservation in South Dakota. He was killed there in an incident that led up to the Wounded Knee conflict. In writing Sitting Bull's biography, Utley relied on the recollections of White Bull (1849–1947), who was the nephew of Sitting Bull. See Vestal, *Warpath.*

A professor at the University of Oklahoma, Stanley Vestal (1877–1957) wrote over twenty books and numerous articles about the historic West.

21. Custer employed Crow scouts during the Little Bighorn expedition. They were released from the battle just before Custer started down Medicine Tail Coulee. Curley (1859–1923), who was one of the Crow scouts, stayed with Custer during the early movements but escaped before the destruction of Custer's troops. His translated account of the Battle of the Little Bighorn appeared in several newspapers. See Utley, *Custer: Cavalier in Buckskin,* 147.

22. Crazy Horse was a major leader in the Sioux Wars of 1876–77 and is considered one of the greatest of the Oglala Sioux. He surrendered in May 1877, only to be killed four months later in a guardhouse scuffle. Until his surrender, he had very few dealings with whites, and there is little reliable information on his life. Mari Susette Sandoz (1896–1966) was one of Nebraska's foremost authors. A novelist and biographer, she wrote extensively about pioneer life and the Plains Indians. Her biography *Crazy Horse: The Strange Man of the Oglalas* is often considered her finest work.

23. Kingsley Bray is senior bookseller at BMA Hammicks Medical Bookshop in Manchester, England. His articles on Plains Indians have appeared in *Nebraska History* and *Montana The Magazine of Western History.* See Bray, *Crazy Horse: A Lakota Life.*

24. No Water shot Crazy Horse in the face because his wife, Black Buffalo Robe Woman, rode off with Crazy Horse.

25. On George Hyde, see chapter 5, note 17.

26. On Dee Brown, see chapter 1, note 13.

27. Utley, *Indian Wars,* 289.

28. Colonel Ranald S. Mackenzie (1840–89) fought in the Red River War, routing a combined Indian force of Kiowas, Cheyennes, and Comanches at the Battle of Palo Duro Canyon on September 28, 1874.

29. Launched in 1874, the Red River War was the U.S. Army's military campaign to drive the Comanche, Kiowa, Southern Cheyenne, and Arapaho tribes back to their reservations in the Indian Territory.

30. In 1863 Brigadier General James H. Carleton ordered Carson to institute a scorched earth policy against the Navajos, burning their fields, orchards, and homes and confiscating or killing their livestock.

31. The Long Walk of the Navajos was an Indian removal effort of General Carleton in 1863 and 1864. The Navajos were marched from their homeland in northern Arizona to a reservation at Bosque Redondo along the Pecos River in eastern New Mexico. The walk was in some ways similar to the Cherokees' Trail of Tears.

32. For an extensive treatment of Wounded Knee and its background, see Utley, *The Last Days of the Sioux Nation.*

33. According to Utley in *Last Days of the Sioux Nation,* Daniel F. Royer, a South Dakota citizen who had no experience with Indians, was appointed agent at the Pine Ridge Reservation in early October 1890 at the height of the Ghost Dance phenomenon. The Oglalas realized that Indians made him uneasy and dubbed him "Young-Man-Afraid-of-Indians." He was unable to get the Oglalas to desist from the Ghost Dance through either persuasion or threats; indeed the Indians began to defy him openly. He then requested that troops be sent to the area to control the Indians, which ultimately led to the Wounded Knee affair. Royer's failure to control the Ghost Dance mania led to his dismissal in January 1891.

34. Lieutenant Colonel Edwin V. Sumner had a long career as a military officer on the frontier. He served in the Mexican War and took over the defense of the New Mexico Territory in 1851. He commanded the Department of the West in 1858 and served in the Civil War. On December 3, 1890, he assumed command of Camp Cheyenne, on the Cheyenne River north of the Pine Ridge Reservation and south and west of the Cheyenne River Reservation, with orders to keep Big Foot under observation and control. Sumner reported that Big Foot was attempting to keep his followers quiet. In late December 1890 Big Foot's followers convinced him to go to Pine Ridge to help restore tranquillity there. General Miles's interpretation of this was that Sumner had allowed Big Foot to escape. Miles began an unsuccessful effort to collect evidence to bring Sumner before a court of inquiry.

35. The Sierra Madre campaign of 1881–86 involved a group of Chiricahua and Warm Springs Apaches who fled the San Carlos Reservation in Arizona four times into the Sierra Madre of northern Mexico, where they operated in part under the leadership of Geronimo. The Apaches raided settlements, primarily in Mexico but also in Arizona and New Mexico, to obtain supplies and ammunition. Obtaining permission to operate in Mexico, Crook used Apache scouts under military officers such as Emmet Crawford and Charles Gatewood to track down the fugitives. Crook finally convinced Geronimo and other leaders to surrender in March 1886, but the next day Geronimo and some of his followers got drunk and fled back into Mexico. The others, under Chihuahua, kept their promise to Crook. Although Crook's terms included a two-year imprisonment in Florida followed by a return to Arizona, General Philip Sheridan demanded unconditional surrender. Rather than violate his agreement, Crook resigned and was replaced by General Miles, who promptly removed all on-reservation Chiricahua and Warm Springs Apaches to imprisonment in Florida. When Lieutenant Gatewood informed Geronimo of the removal, he finally surrendered. See Utley, *Frontier Regulars,* chapter 19.

36. An educated Virginian, Lieutenant Charles Bare Gatewood (1853–96) served under General Crook and General Miles in Arizona and New Mexico. Because of his

effort to understand the Indian culture, he became commander of some of the Apache scouts. In 1886, after Miles's forces were unable to capture Geronimo and his small band of Indians, Gatewood was sent into Mexico to convince Geronimo to surrender. See Gatewood, *Lt. Charles Gatewood & His Apache Wars Memoir.* See also Louis Kraft, *Gatewood and Geronimo.*

37. William Wotherspoon (1850–1921) served in the West during the Indian Wars. From 1891 to 1894 he was head of the Apache prisoners at Mount Vernon barracks in Alabama. He served in the Philippines, became head of the Army War College, and was Army Chief of Staff for several months in 1914.

Chapter 8. The Cheyenne Wars

1. A student of Native American life, George Bird Grinnell (1849–1938) was an American anthropologist, historian, and naturalist. He accompanied George Armstrong Custer's 1874 Black Hills expedition as a naturalist but declined an appointment to the Little Bighorn expedition. Grinnell's best-known works include *The Fighting Cheyennes* (1915) and *The Cheyenne Indians* (1923). For George Bent, see chapter 5, note 17.

2. For Tate's thesis, see the interview in chapter 5.

3. For a brief overview of the Santee Sioux uprising, see the synopsis in chapter 7. For an extended account, see Utley, *Frontiersmen in Blue,* chapter 13.

4. John Evans (1814–97) was governor of the Territory of Colorado. The founder of both Northwestern University and the University of Denver, he is the namesake of Evanston, Illinois; Evans, Colorado; and Mount Evans, Colorado. In 1864 Evans appointed John Chivington as colonel of the Colorado Volunteers and sent him with 800 cavalry troopers to locate the Indians. On November 28, 1864, Chivington carried out the Sand Creek Massacre. In response, President Andrew Johnson asked Evans to resign from his position of governor. For an account of the Sand Creek Massacre, see Greene and Scott, *Finding Sand Creek,* and Hoig, *The Sand Creek Massacre.* For biographical information on of Evans, Chivington, and Byers, see Svaldi, *Sand Creek and the Rhetoric of Extermination.*

John Milton Chivington (1821–92) arrived in Denver in 1860 as a Methodist minister. He became celebrated for his role in the 1862 Battle of Glorieta Pass (see chapter 1, note 2): as a major in the First Colorado Regiment, he destroyed the Texans' supply wagons, which brought an end to the Confederate campaign to capture New Mexico and Colorado. He became infamous for his role in the 1864 Sand Creek Massacre. In later life, he worked as a freight hauler, editor, farmer, and deputy sheriff. He defended his actions at Sand Creek until the end of his life.

William Newton Byers (1831–1903) published Denver's first newspaper, the *Rocky Mountain News,* on April 23, 1859. A friend of Governor John Evans, Byers used the paper to promote Denver's growth as a Rocky Mountain metropolis. When Byers reported on the Sand Creek Massacre in his paper, he justified the attack as a brilliant feat.

5. For an account of the archaeology of the massacre site, see Greene and Scott, *Finding Sand Creek.*

6. Silas Stillman Soule (1838–65) was a soldier in the Colorado infantry and cavalry during the American Civil War. As commander of Company D, First Colorado Cavalry, Captain Soule was present at the Sand Creek Massacre. He refused the orders of his commanding officer, Colonel John Chivington, to fire on defenseless Indians and later testified against Chivington for the atrocities committed by his troops.

7. Carroll, *The Sand Creek Massacre.*

8. See Greene, *Washita,* and Hoig, *The Battle of the Washita.* Philip Henry Sheridan (1831–88) was a U.S. Army officer and a Union general in the Civil War. After the Sand Creek Massacre ignited a general war with the Indians, President Grant appointed Sheridan to head the Department of the Missouri and pacify the Plains Indians. Sheridan served in this position from 1867 to 1869. He was promoted to lieutenant general and commanded the Division of the Missouri (which included the Department of the Missouri) from 1869 to 1883, when he became commanding general of the army. For a biography of Sheridan, see Hutton, *Phil Sheridan and His Army.*

9. Winfield Scott Hancock (1824–86), the Democratic nominee for president of the United States in 1880, was a career U.S. Army officer who was famous for staving off Pickett's Charge at the Battle of Gettysburg. In 1866 Hancock was promoted to major general and was given command of the Military Department of the Missouri. Shortly after he arrived, General Sherman assigned him to lead an expedition to negotiate with the Cheyennes and Sioux. Together with Colonel George Armstrong Custer, commander of the Seventh Cavalry, Hancock led the Seventh on an expedition to give the central Plains Indians a lesson. One of Hancock's acts was to destroy a Cheyenne-Lakota village on the Pawnee Fork in what is today Ness County, Kansas. The bad relations between Hancock and Custer regarding the latter's harsh punishment of deserters resulted in Custer's court-martial for being absent without leave. For information on Hancock's unsuccessful expedition against southern plains tribes, see Greene, *Washita,* 32–33, 40, 43, 72, 74, 191–92.

10. The quotation, from Indian agent Jesse Leavenworth, is from Greene, *Washita,* 24.

11. In the summer of 1868 war parties of Southern Cheyennes, Arapahos, Kiowas and Comanches, Northern Cheyennes, Brulé and Oglala Lakotas, and Pawnees raided white settlements in western Kansas, southeast Colorado, and northwest Texas. Among these raids were those along the Solomon and Saline Rivers in Kansas. These attacks began in August 1868 and resulted in the deaths of fifteen white settlers. Others were wounded, and some women were raped or taken captive. For a description of the Southern Cheyenne warriors' raids on the Solomon and the Saline in the summer of 1868, see Greene, *Washita,* 49–50.

12. Alfred Sully (1821–79), the son of portrait painter Thomas Sully, was a military officer during the Civil War and during the Indian Wars. He drove the Sioux of the

Minnesota rebellion of 1863 into the Black Hills and was active in a campaign against the Northern Cheyennes along the North Platte. By the early fall of 1868 over 100 non-Indians had been killed within twelve months in Major General Philip H. Sheridan's military Department of the Missouri. Sheridan sent 500 soldiers led by Lieutenant Colonel Alfred Sully to attack the Cheyennes. Sully's unsuccessful campaign only incited more Indian raids. See Greene, *Washita,* 64–72.

13. Lavender, *Bent's Fort,* 363, which cites no source for the incident.

14. Major Joel Haworth Elliott (1840–68) was Custer's second in command at Washita. Following distinguished service in the Civil War, he had qualified as a major in the postwar army by brilliant performance on an examination, which was quite an unusual route to advancement. He was the effective commander of the Seventh Cavalry during Custer's suspension. Elliott led the reconnaissance that found Black Kettle's camp at the Washita. During the battle, he and seventeen volunteers became separated from the rest of the command and were killed by the Indians. Custer left the battlefield without locating Elliott's command, leading to considerable criticism. According to Greene, "it is difficult to ascertain what more Custer could have done under the circumstances" (*Washita,* 188).

15. Red Cloud's War of 1866–68 is treated in Utley, *Frontier Regulars,* chapters 7 and 9; and *The Indian Frontier,* chapter 4. For a brief account, see the synopsis in chapter 7.

16. For a discussion of the Battle of Powder River, see the synopsis in chapter 7. For an account of the battle from the perspective of Native American participants, see Greene, *Lakota and Cheyenne,* 3–15. For the military's view of the battle, see Greene, *Battles and Skirmishes,* 11–17.

The Battle of the Little Bighorn is discussed in chapter 7. For an account of the Battle of the Little Bighorn from the perspective of Native American participants, see Greene, *Lakota and Cheyenne,* 31–72. For the military's view of the battle, see Greene, *Battles and Skirmishes,* 47–60.

17. For Crazy Horse, see chapter 7, note 22; Sandoz, *Crazy Horse;* and Bray, *Crazy Horse.*

18. For Sitting Bull, see chapter 7, note 20.

19. Colonel Joseph Reynolds (1822–99) served in both the Mexican War and the Civil War. He led the column of troops under Crook's command at the Battle of Powder River.

20. In "Cheyenne Primacy," Liberty provides new ideas regarding the Sioux (Cheyenne) War of 1876.

21. Colonel Ranald S. Mackenzie (1840–89) was a general in the Union Army during the Civil War. He also served with great distinction in the Indian Wars. He fought in the Red River War, routing a combined Indian force of Kiowas, Cheyennes, and Comanches at the Battle of Palo Duro Canyon on September 28, 1874. Morning Star was a Northern Cheyenne chief, also known by his Lakota Sioux name, Dull Knife.

For an account of Mackenzie's attack on Morning Star's village, see Greene, *Morning Star Dawn,* 106–25.

22. Nelson Appleton Miles (1839–1925) served in the Civil War, the Indian Wars, and the Spanish-American War. He played a significant role in the army's campaigns against the Indian tribes of the Great Plains. In 1874–75 he was field commander in the force that defeated the Kiowas, Comanches, and Southern Cheyennes along the Red River. In 1876–78 he participated in the campaign that patrolled the plains after Custer's defeat at the Battle of the Little Bighorn. For Crook, see chapter 4, note 32.

23. Pierce, *The Most Promising Young Officer.*

24. The Battle of Slim Buttes took place on September 9–10, 1876, in the Dakota Territory. Following a lengthy "starvation march," an advance column of Crook's troops, led by Captain Anson Mills, encountered and charged a mixed Sioux/Cheyenne encampment, driving out the Indians and holding the village until the main column arrived. They then repelled a counterattack by the warriors. This episode marked the first significant victory for the army since Custer's defeat at the Little Bighorn. For a history of the conflict, see Greene, *Slim Buttes.*

25. Greene, *Washita,* 191.

26. The Bear River Massacre is discussed in chapter 9 and note 16; for a history of the massacre, see Madsen, *The Shoshoni Frontier and the Bear River Massacre.*

27. In the Marias River Massacre (also called the Baker Massacre) Piegan Blackfeet Indians were killed by U.S. troops on January 23, 1870. Major Eugene Baker's party attacked the camp of Chief Heavy Runner. Most of the men of the camp were out hunting, so the victims were mainly women and children. For a description of the massacre, see Ege, *"Tell Baker to Strike Them Hard!"* 53, and Hutton, *Phil Sheridan and His Army,* 180–200.

28. The Battle of the Big Hole between the Nez Perces and the U.S. Army occurred on August 9, 1877, during the Nez Perce War of 1877. Colonel John Gibbon's party took the Nez Perces by surprise, and they lost their camp in twenty minutes. See Greene, *Nez Perce Summer,* 124–40.

The Battle of Bear Paw on September 30, 1877, was the final engagement of the Nez Perce War. Chief Joseph was forced to surrender the majority of his tribe to Oliver O. Howard. See Greene, *Nez Perce Summer,* 272–324.

29. Chief Joseph (1840–1904) was the chief of the Wallowa band of Nez Perce Indians during the time of General Oliver Howard's attempt forcibly to remove the Wallowas and the other nontreaty Indians to a reservation in Idaho.

30. Greene, *Evidence and the Custer Enigma,* 15.

31. Walter Mason Camp (1867–1925) interviewed hundreds of both white and Indian participants in the American Indian Wars. Although he wrote only a few brief papers, his interview notes currently housed in various public collections contain important source material for the period.

Eli S. Ricker (1842–1926) interviewed many participants in the wars of the northern plains. He never wrote a book, but his interviews have been collected in *Voices of the American West,* edited by Richard E. Jensen.

On George Bird Grinnell, see note 1 above.

Between 1896 and 1930 the famed photographer Edward S. Curtis (1868–1952) took more than 40,000 photographs, conducted interviews, recorded tribal lore and history, and wrote biographical sketches of tribal leaders. His monumental work *The North American Indian* can be found online in Northwestern University's Digital Library Collection.

32. For a note on John Stands In Timber, see chapter 5, note 16.

Chapter 9. Violence over the Great Basin

1. Blackhawk, "The Displacement of Violence," 725–26.

2. The Athabaskans are late prehistoric and historic indigenous people of North America. Considered ancestral to the Navajos and Apaches, Athabaskans migrated from southwestern Canada into the American Southwest sometime after AD 1400. The precontact civilizations of the region included the Hohokams in Arizona, the Mogollons in southern New Mexico, and the Ancient Puebloans or Anasazis in the Four Corners region.

3. Following half a century of attacks and counterattacks, the Spanish and the Utes established peace in the early 1750s; a second peace treaty in 1786 led to peace among the Utes, the Spanish, and the Comanches. Such treaties allowed for regularized trade and protection from common enemies, such as the Apaches. The treaties gradually unraveled with the advent of Mexican independence, and the Utes were again at war with the New Mexicans after 1844. Following the U.S.-Mexican War, a series of treaties was negotiated between the United States and the Utes, involving skilled diplomats such as the Ute chief Ouray. The unconquered, undefeated Utes negotiated a treaty in 1868 that led to a reservation covering most of western Colorado. Dispossessed of most of this land over the next ten years, the Utes were subsequently confined to much smaller reservations in Utah and southwestern Colorado.

4. Blackhawk, "The Displacement of Violence," 751, cites Hämäläinen, "The Western Comanche Trade Center." Pekka Hämäläinen is a Finnish scholar of the American West. He is currently at the University of California, Santa Barbara. In *The Comanche Empire,* Hämäläinen shows how the Comanches, who were initially a pedestrian group of eastern Shoshones, acquired horses and guns and eventually became the most powerful tribe on the southern plains. By the early 1800s they had established an important trade center on the Arkansas River in southeastern Colorado. They traded with various northern tribes, French and Americans out of Missouri, Spanish out of New Mexico, and tribes to the southeast. The trade began to unravel in the 1830s, due to influences such as the advent of the trade center of brothers William and Charles Bent and the incursion of the Cheyennes and Arapahos into the southern plains.

5. Luis de Rosas was the Spanish governor of New Mexico from 1637 to 1641. He was assassinated by his enemies on January 25, 1642.

6. Navajos and Apaches acquired horses and metals earlier than the Utes and conducted raids on Ute settlements. The Utes sought horses, metals, and guns to defend against these raids as well as raids by the Spanish. This led to cycles of increased violence in the region.

7. Blackhawk, *Violence over the Land,* 7.

8. The Old Spanish Trail, a pack-mule trade route that came into prominence in the 1830s, ran from northern New Mexico to southern California. In addition to legitimate trade, considerable illegal trade in stolen horses and in captives for the New Mexican slave market was conducted over the trail. The captives were typically Paiutes. Utes such as the famous leader Wakara joined with renegade trappers in the raids on Californio and Paiute settlements. For more information on the trail, see Hafen and Hafen, *Old Spanish Trail.*

9. Blackhawk, *Violence over the Land,* 136.

10. Relations between Indians and emigrants on overland trails are discussed in chapter 5. For background, see Tate, *Indians and Emigrants,* and Unruh, *The Plains Across.*

11. Madsen, *The Shoshoni Frontier,* deals with relations and events involving the Mormons, the U.S. government, and the Shoshones, Bannocks, and Paiutes of northern Utah, southern Idaho, and northern Nevada from the Mormon arrival in Utah in the late 1840s through the Bear River Massacre of 1863. Madsen gives evidence that a number of the attacks on emigrant wagon trains during this period involved "White Indians," who were typically escapees from justice in California or renegade ex-trappers.

12. Thomas L. "Peg-leg" Smith (1801–66) was a fur trapper, mountain man, and guide. He began working for John Jacob Astor as a fur trapper in St. Louis, Missouri. Later he accompanied Alexandre Le Grand's expedition into New Mexico. Smith was shot in the right knee by an Indian during the expedition and had to use a wooden leg, which earned him his name. Together with trapper Bill Williams and the Ute leader Wakara, he was involved in a major raid in California in 1840, in which the raiders acquired horses for trade in New Mexico and further east. See Hafen and Hafen, *Old Spanish Trail,* 240–46.

13. Many trappers and traders married into Indian communities. For Kit Carson's marriage to Arapaho and Cheyenne women, see Simmons, *Kit Carson and His Three Wives.* For William Bent's marriage to Owl Woman of the Southern Cheyennes, see Lavender, *Bent's Fort.* For hints of the violence engaged in by the mountain men, see Weber, *The Taos Trappers.*

14. On August 20, 1854, eighteen of the twenty members of the Alexander Ward party were massacred by Shoshones while traveling on the Oregon Trail in western

Idaho. It marked the culmination of Indian activities that led to the closing of the Hudson's Bay Company's Fort Boise and Fort Hall. For an account of the attack from the emigrants' perspective, see Shannon, *The Boise Massacre on the Oregon Trail.* For the Utter Massacre, see chapter 5, note 28.

15. Madsen, *The Shoshoni Frontier,* 17. The source of the estimate is Unruh, *The Plains Across:* "90 percent of all emigrant killings took place west of South Pass, principally along the Snake and Humboldt Rivers and on the Applegate Trail" (185).

16. The extension of Mormon settlements into Shoshone territories set the stage for one of the least-known Indian massacres in U.S. history. On January 29, 1863, Colonel Patrick Edward Connor (1820–91), the commander of a unit of California volunteers, attacked a Shoshone winter camp at the confluence of the Bear River and Beaver Creek in what was then southeastern Washington Territory but is today southern Idaho. Connor and his men killed as many as 300 Indians and destroyed all of the food in the camp, except for a small amount of wheat that they left behind to feed the 160 women and children who were spared. For a biography of Connor, see Madsen, *Glory Hunter.* For a history of the massacre, see Madsen, *The Shoshoni Frontier.*

17. For a treatment of sources on the Bear River Massacre, see Barnes, "The Struggle to Control the Past"; for recent findings on the massacre, see Schindler, "The Bear River Massacre."

The Official Records of the American Civil War are the most extensive collection of primary sources on the history of the war. They include selected firsthand accounts, orders, reports, maps, diagrams, and correspondence drawn from War and Navy Department records for both the Confederate and the Union governments. See Sauers, "The War of the Rebellion (Official Records)."

18. As mentioned in note 3 above, the large reservation in western Colorado that the Utes had negotiated in 1868 was diminished in the 1870s by illegal land seizures and abrogated treaties. Territorial leaders used an uprising at the White River Agency in 1879 to justify a large reduction of Ute lands. See Blackhawk, *Violence over the Land,* 224, and Utley, *Frontier Regulars,* 332–42.

19. For Sarah Winnemucca Hopkins (1844–91), see chapter 5, note 18. Her book *Life among the Piutes* includes a discussion of a number of instances in which the Paiutes turned to the military to redress the ill treatment they had received from settlers and civilian Indian agents.

20. Madsen, *Shoshoni Frontier,* xiii.

21. John G. Neihardt (1881–1973) was a professor of poetry at the University of Nebraska, a literary editor in St. Louis, Missouri, and poet-in-residence and lecturer at the University of Missouri in Columbia. He is best known for *Black Elk Speaks,* the story of an Oglala Sioux medicine man. Black Elk's son Ben translated Black Elk's words from Lakota into English for Neihardt and his daughter to record.

22. Raymond J. DeMallie (1946–) is an American anthropologist at the University of Indiana. His work focuses on the cultural history of the peoples of the northern

plains, particularly the Lakotas. DeMallie, *The Sixth Grandfather: Black Elk's Teaching Given to John G. Neihardt,* makes the transcripts from Neihardt's interviews with Black Elk in 1931 and 1944 available for the first time, offering new insights into Black Elk's life.

23. Brooks, *Captives and Cousins,* is a study of captivity and slavery in the Southwest up to the time of the American takeover. It focuses on captive-taking by plains tribes such as the Comanches, by the Navajos, and by the Spanish in New Mexico. Captive women and children were typically adopted into the social group that had captured them, thus forming networks of kinship and exchange between otherwise hostile communities. In his review in *American Indian Culture and Research Journal,* Blackhawk criticizes Brooks's book for minimizing the violence and trauma associated with captive-taking and for use of questionable sources in ascribing slavery to precontact societies. A key example is Brooks's use of the Pawnee Morning Star ritual, which involved the capture and killing of a young enemy girl. Historical references to the ritual are not found until the nineteenth century, however, and only very tentative archaeological evidence exists for the ritual in the precontact era.

24. See Blackhawk, "The Displacement of Violence." Flores, "Bison Ecology and Bison Diplomacy," is concerned with whether the southern plains tribes, in particular the Comanches, had established a society in ecological equilibrium with the habitat, especially with the bison herds. In the course of explaining the background history, Flores contends that "as full-time bison hunters the Comanches appear to have abandoned all the old Shoshonean mechanisms, such as infanticide and polyandry, that had kept their population in line with available resources" (471).

25. Gutiérrez, *When Jesus Came, the Corn Mothers Went Away,* is a social history of the Southwest viewed through the lens of the institution of marriage in the preconquest Pueblo world, in the postcontact era up to the time of the Pueblo Revolt, and in Spanish New Mexico after the revolt (which included Spanish-Indian marriages leading to *genízaro* culture). The first chapter is an effort to outline precontact Puebloan culture. Gutiérrez warns the reader that this chapter "may at times seem based more on unsubstantiated assertions than on an extensive documentary base" (xxx). In his review of *Captives and Cousins,* Blackhawk points to commentaries by Indian scholars claiming that Gutiérrez's "portrait of Pueblo societies is problematic on multiple levels," including use of "twentieth-century ethnographies to reconstruct early Pueblo history" (86).

DeLay, *War of a Thousand Deserts,* gives the history of the raids by Comanches and neighboring tribes into northern Mexico prior to the U.S.-Mexican War. His thesis is that these raids so weakened the Mexican communities that they set the stage for victory by the U.S. troops. He points out that the destructiveness of these campaigns worked counter to the economic motivation for the raids: in addition to stealing horses and material goods and acquiring captives, the raiders often went to extremes to kill Mexicans, slaughter livestock, and set fire to buildings. DeLay argues that this behavior was motivated by a desire for vengeance. See also DeLay, "Independent Indians and the U.S.-Mexican War."

26. See Hämäläinen, "The Western Comanche Trade Center."

27. Álvar Núñez Cabeza de Vaca (ca. 1490/1507–ca. 1557/59) was a Spanish conquistador. He was one of the four survivors of the Pánfilo de Narváez expedition, which was shipwrecked in 1528 on what is now Galveston Island. For the next eight years, he explored what is now Texas and the Southwest. His account of these explorations, *La Relación,* was first published in 1542.

Concluding Comments

1. Dodge, *Our Wild Indians,* 622.

2. McCarthy, *No Country for Old Men,* 63.

3. For a brief discussion of the massacre, see chapter 8, note 27. The Marias River Massacre is treated in more detail in Welch with Stekler, *Killing Custer.* Welch's historical novel *Fools Crow* culminates with the massacre. See also Utley, *Frontier Regulars,* 191.

4. The Clear Lake, Burnt Ranch, and Indian Island massacres are discussed in the interview with Albert Hurtado in chapter 6. For a discussion of other massacres in California during the 1850s, see Secrest, *When the Great Spirit Died.*

5. In the spring of 1871 in the vicinity of Fort Belknap, Texas, a band of Kiowas including Satanta and Satank attacked a wagon train belonging to Henry Warren, a government contractor. Of the six men killed, one was burned alive and all were scalped. A smaller party that preceded the Warren train that included General Sherman narrowly escaped attack. Following a scuffle at Fort Sill, Satanta, Satank, and Big Tree were arrested and sent for trial in Texas courts. See Utley, *Frontier Regulars,* 210–11. For a semifictional version, see Capps, *The Warren Wagontrain Raid.*

6. Utley, *Frontiersmen in Blue,* 265. For an extended history of the revolt, see Keenan, *The Great Sioux Uprising.*

7. Tate, *Indians and Emigrants,* x. See also Unruh, *The Plains Across,* a classic history of overland migration.

8. The Cutthroat Massacre occurred in the spring of 1833, when a war party of Osage Indians attacked a village of Kiowas in Oklahoma, killing a large number of women and children. Most of the Kiowa warriors were absent on a raid against the Utes. The Osages cut the heads off the dead bodies and left them in cooking pots. See Mooney, *A Calendar History of the Kiowa Indians,* 257, and Hoig, *Tribal Wars of the Southern Plains,* 102–104.

9. For mutual attacks involving the Apaches, Yavapais, and Navajos, see the narratives of Anna Price, Palmer Valor, and Joseph Hoffman in Basso, *Western Apache Raiding and Warfare.* For background on Goodwin's interviews, see chapter 1, note 10.

10. For Haun's Mill, see chapter 3, note 13. For a thoughtful history of the 1838

conflict between the Mormons and the Missourians, see LeSeur, *The 1838 Mormon War in Missouri.*

11. The long history of mutual attacks by Apaches and Hispanic Arizonans is recounted in Officer, *Hispanic Arizona, 1536–1856;* Jacoby, *Shadows at Dawn;* and Haley, *Apaches.* For accounts by Apache participants, see Basso, *Western Apache Raiding and Warfare.*

12. As related in the epilogue in Bagley, *Blood of the Prophets,* a meeting in 1988 at Mountain Meadows by massacre descendants resulted in a granite monument at the site, listing the names of the victims and survivors. The descendants have formed the Mountain Meadows Association to commemorate the massacre.

13. Hurtado, *Indian Survival on the California Frontier,* 218.

14. Ebright and Hendricks, *The Witches of Abiquiu,* use the Abiquiu witchcraft outbreak in the mid-1700s to shed light on the history of the northern New Mexico *genízaros.*

15. A recent exposition along these lines is Stannard, *American Holocaust.*

16. For an examination of how disease and population decline affected California mission Indians, see Hackel, *Children of Coyote.*

17. Utley and Washburn, *Indian Wars,* 157.

18. Tate, *Indians and Emigrants,* 131–32.

19. Madsen, *The Shoshoni Frontier,* 58–59.

20. Utley, *Frontiersmen in Blue,* 265.

21. For the torture of Mangas Coloradas, see ibid., 21–23; for the atrocities committed by the soldiers at Sand Creek, see the appendix in Hoig, *The Sand Creek Massacre;* for rape at Bear River, see Madsen, *The Shoshoni Frontier,* 193; for a discussion of scalp hunting in the Southwest, see Thrapp, *The Conquest of Apacheria,* 8–10.

22. Samuel Chamberlain, who claimed to be a member of John Glanton's gang, includes a description of the scalp hunters' activities in his memoir, *My Confession.* Cormac McCarthy's novel *Blood Meridian,* much of which comes from Chamberlain's account, features a fictionalized version of Glanton.

23. In Basso, *Western Apache Raiding and Warfare,* Palmer Valor tells of a war party that killed twenty Mexicans in revenge for two Apaches killed in an earlier raid to steal horses (45–46). He also recounts a case where the revenge warfare took place during a raid (60–62).

24. See chapter 4, "The Politics of Vengeance," in DeLay, *War of a Thousand Deserts;* see also DeLay, "Independent Indians and the U.S.-Mexican War" (44–48).

25. Twain, *Roughing It,* 169.

26. Bagley, *Blood of the Prophets*, xvi.

27. For a discussion of John Higbee's document detailing a "true account of the tragedy" (written under the alias "Bull Valley Snort"), see Bagley, *Blood of the Prophets*, 326–29.

Bibliography

Abbey, Edward. *The Monkey Wrench Gang*. Philadelphia: Lippincott, 1975.

Ambrose, Stephen E. *Crazy Horse and Custer: The Parallel Lives of Two American Warriors.* New York: Random House, 1996.

Arnold, Elliott. *The Camp Grant Massacre.* New York: Simon and Schuster, 1976.

Backus, Anna Jean. *Mountain Meadows Witness: The Life and Times of Bishop Philip Klingensmith.* Hurricane, Utah: AJB Distributing, 2004.

Bagley, Will. *Blood of the Prophets: Brigham Young and the Massacre at Mountain Meadows.* Norman: University of Oklahoma Press, 2002.

———. *So Rugged and Mountainous: Blazing the Trails to Oregon and California, 1840–1848.* Norman: University of Oklahoma Press, 2010.

Ball, Eve, with Nora Henn and Lynda A. Sanchez. *Indeh: An Apache Odyssey.* Norman: University of Oklahoma Press, 1988.

Ball, Eve, and James Kaywaykla. *In the Days of Victorio: Recollections of a Warm Springs Apache.* Tucson: University of Arizona Press, 1970.

Barnes, John. "The Struggle to Control the Past: Commemoration, Memory, and the Bear River Massacre of 1863." *Public Historian* 30 (2008): 81–104.

Barnett, Louise. *The Ignoble Savage: American Literary Racism, 1790–1890.* Westport, Conn.: Greenwood Press, 1975.

Basso, Keith H., ed. *Western Apache Raiding and Warfare: From the Notes of Grenville Goodwin.* Tucson: University of Arizona Press, 1971.

Belshaw, Maria Parsons, and George Belshaw. *Crossing the Plains to Oregon in 1853.* Edited and with an introduction by Michael L. Tate. Fairfield, Wash.: Ye Galleon Press, 2000.

Bettelyoun, Susan Bordeaux, Josephine Waggoner, and Emily Levine, eds. *With My Own Eyes: A Lakota Woman Tells Her People's History.* Lincoln: University of Nebraska Press, 1999.

Betzinez, Jason, with Wilbur Sturtevant Nye. *I Fought with Geronimo.* Lincoln: University of Nebraska Press, 1987.

Bigler, David L. *Forgotten Kingdom: The Mormon Theocracy in the American West, 1847–1896.* Spokane, Wash.: Arthur H. Clark, 1998.

Bigler, David L., and Will Bagley, eds. *Innocent Blood: Essential Narratives of the Mountain Meadows Massacre.* Norman: Arthur H. Clark, 2008.

Blackhawk, Ned. *The Shoshone.* Austin, Tex.: Raintree, 2000.

———. Review of *Captives and Cousins*, by James Brooks. *American Indian Culture and Research Journal* 28 (2004): 85–90.

———. *Violence over the Land: Indians and Empires in the Early American West.* Cambridge, Mass.: Harvard University Press, 2006.

———. "The Displacement of Violence: Ute Diplomacy and the Making of New Mexico's Eighteenth-Century Northern Borderlands." *Ethnohistory* 54 (2007): 723–55.

Boorstin, Daniel. *The Americans: The National Experience.* New York: Vintage, 1967.

Bourke, John G. *On the Border with Crook.* Lincoln: University of Nebraska Press, 1971.

Bray, Kingsley. *Crazy Horse: A Lakota Life.* Norman: University of Oklahoma Press, 2006.

Brooks, James F. *Captives and Cousins: Slavery, Kinship, and Community in the Southwest Borderlands.* Chapel Hill: University of North Carolina Press, 2002.

Brooks, Juanita. *The Mountain Meadows Massacre.* Stanford: Stanford University Press, 1950. (Paperback edition with foreword by Jan Shipps, 1991.)

———. *Emma Lee.* Logan: Utah State University Press, 1984.

———. *John Doyle Lee: Zealot, Pioneer Builder, Scapegoat* (1961). Salt Lake City: Howe Brothers, 1985.

Brown, Dee Alexander. *Bury My Heart at Wounded Knee: An Indian History of the American West.* New York: Henry Holt, 1970.

Browning, Sinclair. *Enju: The Life and Struggles of an Apache Chief from the Little Running Water.* Lincoln, Nebr.: iUniverse, 2000.

Cabeza de Vaca, Álvar Núñez. *Cabeza de Vaca's Adventures in the Unknown Interior of America.* Translation of *La Relación* by Cyclone Covey. Albuquerque: University of New Mexico Press, 1983.

Capps, Benjamin. *The Warren Wagontrain Raid: The First Complete Account of an Historic Indian Attack and Its Aftermath.* Dallas: Southern Methodist University Press, 1989.

Carleton, J. H. *The Mountain Meadows Massacre: A Special Report by J. H. Carleton BVT, Major U.S.A. Captain 1st Dragoons 1859.* Spokane, Wash.: Arthur Clark, 1995.

Carroll, John M., comp. *The Sand Creek Massacre: A Documentary History.* New York: Sol Lewis, 1973.

Cates, Nancy Huff. "The Mountain Meadow Massacre: Statement of One of the Few Survivors." *Daily Arkansas Gazette*, September 1, 1875, 66:240, 3/1.

Chamberlain, Samuel E. *My Confession.* New York: Harper and Brothers, 1956.

Clappe, Louise Amelia Knapp Smith. *The Shirley Letters: Being Letters Written in 1851–1852 from the California Mines* (1922). Ed. Marlene Smith-Baranzini. Berkeley: Heyday Books, 1998.

Clark, Doris, and Hal Clark. *The Oatman Story.* Las Vegas: self-published, 2002.

Clum, John P. "Es-kin-in-zin." *New Mexico Historical Review* 3, no. 4 (1928): 399–420.

———. "Es-kin-in-zin." *New Mexico Historical Review* 4, no. 1 (1929): 1–27.

Colwell-Chanthaphonh, Chip. *Massacre at Camp Grant: Forgetting and Remembering Apache History.* Tucson: University of Arizona Press, 2007.

———. *Inheriting the Past: The Making of Arthur C. Parker and Indigenous Archaeology.* Tucson: University of Arizona Press, 2009.

Colwell-Chanthaphonh, Chip, Julie Hollowell, and Dru McGill. *Ethics in Action: Case Studies in Archaeological Dilemmas.* Washington, D.C.: SAA Press, 2008.

Cook, Noble David. *Born to Die: Disease and New World Conquest, 1492–1650.* Cambridge: Cambridge University Press, 1998.

Cook, Sherburne F. *The Population of the California Indians, 1769–1970.* Berkeley: University of California Press, 1976.

Curtis, Edward S. *The North American Indian.* http://curtis.library.northwestern.edu.

Davis, Britton. *The Truth about Geronimo.* Lincoln: University of Nebraska Press, 1976.

DeLay, Brian. "Independent Indians and the U.S.-Mexican War." *American Historical Review* 112 (2007): 35–68.

———. *War of a Thousand Deserts: Indian Raids and the U.S.-Mexican War.* New Haven: Yale University Press, 2009.

DeMallie, Raymond J., ed. *The Sixth Grandfather: Black Elk's Teaching Given to John G. Neihardt.* Lincoln: University of Nebraska Press, 1985.

Denton, Sally. *American Massacre: The Tragedy at Mountain Meadows, September 1857.* New York: Alfred A. Knopf, 2003.

Derounian-Stodola, Kathryn Zabelle. "The Indian Captivity Narratives of Mary Rowlandson and Olive Oatman." *Studies in the Literary Imagination* 27 (1994): 33–46.

———. "The Captive and Her Editor: The Ciphering of Olive Oatman and Royal B. Stratton." *Prospects: An Annual of American Cultural Studies* 23 (1998): 171.

———, ed. *Women's Indian Captivity Narratives.* New York: Penguin, 1998.

Dobie, J. Frank. *Coronado's Children: Tales of Lost Mines and Buried Treasure of the Southwest.* Austin: University of Texas Press, 1978.

———. *Apache Gold and Yaqui Silver.* Austin: University of Texas Press, 1985.

Dodge, Bertha S. *The Road West: Saga of the 35th Parallel.* Albuquerque: University of New Mexico Press, 1980.

Dodge, Colonel Richard Irving. *Our Wild Indians: Thirty-three Years' Personal Experience among the Red Men of the Great West.* Hartford: A. D. Worthington, 1884.

Donahue, Michael. *Drawing Battle Lines: The Map Testimony of Custer's Last Fight.* El Segundo, Calif.: Upton and Sons, 2008.

Duffus, R. L. *The Santa Fe Trail.* Albuquerque: University of New Mexico Press, 1972.

Ebright, Malcolm, and Rick Hendricks. *The Witches of Abiquiu: The Governor, the Priest, the Genízaro Indians, and the Devil.* Albuquerque: University of New Mexico Press, 2006.

Ege, Robert J. *"Tell Baker to Strike Them Hard!": Incident on the Marias, 23 Jan. 1870.* Fort Collins: Old Army Press, 1970.

Ewers, John C. *The Blackfeet: Raiders of the Northwestern Plains.* Norman: University of Oklahoma Press, 1976.

Ferguson, T. J., and Chip Colwell-Chanthaphonh. *History Is in the Land: Multivocal Tribal Traditions in Arizona's San Pedro Valley.* Tucson: University of Arizona Press, 2006.

Fielding, Robert Kent. and Dorothy S. Fielding. *The Tribune Reports of the Trials of John D. Lee for the Massacre at Mountain Meadow.* Higganum, Conn.: Kent's Books, 2000.

Flores, Dan. "Bison Ecology and Bison Diplomacy: The Southern Plains from 1800 to 1850." *Journal of American History* 78, 468 (1991): 465–85.

Freeman, Judith. *Red Water.* New York: Pantheon, 2002.

French, Richard. *Four Days from Fort Wingate: The Lost Adams Diggings.* Caldwell, Idaho: Caxton Press, 1994.

Fuller, Emeline L. *Left by the Indians.* Fairfield, Wash.: Ye Galleon Press, 1992.

Galvin, Lynn. "Cloudwoman: The Life of Olive Oatman, An Old California Indian Captive." *Californians* 13 (April 1996): 10–19.

Gatewood, Charles. *Lt. Charles Gatewood & His Apache Wars Memoir.* Lincoln: University of Nebraska Press, 2005.

Geronimo. *Geronimo: His Own Story. As Told to S. M. Barrett.* New York: Penguin/ Meridian Books, 1996.

Gifford, Edward, and Gwendoline Harris Block. *Californian Indian Nights.* Lincoln: University of Nebraska Press, 1990.

Goodwin, Grenville. *Myths and Tales of the White Mountain Apache.* Tucson: University of Arizona Press, 1994.

Goodwin, Grenville, and Neil Goodwin. *The Apache Diaries: A Father-Son Journey.* Lincoln: University of Nebraska Press, 2000.

———. *Like a Brother: Grenville Goodwin's Apache Years, 1928–1939.* Tucson: University of Arizona Press, 2004.

Gould, Richard. "Indian and White Versions of 'The Burnt Ranch Massacre.'" *Journal of Folklore Institute* 3, no. 1 (1966): 30–42.

Grayson, Elizabeth. *So Wide the Sky: A Heart-Soaring Novel of Destiny, Love, Courage and Family.* New York: Avon, 1997.

Greene, Candice C., and Russel Thornton, eds. *The Year the Stars Fell: Lakota Winter Counts in the Smithsonian.* Washington, D.C.: Smithsonian Institution, 1997.

Greene, Jerome. *Slim Buttes: An Episode of the Great Sioux War.* Norman: University of Oklahoma Press, 1982.

——— (comp. and ed.). *Lakota and Cheyenne: Indian Views of the Great Sioux War, 1876–1877.* Norman: University of Oklahoma Press, 1994.

———. *Evidence and the Custer Enigma: A Reconstruction of Indian-Military History.* Silverthorne, Colo.: Outbooks, 1995.

———. (com. and ed.). *Battles and Skirmishes of the Great Sioux War, 1876–1877: The Military View.* Norman: University of Oklahoma, 1996.

———. *Nez Perce Summer, 1877: The U.S. Army and the Nee-Me-Poo Crisis.* Helena: Montana Historical Society Press, 2000.

———. *Morning Star Dawn: The Powder River Expedition and the Northern Cheyennes, 1876.* Norman: University of Oklahoma Press, 2003.

———. *Washita: The U.S. Army and the Southern Cheyennes, 1867–1869.* Norman: University of Oklahoma Press, 2004.

———. *Stricken Field: A History of the Little Bighorn Battlefield.* Norman: University of Oklahoma Press, 2008.

Greene, Jerome A., and Douglas D. Scott. *Finding Sand Creek: History, Archeology, and the 1864 Massacre Site.* Norman: University of Oklahoma Press, 2004.

Gregg, Josiah. *Commerce of the Prairies.* Norman: University of Oklahoma Press, 1954.

Grinnell, George Bird. *The Fighting Cheyennes* (1915). Norman: University of Oklahoma Press, 1956.

———. *The Cheyenne Indians, Vol. 1: History and Society* (1923). Lincoln: Bison Books, 1972.

———. *The Cheyenne Indians, Vol. 2: War, Ceremonies, and Religion.* Lincoln: Bison Books, 1972.

Gutiérrez, Ramón A. *When Jesus Came, the Corn Mothers Went Away: Power, Sexuality and Marriage in New Mexico, 1500–1846.* Stanford: Stanford University Press, 1991.

Hackel, Steven W. *Children of Coyote, Missionaries of St. Francis: Indian-Spanish Relations in Colonial California, 1769–1850.* Chapel Hill: University of North Carolina Press, 2005.

Hafen, Leroy R., and Ann W. Hafen. *Old Spanish Trail: Santa Fé to Los Angeles.* Lincoln: University of Nebraska Press, 1993.

Haley, James L. *Apaches: A History and Culture Portrait.* Garden City, N.Y.: Doubleday, 1981.

Hall, Oakley. *Warlock.* Lincoln: University of Nebraska Press, 1980.

———. *Apaches.* New York: Simon and Schuster, 1986.

———. *Separations.* Reno: University of Nevada Press, 1997.

Hämäläinen, Pekka. "The Western Comanche Trade Center: Rethinking the Plains Indian Trade System." *Western Historical Quarterly* 29 (1998): 485–513.

———. *The Comanche Empire.* New Haven: Yale University Press, 2008.

Harte, Bret. "The Luck of Roaring Camp." In Bret Harte, *The Luck of Roaring Camp and Other Tales,* 7–17. New York: Dodd, Mead, 1961.

Hastings, Lansford W. *The Emigrants' Guide to Oregon and California.* Winnipeg: Stackpole Books, 2001.

Havnes, Mark. "Housing Lots Sprout near Mountain Meadows Site." *Salt Lake Tribune,* October 21, 2007.

Heard, Joseph. *White into Red: A Study of the Assimilation of White Persons Captured by Indians.* Metuchen, N.J.: Scarecrow, 1973.

Heizer, Robert F., ed. *Collected Documents of the Causes and Events in the Bloody Island Massacre of 1850.* Berkeley: University of California Press, 1973.

———, ed. *The Destruction of California Indians.* Santa Barbara: Peregrine Smith, 1974.

Heizer, Robert F., and Albert E. Elsasser. *The Natural World of the California Indians.* Berkeley: University of California Press, 1980.

Hill, Rita. *Then and Now: Here and around Shakespeare.* Lordsburg, N.Mex.: Privately printed, 1998.

Hoig, Stan. *The Sand Creek Massacre.* Norman: University of Oklahoma Press, 1961.

———. *The Battle of the Washita: The Sheridan-Custer Indian Campaign of 1867–69.* Lincoln: University of Nebraska Press, 1976.

———. *Tribal Wars of the Southern Plains.* Norman: University of Oklahoma Press, 1993.

Holliday, J. S. *The World Rushed In: The California Gold Rush Experience.* Norman: University of Oklahoma Press, 2002.

Hopkins, Sarah Winnemucca. *Life among the Piutes: Their Wrongs and Claims* (1883). Whitefish, Mont.: Kessinger, 2007.

Hurtado, Albert. *Indian Survival on the California Frontier.* New Haven: Yale University Press, 1988.

———. "California Indian Demography, Sherburne F. Cook and the Revision of American History." *Pacific Historical Review* 58 (August 1989): 323–43.

———. "California Indians and the Workaday West: Labor, Assimilation, and Survival." *California History* 69 (Spring 1990): 2–11, 77–79.

———. "Sexuality in the California Missions: Cultural Perceptions and Sad Realities." *California History* 71 (Fall 1992): 371–85, 451–53.

———. *Intimate Frontiers: Sex, Gender, and Culture in Old California.* Albuquerque: University of New Mexico Press, 1999.

———. "Clouded Legacy: Indians and the California Gold Rush." In *Riches for All: The California Gold Rush as a World Event,* ed. Kenneth N. Owens, 90–117. Lincoln: University of Nebraska Press, 2002.

———. *John Sutter: A Life on the North American Frontier.* Norman: University of Oklahoma Press, 2006.

———. "Empires, Frontiers, Filibusters, and Pioneers: The Transnational World of John Sutter." *Pacific Historical Review* 77 (February 2008): 19–47.

Hutton, Paul A. *Phil Sheridan and His Army.* Lincoln: University of Nebraska Press, 1985.

Hyde, George. *Red Cloud's Folk: A History of the Oglala Sioux Indians.* Norman: University of Oklahoma Press, 1937.

———. *The Pawnee Indians.* Norman: University of Oklahoma Press, 1951.

———. *A Sioux Chronicle.* Norman: University of Oklahoma Press, 1956.

———. *Life of George Bent, Written from His Letters.* Norman: University of Oklahoma Press, 1983.

Jacoby, Karl. *Shadows at Dawn: A Borderlands Massacre and the Violence of History.* New York: Penguin Press, 2008.

Josephy, Alvin M., Jr. *The Civil War in the American West.* New York: Alfred A. Knopf, 1991.

Keenan, Jerry. *The Great Sioux Uprising: Rebellion on the Plains, August–September, 1862.* Cambridge, Mass.: Da Capo Press, 2003.

Kraft, Louis. *Gatewood and Geronimo.* Albuquerque: University of New Mexico Press, 2000.

Kroeber, Albert. *Handbook of the Indians of California* (1925). Reprint. Berkeley: California Book, 1967.

Kroeber, A. L., and Clifton B. Kroeber. "Olive Oatman's First Account of Her Captivity among the Mohave." *California Historical Society Quarterly* 41 (1962): 309–17.

Kroeber, Theodora. *Ishi: The Last of His Tribe.* Berkeley: Parnassus Press, 1964.

Lavender, David. *Bent's Fort.* Lincoln: University of Nebraska Press, 1972.

Lawrence, Deborah, and Jon Lawrence. "Interview with Oakley Hall." *Desert Tracks: Newsletter of the Southwest Chapter of the Oregon-California Trails Association* (June 2007): 9–20.

———. "A Tour of Shakespeare with Manny Hough." *Desert Tracks: Newsletter of the Southwest Chapter of the Oregon-California Trails Association* (January 2009): 16–19.

Lee, John D. *A Mormon Chronicle: The Diaries of John D. Lee, 1848–1876.* Edited by Robert Glass Cleland and Juanita Brooks. San Marino, Calif.: Huntington Library, 1955.

———. *Journals of John D. Lee, 1846–47 and 1859.* Edited by Charles Kelly. Salt Lake City: University of Utah Press, 1984.

———. *Mormonism Unveiled: The Life and Confession of John D. Lee and the Life of Brigham Young.* Reprint, facsimile issue. Albuquerque: Fierra Blanca, 2001.

Leonard, Elmore. *The Tonto Woman and Other Western Stories.* New York: Penguin Books, 2000.

LeSeur, Stephen C. *The 1838 Mormon War in Missouri.* Columbia: University of Missouri Press, 1987.

Liberty, Margot. "Cheyenne Primacy: The Tribes' Perspective as Opposed to That of the United States Army; A Possible Alternative to 'The Great Sioux War of 1876.'" Friends of the Little Bighorn Battlefield, 2006 (friendslittlebighorn.com/cheyenneprimacy.htm).

Linderman, Frank B. *Plenty Coups: Chief of the Crows.* Lincoln: University of Nebraska Press, 1962.

———. *Pretty Shield: Medicine Woman of the Crows.* Lincoln: University of Nebraska Press, 1972.

Madsen, Brigham D. *The Shoshoni Frontier and the Bear River Massacre.* Salt Lake City: University of Utah Press, 1985.

———. *Glory Hunter: A Biography of Patrick Edward Connor.* Salt Lake City: University of Utah Press, 1990.

Marshall, Joseph, III. *On Behalf of the Wolf and the First Peoples.* Santa Fe, N.Mex.: Red Crane Books, 1995.

McCarthy, Cormac. *Blood Meridian: Or the Evening Redness in the West* (1985). New York: Vintage, 1992.

———. *No Country for Old Men.* New York: Alfred A. Knopf, 2005.

McGinty, Brian. *The Oatman Massacre: A Tale of Desert Captivity and Survival.* Norman: University of Oklahoma Press, 2005.

McMurtry, Larry. *Crazy Horse.* New York: Penguin Putnam, 1999.

Mifflin, Margot. *Bodies of Subversion: A Secret History of Women and Tattoo.* New York: Juno Books, 1997.

———. *The Blue Tattoo: The Life of Olive Oatman.* Lincoln: University of Nebraska Press, 2009.

Mooney, James. *A Calendar History of the Kiowa Indians.* Washington, D.C.: Smithsonian Institution Press, 1979.

Munro, Pamela. *Mojave Syntax.* New York: Garland, 1976.

———. *A Mohave Dictionary.* Los Angeles: Department of Linguistics, UCLA, 1992.

Neihardt, John G. *Black Elk Speaks: Being the Life Story of a Holy Man of the Oglala Sioux.* Lincoln: University of Nebraska Press, 1961.

Nunis, Doyce B., Jr., ed. *The Bidwell-Bartleson Party: 1841 California Emigrant Adventure: The Documents and Memoirs of the Overland Pioneers.* Santa Cruz, Calif.: Western Tanager Press, 1992.

Nye, Wilbur Sturtevant. *Bad Medicine and Good: Tales of the Kiowa.* Norman: University of Oklahoma Press, 1962.

———. *Plains Indian Raiders: The Final Phases of Warfare from the Arkansas to the Red River.* Norman: University of Oklahoma Press, 1968.

Officer, James E. *Hispanic Arizona, 1536–1856.* Tucson: University of Arizona Press, 1987.

Oury, William S. "Article on Camp Grant Massacre." 1885. Manuscript on file, Arizona Historical Society, Tucson.

Owens, Kenneth N., ed. *John A. Sutter, Sr., and His Grants, by John A. Laufkotter.* 2nd ed. Sacramento: Sacramento Book Collectors Club, 2004.

Paul, R. Eli. *Blue Water Creek and the First Sioux War, 1854–1856.* Norman: University of Oklahoma Press, 2004.

Pettid, Edward J. "The Oatman Story." Unpublished manuscript, n.d. Special Collections, University of Arizona Library, Tucson.

———. "The Oatman Story: A Frontier Tragedy." *Arizona Highways* 44, no. 11 (1968): 4–9.

———, ed. "Olive Ann Oatman's Lecture Notes and the Oatman Bibliography." *San Bernardino Museum Association Quarterly* 16 (Winter 1968): entire issue.

Pierce, Michael D. *The Most Promising Young Officer: A Life of Ranald Slidell Mackenzie.* Norman: University of Oklahoma Press, 1993.

Prater, Jeffrey. "John Ford's Cavalry Trilogy: Myth or Reality?" Master's thesis. General Staff College, Fort Leavenworth, Kans., 1989.

Purcell, Jack. *The Lost Adams Diggings: Myth, Mystery and Madness.* Olathe, Kans.: NineLives Press, 2003.

Ricker, Eli S. *Voices of the American West, Volume 1: The Indian Interviews of Eli S. Ricker, 1903–1919; Volume 2: The Settler and Soldier Interviews of Eli S. Ricker, 1903–1919.* Edited by Richard E. Jensen. Lincoln: University of Nebraska Press, 2005.

Rister, Carl Coke. *Comanche Bondage: Dr. John Charles Beale's Settlement of La Villa de Dolores on Las Moras Creek in Southern Texas of the 1830's, with an Annotated Reprint of Sarah Ann Horn's Narrative of Her Captivity among the Comanches, Her Ransom by Traders in New Mexico, and Return via the Santa F. Trail.* Lincoln: University of Nebraska Press, 1989.

Roberts, David. *Once They Moved like the Wind: Cochise, Geronimo, and the Apache Wars.* New York: Simon and Schuster, 1993.

———. *The Pueblo Revolt: The Secret Rebellion That Drove the Spaniards Out of the Southwest.* New York: Simon and Schuster, 2004.

Robinson, W. W., Jr. "Appendix A b, No. 3." In *Annual Report of the Commissioner of Indian Affairs to the Secretary of the Interior for the Year 1871,* 74–76. Washington, D.C.: Government Printing Office, 1872.

Roessel, Ruth W. *Navajo Stories of the Long Walk Period.* Tsaile, Ariz.: Navajo Community College Press, 1973.

Romo, Rene. "Hail to the Chief." *Albuquerque Journal,* October 10, 2004.

Root, Virginia. *Following the Pot of Gold at the Rainbow's End in the Days of 1850: The Life of Mrs. Susan Thompson Lewis Parrish of El Monte, California.* Edited by Leonore Rowland. Downey, Calif.: Elena Quinn, 1960.

Rosenus, Alan. *General Vallejo and the Advent of the Americans.* Berkeley: Heyday Books, 1999.

Rowlandson, Mary. *The Sovereignty and Goodness of God, with Related Documents.* Edited by Neal Salisbury. Boston: Bedford, 1997.

Sandoz, Mari. *Crazy Horse: The Strange Man of the Oglalas.* Lincoln: University of Nebraska Press, 1992.

———. *Old Jules* (1935). Lincoln: Bison Books, 2005.

Sauers, Richard A. "The War of the Rebellion (Official Records)." In *Encyclopedia of the American Civil War: A Political, Social, and Military History,* edited by David S. Heidler and Jeanne T. Heidler, 2060–61. New York: W. W. Norton, 2000.

Schellie, Don. *Vast Domain of Blood: The Story of the Camp Grant Massacre.* Los Angeles: Westernlore Press, 1968.

Schindler, Harold. *Orrin Porter Rockwell: Man of God, Son of Thunder* (1966). 2nd ed. Salt Lake City: University of Utah Press, 1983.

———. "The Bear River Massacre: New Historical Evidence." *Utah Historical Quarterly* 67 (1999): 300.

Secrest, William B. *When the Great Spirit Died: The Destruction of the California Indians, 1850–1860.* Sanger, Calif.: Word Dancer Press, 2002.

Shannon, Donald H. *The Utter Disaster on the Oregon Trail: The Utter and Van Ornum Massacres of 1860.* Caldwell, Idaho: Snake Country Publishing, 1993.

———. *The Boise Massacre on the Oregon Trail: Attack on the Ward Party in 1854 and Massacres of 1859.* Caldwell, Idaho: Snake Country Publishing, 2004.

———. *Massacre Rocks and City of Rocks: 1862 Attacks on Emigrant Trains.* Caldwell, Idaho: Snake Country Publishing, 2008.

Simmons, Marc. *Murder on the Santa Fe Trail: An International Incident, 1843.* El Paso: Texas Western Press, 1987.

———. *Massacre on the Lordsburg Road: A Tragedy of the Apache Wars.* College Station: Texas A&M University Press, 1997.

———. *Following the Santa Fe Trail: A Guide for Modern Travelers.* 3rd ed. Santa Fe: Ancient City Press, 2001.

———. *Millie Cooper's Ride: A True Story from History.* Albuquerque: University of New Mexico Press, 2002.

———. *Kit Carson and His Three Wives: A Family History.* Albuquerque: University of New Mexico Press, 2003.

———. *Friday, the Arapahoe Boy: A Story from History.* Albuquerque: University of New Mexico Press, 2004.

Slotkin, Richard. *Regeneration through Violence: The Mythology of the American Frontier, 1600–1860.* Middletown, Conn.: Wesleyan University Press, 1973.

Stands In Timber, John, and Margot Liberty. *Cheyenne Memories.* New Haven: Yale University Press, 1967.

Stannard, David E. *American Holocaust: The Conquest of the New World.* Oxford: Oxford University Press, 1992.

Stratton, R. B. *Captivity of the Oatman Girls.* New York: Carlton and Porter, 1857. Reprint, with foreword by Wilcomb Washburn. Lincoln: University of Nebraska Press, 1983.

Svaldi, David. *Sand Creek and the Rhetoric of Extermination: A Case Study in Indian-White Relations.* Lanham, Md.: University Press of America, 1989.

Tate, Michael L. "Comanche Captives: People between Two Worlds." *Chronicles of Oklahoma* 72 (1994): 228–63.

———. *The Frontier Army in the Settlement of the West.* Norman: University of Oklahoma Press, 2001.

———. *Indians and Emigrants: Encounters on the Overland Trails.* Norman: University of Oklahoma Press. 2006.

———. *The American Army in Transition, 1865–1898.* Santa Barbara: Greenwood Press, 2007.

———. "The Artist and the Entrepreneur: William Quesenbury and John Wesley Jones on the California Trail." *Overland Journal* 25 (2007): 187–201.

Thrapp, Dan L. *The Conquest of Apacheria.* Norman: University of Oklahoma Press, 1967.

Tinnemeyer, Andrea. "Rescuing the Past: The Case of Olive Oatman." In *María Amparo Ruiz de Burton: Critical and Pedagogical Perspectives,* edited by Anne Goldman and Amelia De La Luz Montes, 169–83. Lincoln: University of Nebraska Press, 2004.

Turley, Richard E. "The Mountain Meadows Massacre." *Ensign* (September 2007): 14–21.

Twain, Mark. *Roughing It.* New York: Penguin, 1981.

Uldall, Hans Jørgen, and William Shipley. *Nisenan Texts and Dictionary.* University of California Publications in Linguistics, vol. 46. Berkeley: University of California Press, 1966.

Underhill, Ruth M. *A Papago Calendar Record. University of New Mexico Bulletin.* Anthropological Series, vol. 2, no. 5 (1938).

———. *Social Organization of the Papago Indians.* Columbia: Columbia University Press, 1939.

United States War Department. *The War of the Rebellion: A Compilation of the Official Record of the Union and Confederate Armies.* Washington, D.C.: Government Printing Office, 1880–1901 (online at http://digital.library.cornell.edu/m/moawar/waro.html).

Unruh, John D., Jr. *The Plains Across: The Overland Emigrants and the Trans-Mississippi West, 1840–1860.* Urbana: University of Illinois Press, 1979.

Utley, Robert. *The Last Days of the Sioux Nation.* New Haven: Yale University Press, 1963.

———. *Frontiersmen in Blue: The United States Army and the Indian, 1848–1865.* Lincoln: University of Nebraska Press, 1967.

———. *Frontier Regulars: The United States Army and the Indian, 1866–1891.* Lincoln: University of Nebraska Press, 1973.

———. *The Indian Frontier of the American West, 1846–1890.* Albuquerque: University of New Mexico Press, 1984.

———. "On Digging Up Custer Battlefield." *Montana The Magazine of Western History* 36, no. 2 (1986): 80–82.

———. *The Lance and the Shield: The Life and Times of Sitting Bull.* New York: Henry Holt, 1993.

———. *Custer and the Great Controversy: The Origin and Development of a Legend.* Lincoln: University of Nebraska Press, 1998.

———. *Custer: Cavalier in Buckskin.* Norman: University of Oklahoma Press, 2001.

Utley, Robert M., and Wilcomb E. Washburn. *Indian Wars.* New York: Mariner Books, 2002.

Valkenburgh, Richard van. "Apache Ghost Guards Aravaipa." *Desert Magazine* 11, no. 6 (1948): 16–20.

Vestal, Stanley. *Sitting Bull--Champion of the Sioux: A Biography.* Boston: Houghton Mifflin, 1932.

———. *Warpath: The True Story of the Fighting Sioux Told in a Biography of Chief White Bull.* Lincoln: University of Nebraska Press, 1984.

Vitale, Gary C. "Whatever Happened to James Colin Brewster, the Boy Mormon Prophet?" *Desert Tracks: Newsletter of the Southwest Chapter of the Oregon-California Trails Association* (December 2007): 9–16.

Walker, Ronald W., Richard E. Turley, and Glen M. Leonard. *Massacre at Mountain Meadows.* Oxford: Oxford University Press, 2008.

Wallace, Andrew, and Richard H. Hevly, eds. *From Texas to San Diego in 1851: The Overland Journal of S. W. Woodhouse, Surgeon-Naturalist of the Sitgreaves Expedition.* Lubbock: Texas Tech University Press, 2007.

Ware, Joseph E. *The Emigrants' Guide to California.* Cambridge, Mass.: Da Capo Press, 1972.

Waterfall, Richard. "Vengeance at Sunrise: The Camp Grant Massacre, 30 April 1871." *Journal of the West* 21, no. 3 (1992): 110–18.

Weber, David. *The Taos Trappers: The Fur Trade in the Far Southwest, 1540–1846.* Norman: University of Oklahoma Press, 1971.

———. *Richard H. Kern: Expeditionary Artist in the Far Southwest, 1848–1853.* Albuquerque: University of New Mexico Press, 1985.

———. The *Spanish Frontier in North America.* New Haven: Yale University Press, 1992.

———. *Bárbaros: Spaniards and Their Savages in the Age of Enlightenment.* New Haven: Yale University Press, 2005.

Welch, James. *Fools Crow.* New York: Penguin, 1987.

Welch, James, with Paul Stekler. *Killing Custer: The Battle of Little Bighorn and the Fate of the Plains Indians.* New York: W. W. Norton, 2007.

West, Elliott. *The Contested Plains: Indians, Goldseekers and the Rush to Colorado.* Lawrence: University Press of Kansas, 1998.

Woodin, Debbie. "Whatever Happened to Charley McComas?" *Joplin Globe*, October 31, 2004.

Worrall, Simon. *The Poet and the Murderer: A True Story of Literary Crime and the Art of Forgery.* New York: Dutton Books, 2002.

Zanjani, Sally. *Sarah Winnemucca.* Lincoln: Bison Books, 2004.

Zesch, Scott. *The Captured: A True Story of Abduction by Indians on the Texas Frontier.* New York: St. Martin's Griffin, 2005.

Index

References to illustrations appear in italics.

www.ingramcontent.com/pod-product-compliance
Lightning Source LLC
LaVergne TN
LVHW090728201026
850618LV00022B/99/J
* 9 7 8 0 8 0 6 1 4 1 2 6 8 *